T0271297

On July 1, 1997, Hong Kong, the last vestige of British imperialism in China, will be restored to Chinese sovereignty, symbolizing the end of China's age of humiliation. The essays in this volume, prepared by several of the world's leading specialists on Chinese commerce, finance, law, and international relations, explain what reversion will mean to the people of Hong Kong and to those of us who invest, trade, and shop there. Will a Hong Kong ruled from Beijing continue to be a safe haven for those who live there and those who earn their fortunes there?

Deng Xiaoping once promised that China would leave the city alone for fifty years, presumably to enjoy relative political freedom and the blessings of unfettered capitalism well into the twenty-first century. Skepticism about Deng's promise, never absent, was reinforced when he ordered the crushing of dissent in China in June 1989, resulting in the Tiananmen massacre.

The contributors to this volume note that Chinese leaders have shown only limited comprehension of what the continued success of Hong Kong will require. Nonetheless, they are agreed that China will try to maintain Hong Kong's role in the international economic system and that the prognosis for the short run is good. In the long run, they fear that Beijing will inadvertently strangle the goose that lays the golden egg.

Hong Kong Under Chinese Rule

Hong Kong Under Chinese Rule

The Economic and Political Implications of Reversion

Edited by

WARREN I. COHEN
*University of Maryland, Baltimore County,
and the Woodrow Wilson International Center for Scholars*

LI ZHAO
Woodrow Wilson International Center for Scholars

CAMBRIDGE
UNIVERSITY PRESS

PUBLISHED BY THE PRESS SYNDICATE OF THE UNIVERSITY OF CAMBRIDGE
The Pitt Building, Trumpington Street, Cambridge CB2 1RP, United Kingdom

CAMBRIDGE UNIVERSITY PRESS
The Edinburgh Building, Cambridge CB2 2RU, United Kingdom
40 West 20th Street, New York, NY 10011-4211, USA
10 Stamford Road, Oakleigh, Melbourne 3166, Australia

First published 1997

Typeset in Times Roman

Library of Congress Cataloging-in-Publication Data

Hong Kong Under Chinese rule : the economic and political implications
of reversion / edited by Warren I. Cohen, Li Zhao.

p.   cm.

Includes index.

ISBN 0-521-62158-5. – ISBN 0-521-62761-3 (pbk.)

1. Hong Kong – Economic conditions.   2. Hong Kong – Politics and
government.   3. Hong Kong – Foreign relations.   I. Cohen, Warren I.
II. Zhao, Li, d1970–   .
HC470.3.H675   1997
338.95125 – dc21   97-8295
                                                          CIP

*A catalog record for this book is available from
the British Library.*

ISBN 0 521 62158 5 hardback
ISBN 0 521 62761 3 paperback

Transferred to digital printing 2004

Contents

v

Contents

Contributors

Edgardo Barandiaran is a senior economist at the World Bank Resident Mission in China.

Philip Bowring is a columnist for the *International Herald Tribune* and consultant to *Kleinwort Benson Securities Asia.*

Joseph Y. S. Cheng is a professor of political science at the City University of Hong Kong.

Jacques deLisle is an assistant professor at the University of Pennsylvania Law School.

James V. Feinerman is a professor of law at the Georgetown University Law Center.

Yasheng Huang is an assistant professor of political science at the University of Michigan.

Kevin P. Lane is an assistant professor of government at Franklin and Marshall College.

Kenneth Lieberthal is the Arthur Thurnau Professor of Political Science and William Davidson Professor of Business Administration at the University of Michigan.

Ronald N. Montaperto is a senior fellow at the National Defense University.

Tsang Shu-ki is a professor of economics at the Hong Kong Baptist University.

Contributors

Nancy Bernkopf Tucker is a professor of history in the School of Foreign Service at Georgetown University.

Changqi Wu is an assistant professor of economics at the Hong Kong University of Science and Technology.

Michael Yahuda is a professor of international relations at the London School of Economics and Political Science.

Introduction

ON July 1, 1997, Hong Kong, the last vestige of British imperialism in China, will be restored to Chinese sovereignty. One hundred and fifty-five years will have passed since the end of the Opium War, when the British forced the Chinese to cede the island of Hong Kong; one hundred and thirty-seven years will have passed since they took Kowloon; and ninety-nine years will have passed since the British forced the Chinese to grant them a "lease" over the New Territories, a few square miles of the mainland across from the island. For Great Britain, the lowering of the Union Jack on June 30, 1997, will be further evidence (hardly needed) of imperial decline. For China, as the People's Liberation Army marches in the next day, as the red flag with five gold stars is raised over Hong Kong, the moment will symbolize the end of China's age of humiliation, further evidence of China's emergence as a Great Power, another step toward Chinese hegemony over East Asia.

What will the reversion of Hong Kong mean to the people of Hong Kong – and to the rest of us – who invest, trade, and shop there? Over the last fifty years Hong Kong has served as a refuge for those who fled communism in China, who escaped from the political oppression and economic hardship they experienced under the rule of Mao Zedong. It became the greatest entrepot and financial center on the Asian mainland. Billions of dollars in foreign investment flowed there from Europe, Japan, and the United States. A stunning percentage of the world's trade passed through its magnificent harbor. Known for its natural beauty, its restaurants, and its tax-free shops offering unsurpassed bargains, Hong Kong became an obligatory stop for tourists from all over the world. Will a Hong Kong ruled from Beijing continue to be a safe haven for those who live there and for those who earn their fortunes there?

1

Warren I. Cohen

Thirteen years ago, the Chinese made the British an offer they couldn't refuse, winning Margaret Thatcher's acquiescence to the surrender of Hong Kong. At the time, Deng Xiaoping spoke of one country, China, with two discrete systems: one communist (with Chinese characteristics, to be sure), for most of China, and one capitalist, for Hong Kong. He promised to leave the city alone for fifty years, presumably so that it could enjoy relative political freedom and the blessings of unfettered capitalism well into the twenty-first century. Skepticism about Deng's promise, never absent, was reinforced when he ordered the crushing of dissent in China in June 1989, resulting in the Tiananmen massacre. The level of anxiety concerning China's intentions in Hong Kong has increased in recent years as the People's Republic of China has opposed and undermined the efforts of Governor Christopher Patten to speed democratic reforms for a city so recently ruled by imperial fiat. Doubts that Thatcher and her minions had provided adequate protection for the rights of their erstwhile subjects mounted.

What will become of Hong Kong after reversion? On July 1, 1996, a workshop organized by my colleague Li Zhao, program associate of the Asia Program of the Woodrow Wilson International Center for Scholars, met to address that question. Analysts came from China, Great Britain, Hong Kong, and the United States to discuss Hong Kong's future under Chinese rule. The central focus of the workshop, like that of this volume, was on the impact Chinese control was likely to have on the city's role in the international economic system – how the international business community would be affected. Issues of trade, finance, and political economy, and concerns about Chinese respect for the rule of law dominated the discussion. The shifting attitudes of the citizens of Hong Kong were examined closely. Participants also weighed the significance of reversion for China and the United States, and attempted to provide signposts that indicate probable outcomes.

This volume is composed of several of the essays presented at the July 1, 1996, workshop and several additional papers commissioned to explore questions that arose at that workshop. It is intended to serve as a guide to those with a professional interest in events in Hong Kong over the next several years.

In Chapter 1, Philip Bowring of the *International Herald Tribune* explains what it is that makes Hong Kong work – how Hong Kong came to be a great international commercial center – and sketches the "critical mass" that he deems essential to the continuation of the city's preeminence in East Asia. He argues that "openness to the outside world and competent – but minimalist –

2

government" are fundamental. Bowring has few peers as an observer of the city, and his contribution constitutes an excellent overview of the problems ahead.

For many, the critical question has been whether Beijing understands the extent to which respect for the rule of law provides the foundation for Hong Kong's prosperity. In Chapter 2, Jacques deLisle of the University of Pennsylvania Law School and Kevin P. Lane of Franklin and Marshall College examine Chinese business and legal practices and postulate three possible models of a rule of law for Hong Kong. The first, which they call the "China Model," derives from inspection of the booming areas of the mainland, "where the economy has thrived despite a limited vision, and even weaker realization, of the rule of law." The second model, which deLisle and Lane label the "Singapore Model," requires a "robust system of legality for economic affairs" and "competent, honest officials," but little beyond business law – specifically, little to warm the hearts of advocates of democracy and human rights. Their third model, called the "Augmented Hong Kong Model," goes beyond the Singapore Model, requiring that laws must protect civil liberties and political rights. deLisle and Lane conclude an exhaustive study of the issues by suggesting a solution that might be acceptable to all, "something more than the China Model, something less than the Augmented Hong Kong Model, and something other than the Singapore Model." This solution is, perhaps, something more than the Chinese will grant – and there can be no doubt that the ultimate decision will be made in Beijing. The authors also warn that fundamentally different Chinese and Western views on what constitutes sovereignty might lead to incompatible views on what constitutes the rule of law.

In Chapter 3, James V. Feinerman, professor at the Georgetown University Law Center, examines the legal and constitutional issues that have emerged since the United Kingdom and the People's Republic of China signed the Joint Declaration on Hong Kong in December 1984. Feinerman, one of America's leading authorities on Chinese law, reviews the legal framework of reversion, looking at the Chinese constitution as well as the international agreements Beijing has signed. He considers the difference between Chinese and British interpretations of the Joint Declaration and analyzes the laws that Beijing has passed in preparation for the reassertion of Chinese sovereignty. In particular, he discusses the controversies over the Provisional Legislative Council and the Court of Final Appeal, and he expresses his concerns about Beijing's obvious antipathy toward democratic reform and apparent lack of respect for the rights of the people of Hong Kong.

Yasheng Huang, a Chinese national now teaching at the University of Michigan, has emerged in recent years as the foremost explicator of China's political economy. In Chapter 4, he describes the existing integration of the Chinese and Hong Kong economies and indicates how this process is likely to develop after reversion. Huang distinguishes the trade and investment between Hong Kong and China from control by mainland firms over assets located in Hong Kong. He sees the two types of integration as having different implications for government–business relations, and he is apprehensive about the long-term survival of Hong Kong's laissez-faire institutions.

In Chapter 5, Changqi Wu of the Hong Kong University of Science and Technology focuses more sharply on economic issues, and broadens the scope of the question of integration by including Taiwan. Based on his conception of Greater China, he discusses the comparative economic advantages of China, Hong Kong, and Taiwan and how the three economies have integrated over the past eighteen years. His statistics demonstrate the centrality of Hong Kong. Of particular interest is his point about the lack of a well-developed legal system in mainland China, necessitating the use of informal structures, such as "kinship," to protect business transactions there. As a result, most foreign capital in China comes from Hong Kong and Taiwan. He suggests that reversion will provide Hong Kong with new opportunities to strengthen its economic position in Greater China.

In Chapter 6, Edgardo Barandiaran, senior economist of the World Bank Resident Mission in China, and Tsang Shu-ki of Hong Kong Baptist University explore monetary relations between Hong Kong and China. They discuss the Hong Kong and Chinese monetary systems and the ways in which they are changing. Their focus is the question of whether two separate currencies, the Hong Kong dollar (HK$) and the Chinese Renminbi (RMB), will coexist after reversion. They note the perception of the HK$ as stable and convertible and the lower regard the international business community has for the RMB – although it is assumed that the RMB will ultimately become both stable and convertible as well. Similarly, they discuss the differences in banking systems and the possible outcomes.

In Chapter 7, Joseph Cheng of the City University of Hong Kong analyzes the attitudes of various participants in Hong Kong political affairs, including senior government officials, political party leaders, leaders of non-governmental organizations, journalists, academics, leading businesspeople, and Chinese appointees to various organizations that are preparing the government for reversion. He also uses polls to indicate the changing opinions of the broader

Hong Kong public. In brief, he has found much to please the rulers of the People's Republic of China: declining support for Governor Chris Patten and his reforms, and growing confidence among the people of Hong Kong that the transfer of power on July 1, 1997, poses little threat to them. He has concluded that the people have lowered their expectations for the future, and that they have accepted the idea that the People's Liberation Army will be stationed in their city and the fact that they have had no say in the selection of Tung Chee-hwa as the first Chief Executive of the Hong Kong Special Administrative Region of the People's Republic of China. They are anxious about the likely erosion of the rule of law and of press freedom, but they have lived without democracy these many years and will give Beijing the benefit of the doubt for now.

In the course of the 1996 workshop, Charles Freeman, recently retired as the Department of State's leading specialist on Chinese affairs, asked about the role of the People's Liberation Army (PLA) in Hong Kong after reversion. In Chapter 8, Ronald N. Montaperto of the National Defense University, a prominent American student of the PLA, addresses that question and discusses the larger strategic and military implications of reversion. His is one of the more reassuring contributions. He views the coming PLA presence in Beijing as merely "an outward and visible symbol of the restoration of Chinese sovereignty over territories extorted from a succession of weak governments by militarily stronger Western powers." Montaperto insists that control of Hong Kong will not have a major impact on China's military position in the region; Hong Kong facilities will not increase the PLA's ability to concentrate force in any of the areas of greatest concern to Chinese leaders. He indicates that Beijing has powerful incentives to minimize Hong Kong's connection with the PLA. His only fear is the possibility, however remote, that the PLA might be used to suppress a mass demonstration in Hong Kong, triggering a worldwide reaction such as followed the Tiananmen massacre of 1989.

Chapter 9 discusses the implications of reversion for China's integration into the international community. Michael Yahuda of the London School of Economics and Political Science, author of the 1996 book *Hong Kong: China's Challenge* and distinguished former fellow of the Wilson Center, stresses the importance of reversion. He details the benefits China would derive from a smooth transition followed by successful management of Hong Kong's autonomy. Although he is cautiously optimistic about the city's future, he readily concedes that "China's leaders have yet to show an understanding of its system" and he fears that their experience offers little preparation.

Warren I. Cohen

Chapter 10 is contributed by Nancy Bernkopf Tucker of Georgetown University, another former Wilson fellow and author of the standard work on America's role in Hong Kong, *Taiwan, Hong Kong, and the United States, 1945–1992: Uncertain Friendships.* She provides insights into a critical international question: How will reversion affect Chinese–American relations? Americans have much to lose if reversion goes badly, but the United States has no legal standing in the affair and, therefore, little leverage. Few Americans are even aware of this issue – and fewer care. Tucker reminds us that the U.S.– Hong Kong Policy Act of 1992 indicated congressional concern about whether China will honor its pledges to the British and to the people of Hong Kong. She also details the enormous stake the American business community has in Hong Kong, indicating the economic importance of the city to Americans. She explains how events in Hong Kong might affect Taiwan and ultimately Chinese–American relations, and how tensions between Beijing and Washington may play a role in the future of Hong Kong.

In Chapter 11, the University of Michigan's Kenneth Lieberthal, the eminent American analyst of Chinese politics, identifies signposts for the post-reversion era – indications of whether Beijing is willing and able to abide by the Basic Law, the constitution for post–July 1997 Hong Kong. Like most of the authors in this volume and most participants in the 1996 workshop, Lieberthal expects sincere effort by the Chinese to ensure that Deng Xiaoping's "one country, two systems" formula works. Like most of the others, he is concerned about "the inevitable difficulties of making two very distinctive systems deal effectively with each other," of uncomprehending Chinese officials unintentionally destroying what Bowring called the critical mass essential to Hong Kong's continued prosperity. Lieberthal wants to see what sort of institutional presence Hong Kong will have in Beijing; whether Hong Kong can lobby successfully at the seat of power in China. He looks to the development in Hong Kong of counterparts to Beijing's governing bodies, essential for coordinating policy between the city and the center. Noting that the Hong Kong civil service, arguably the finest in the world, is far more professional than its Chinese counterpart, Lieberthal wants us to watch for pressures to change it. He wants us to watch for attempts to make it more susceptible to mainland political pressure, more susceptible to *guanxi* (personal relationships). He wants to know what kind of political supervision will be imposed on the city and how Beijing will cope with potential subversion, whether from Taiwan's operatives or from advocates of democracy such as Martin Lee. Lieberthal foresees changes in government institutions, some of which have already been indicated, and – like

6

Feinerman, deLisle, and Lane in particular – he is concerned about the future legal system.

The die is cast. Reversion is fast upon us, and there is little outsiders can do to influence its course. The people of Hong Kong and foreigners with a stake in the city will be dependent upon the wisdom and skill with which Beijing and its representatives manage the takeover. To date, Chinese leaders have shown only limited comprehension of what the continued success of Hong Kong will require, and there is nothing about the way in which they have handled their own affairs to inspire confidence. Nonetheless, virtually all analysts agree that China will try to maintain Hong Kong's role in the international economic system and that the prognosis for the short run is favorable. In the long run, many of the same analysts fear that Beijing will inadvertently strangle the goose that lays the golden egg. On the other hand, the people of Hong Kong, the city's main asset, have demonstrated that they have the ability and the resilience to overcome extraordinary adversity. Their best hope is that they can preserve their system long enough for the Chinese to learn how it works and for the Hong Kong model to prevail in China. In this endeavor, the watchfulness and support of the international community, businesspeople and human rights advocates alike, may prove decisive. The essays in this volume will provide readers with the basis for informed action.

The editors are grateful to the Woodrow Wilson Center for providing federal conference funds for the July 1, 1996, workshop and to Benjamin Self and Kimberley Lays for their assistance at the workshop. They also wish to thank Mary-Lea Cox for her editorial assistance.

1

Hong Kong as an International Commercial Center

PHILIP BOWRING

HONG Kong's most enduring characteristic has been its remarkable ability to re-invent itself. As old flowers start to fade, new buds appear and grow bigger than their predecessors.

The secret of this rejuvenation has always been in the diversity of interests and enterprises that have found a home here. Though Hong Kong remains a small place, it has always been just about big enough and diverse enough to have "critical mass" – that hard-to-define state which acts as a natural magnet for enterprising people and for new ventures which prosper quickly in proximity to older and more established enterprises. Over time, the principal activities change, but there is still an accretion of functions. The older functions shrink in relation to the larger total mass.

Critical mass cannot be taken for granted. Its sustenance is openness to the outside world and competent – but minimalist – government at home. Call it a colony (as was the case and technically still is); a territory (as it currently prefers); a Special Administrative Region, or SAR (which it is soon to become) – the key to Hong Kong's success has been, and will remain, that it is a rather peculiar institution which thrives on the contradictions around it.

Hong Kong has only one natural advantage: its harbor. Effective and magnificent though it may be, this harbor is not a unique attribute on the south China coast. History has proved a much more important advantage. The history began in Macao – 300 years before the British grabbed Hong Kong – with the desire of the emperor in Beijing to keep the barbarian traders confined to a remote and inhospitable part of the empire. This defined the geography of China's links with the West and thus, over the past 150 years, has been the key to China's interaction with successive world leaders, Great Britain, and the

United States. Hong Kong's global orientation has given a new dimension to China. The territory has been the often unwitting intermediary in the dramatic expansion of Chinese communities outside China, particularly in Southeast Asia but also in the western hemisphere.

Hong Kong is not only the historic meeting point of East and West, of China and non-China. It is also where the descendants of the Sons of the Yellow Emperor, who had the courage or desperation to leave China and seek a better life elsewhere, interact with their erstwhile motherland. It has always been easier for the two to meet on this foreign-ruled turf, which, too, remains inalienably Chinese.

The overseas Chinese have always been proud of being Chinese, while seldom finding it easy to be proud of China. The people of Hong Kong face this problem in an acute form as race and national identity are forged into one in 1997, whether they like it or not.

Such non-mainland Chinese, whether compatriots or nationals of other countries, have also played a major role in the post-1945 transformation of East Asia. Indeed, at a time when China itself was still traveling down diverse dead-end routes to modernization, non-mainland Chinese were second only to Japan in contributing to the regional renaissance that was taking place at that time, acting as the key link in commercial development, capital accumulation, and technology transfer, from west to east and north to south. Hong Kong was the main contact point, the dealing room, the "neutral zone" where all varieties of Chinese, and many varieties of foreigners, could feel at home. And so it remains.

Hong Kong's change of political status removes some of that "neutral" quality and indeed confronts the leaders in Beijing with some of the issues which led it in 1557 to lease a tiny patch of Guangdong to some hairy Portuguese. Hong Kong is all about China's relations with the outside world, especially the Western world, and the relations between mainland and overseas Chinese, and among the overseas Chinese themselves.

What has this history meant in practical terms? Essentially it has defined Hong Kong's commercial role, which in turn defines Hong Kong. Here are the strands in modern-day commercial Hong Kong in approximate sequential order.

1. China trade (of which opium was an important, but not a principal, part) might have originally meant, simply, trade as in earlier days when Portuguese, Dutch, and British fought not for control of land but for mastery of Asian trade,

and when the Chinese looked on with puzzlement. By the time the British acquired Hong Kong in 1842, the flag had begun to follow trade, whether in the name of forceful trade promotion, sheer patriotism, or "piracy" prevention. By the turn of the century, the enforced opening of China had brought dramatic trade growth (and real economic growth) to parts of China, with the lion's share of the "treaty port" trade going to Shanghai and Hong Kong via local compradores. However, despite its early start in establishing links to the British empire and to Southeast Asia and overseas Chinese, Hong Kong was overshadowed by "international" Shanghai, on the central coast, at the mouth of the Long River (Yangze), gateway to the heart of China, location of its new industries, and birthplace of modern Chinese capitalism. The scale and grandeur of old Shanghai are still visible: It dwarfed the Hong Kong of the era. Shanghai was truly international, ultramodern, and slick. Hong Kong, by comparison, was small, stuffy, and colonial – but it thrived on southern China trade and links to European-controlled Southeast Asia.

That pattern returned after 1945, when Hong Kong escaped being handed over to the crumbling Kuomintang. Soon after, however, the Chinese Revolution and the Korean War killed much of the entrepot trade. Hong Kong remained a gateway of sorts to Maoist China, but trade was so negligible that new paths to prosperity had to be found.

It was not until Deng Xiaoping came to power in 1978 that Hong Kong began to regain its China entrepot role. At that time, 80 percent of Hong Kong's exports were domestic manufactures, 20 percent reexports. By the early 1990s, those figures had been reversed. Hong Kong had become the intermediary for a China which was moving toward the upper ranks of global traders.

2. Trade is not so much about movement of goods as it is about the organization of the movement of goods. The presence of ships attracts facilities for unloading, providers of victuallers and chandlery, boat repair, warehousing, as well as office-based services such as agency trading, forwarding, banking, ship management, and insurance. Hong Kong moved rapidly up this chain, acquiring what constituted, by the standards of the still relatively uncomplex and slow-moving nineteenth-century world, critical mass as an entrepot – as well as a seat of British naval presence in the Far East. The development of banking led to Hong Kong establishing its own currency, which in turn attracted capital from less stable regions – whether China itself or the Philippines (the latter in the late Spanish period). Hong Kong was not as important to Great Britain (and global trade) as Singapore, but it had critical mass as an entrepot.

3. This commercial infrastructure was the key to Hong Kong's astonishing development as a manufacturing center post-1949. The shipping, banking, and trading firms were already in place to serve the manufacturers fleeing Shanghai with their machinery, know-how, and capital. A flood of refugees, which continued in periodic waves until the mid-1960s, provided an abundant supply of cheap labor and the combination of low expectations and strong ambition typical of migrants. Great Britain and the United States initially provided easy market access, beginning a trend toward relocation of manufacturing away from advanced countries – a trend which also characterizes the modern global economy – and Hong Kong quickly learned new skills in merchandizing, enabling manufacturers to move into new products, such as plastic flowers or toys, which were not capital intensive but required adaptability and quick response time and could exploit a flexible labor force and frequent, reliable shipping services. By the early 1970s, manufacturing constituted nearly 30 percent of Hong Kong's employment.

4. From around 1980, manufacturing went into steep decline as factories moved to lower labor and land costs across the border. However, this was beneficial to the economy as a whole: Higher value-added business stayed in Hong Kong, and foreign – especially U.S. – desire to bring China into the global trading system enabled Hong Kong–based manufacturers and merchandisers to achieve huge increases in total output by using nearby Guangdong as their production base. This reintegration of the Hong Kong and China economies suggested that Hong Kong had become largely dependent on the mainland. However, the trade was Hong Kong–driven and relied on foreign markets. The export performance of Chinese state enterprises has been pitiful compared with that of the foreign- (including Hong Kong and Taiwan) invested enterprises. Hong Kong benefited greatly from the relocation of much Taiwanese manufacturing to the mainland, and from the fact that lack of direct links ensured that physical trade, as well as the organization of the investment, had to be conducted through Hong Kong.

5. A combination of Hong Kong's port, its banking facilities, and a tax regime which taxed only profits "arising in or derived from" the territory also made it an ideal center for ship owners and managers. At one time Hong Kong was the home of two of the largest ship owners in the world: Y. K. Pao and C. Y. Tung. Both were from Ningpo, the port on the Zhejiang coast south of Shanghai. Pao was essentially a banker acting as a tax-efficient intermediary between Japanese shipbuilders, who provided good credit terms to foreign buy-

ers, and Japanese operators (especially in oil tankers), who wanted long-term charters. Tung was a more active ship manager, especially in the container business. Hong Kong was also the regional center for many foreign lines.

Despite the growth in world trade and the rapid expansion of Hong Kong's port output, its relative position in global shipping has waned because of the changing structure of the industry and the huge expansion of Korean, Taiwanese, and Chinese fleets. Hong Kong owners are still significant but are not the force they once were. Despite the rapid growth of China trade, much ship management has also moved elsewhere, particularly to Singapore, for a variety of reasons. However, the presence of the China Ocean Shipping Corporation (COSCO) will ensure that China remains a center for ship management and brokering.

6. Banking develops naturally from trade. With its political stability and its lack of exchange controls, Hong Kong has served as banker to the traders of much of the region. This was particularly the case between 1950 and 1980. The Communist takeover in China, the Korean War, the unsettled conditions in Southeast Asia following decolonization – all enhanced Hong Kong's position as a refuge for money. It also had a relatively stable currency based on a silver standard until the 1930s and a sterling peg until 1970; after an unstable decade of floating, it has had a U.S. dollar peg since 1980.

This existing regional banking role enabled Hong Kong – like Singapore – to capitalize on the dramatic development of international banking which began around 1965 and involved large movements in capital, not merely trade finance. The extension of the Eurodollar market to Asia was spurred by U.S. involvement in Vietnam and, between 1973 and 1983, by the recycling of the petrodollars made necessary by the huge trade account imbalances resulting from the dramatic rise in oil prices during that period.

The development of Hong Kong as an international financial center stalled in the mid-1980s because of a banking crisis induced by the bursting of the territory's real estate bubble, costing foreign banks, and the Hong Kong government, heavily in write-offs and rescues. Those problems were soon followed by the stock market crash of 1987, which closed the Hong Kong stock market for a week and wiped out the Hong Kong Futures Exchange.

The 1980s also saw rapid progress to financial liberalization in many countries, ranging from Great Britain to Thailand. Foreign-exchange restrictions were lifted, and new intermediaries came into being. Vibrant stock markets emerged in Thailand, Taiwan, and Korea; older stock markets, such as that in Malaysia, grew rapidly. "Privatization" became a buzzword. By the beginning of the 1990s, American money managers noticed these developments and began to move into Asia, following in the footsteps of London-based groups which already had a foothold. The Hong Kong was the first choice for Asian regional operations because of its own large and active market, good communications, ease of access to work permits, and the presence of a large pool of English-speaking lawyers, accountants, and other professionals with practices similar to those in the great Anglophone centers of finance: New York and London.

Hong Kong was the distribution point for the wave of foreign portfolio capital that hit Asia in 1992 and 1993, paused a while, then hit again in 1996. A good proportion of that money stayed in Hong Kong. Because the foreign brokers and fund managers were all there, it picked up far more than its fair (relative to the size of its economy) share of portfolio flows – perhaps 35 percent of the total amount flowing into the combined markets of Malaysia, Singapore, Thailand, Korea, Indonesia, Philippines, Taiwan, China, and India.

7. The past decade has seen an increased internationalization of business. Foreign direct investment has grown far more rapidly than trade as brand names have sought global presence and as surplus capital from Japan and Taiwan has moved to lower-income, faster-developing regions of Southeast Asia and China. The biggest recipient has been China itself, followed by three countries with which Hong Kong has close links: Malaysia, Thailand, and Indonesia. The territory has thus expanded its role as a base from which multinational manufacturers and service providers such as credit card issuers, life insurance companies, engineering and management consultancies, fast-food franchisers, and courier services conduct regional operations.

8. Hong Kong has always been a tourist destination in its own right; however, the past decade has seen the very rapid growth of its role in the travel industry. As gateway, it benefited from the opening of China. It benefited from the liberalization of travel and foreign exchange in Korea and Taiwan, from rapid income growth in Southeast Asia, and, most recently, from an influx of mainland tourists. The very rapid growth of air cargo volume helped by the boom in the electronics industry has also benefited Hong Kong – although tardy development of its new airport has stopped it from exploiting its full potential as a regional hub for air traffic of all sorts.

This historical summary of Hong Kong's development as an international center defines the interaction of the different pieces which make up the critical mass. Hong Kong is now so big and important that it cannot be easily undermined. It has been particularly fortunate over the past decade, as reflected in the

Hang Seng (stock market) index, which has risen from 2,000 to 13,000. Indeed, Hong Kong approaches 1997 on a high note. From its tumultuous history, Hong Kong has emerged stronger and wiser because of its openness and adaptability. Over the next few years, the questions confronting Hong Kong are whether the external environment will remain friendly, and whether Hong Kong's openness and adaptability will enable it to survive change under a very different sovereign power which sees it not as London does – as a distant, exotic flower – but as a part of the motherland.

The most important single issue both for foreign business and for the local population is the maintenance of Hong Kong's economic freedom, notably a convertible currency and free movement of capital. A related issue is the Hong Kong currency's peg to the U.S. dollar. Though there is no direct connection between the peg and convertibility, the peg has come to symbolize Hong Kong's stability. Many foreign banks have taken on massive unhedged exposure to the Hong Kong dollar on the assumption that the peg will be maintained. Other banks are "ring fencing" their Hong Kong operations so that, in the event of systemic failure, their head offices will not be liable for the foreign currency liabilities of their Hong Kong branches. This kind of failure is too remote for many to worry about. However, the possibility of a significant premium developing for Hong Kong foreign currency deposits over the London Interbank Offered Rate (LIBOR) cannot be ruled out, and would obviously damage Hong Kong's international role.

At the formal level, two key documents relate to the future of currency, banking, and fiscal issues. The first is the Sino-British Joint Declaration of 1984, which establishes the transfer of sovereignty and the basis for the future of Hong Kong for fifty years after 1997. The second document is the Basic Law for the Hong Kong Special Administrative Region, the Chinese law which builds on the Joint Declaration and will effectively serve as the constitution for post-1997 Hong Kong.

The key passage of the Joint Declaration states: "The Hong Kong Special Administrative Region will retain the status of an international financial center and its markets for foreign exchange, gold, securities and futures will continue. There will be free flow of capital. The Hong Kong dollar will continue to circulate and be freely convertible." An annex to the Joint Declaration provided by China elaborated as follows: "A freely convertible currency and the right to manage the Exchange Fund, which provides backing for the note issue and is used to regulate the exchange value of the currency, are the essential elements of Hong Kong's monetary system." The annex also promised that the Hong

Kong SAR would "determine its own fiscal policy and manage and dispose of its financial resources in accordance with Hong Kong's own needs."

The Basic Law for the future Hong Kong SAR was adopted by China's National Peoples Congress in 1990. Relevant articles are:

Article 109:
The government of the HK SAR shall provide an appropriate economic and legal environment for the maintenance of the status of Hong Kong as an international financial center.

Article 110:
The government of the HK SAR shall, on its own, formulate monetary and financial policies, safeguard the free operation of financial business and financial markets and regulate and supervise them in accordance with law.

Article 111:
The HK dollar, as the legal tender in the HK SAR, shall continue to circulate. The authority to issue HK currency shall be vested in the government of the HK SAR. The issue of HK currency must be backed by a 100 percent reserve fund.

Article 112:
No foreign exchange control policies shall be applied in the HK SAR. The HK dollar shall be freely convertible. Markets for foreign exchange, gold, securities, futures and the like shall continue. The government of the SAR shall safeguard the free flow of capital within, into and out of the Region.

Article 113:
The Exchange Fund of the HK SAR shall be managed and controlled by the government of the Region, primarily for regulating the exchange value of the HK dollar.

The essential goals of the Basic Law and Joint Declaration promises are threefold:

1. Continuation of a separate currency for Hong Kong
2. Currency convertibility and free movement of capital
3. Autonomy in management of currency and Exchange Fund

At no point in either document is there any mention of a currency peg or even hints at desirable exchange-rate policy. The general thrust is maintenance of the status quo, with Hong Kong being given the right to manage its own affairs. Both documents are reassuring to the financial sector.

If there are to be problems in the future, they are likely to reside in implementation or interpretation rather than in the documents themselves. Perhaps the biggest single problem is that China views law rather differently from the way Western societies view it – or at least those societies influenced by Anglo-Saxon-derived traditions. For the Chinese, law is not an immutable undertaking whose literal meaning must be defined and enforced, but a point of departure for bargaining.

A peculiarity of post–June 1997 Hong Kong is that a sovereign part of China will have a currency overtly pegged to the currency of another country and with a variable exchange rate against the national currency. Milton Friedman is among those who have argued that this will simply be impossible to maintain in a country as big as China, with its strong, even prickly, sense of its own identity. Friedman forecast that, within two years of the handover, the Hong Kong dollar will be absorbed by the Yuan and Hong Kong's reserves will be taken over by China. Friedman was making a political or historical judgment, not an economic one. His argument may be extreme, but so, too, may the argument that postulates a Hong Kong dollar pegged to the U.S. currency at 7.80 lasting well into the twenty-first century.

There is nothing in the Joint Declaration or Basic Law, however, that requires the Hong Kong dollar to be pegged to the U.S. dollar or any other currency. Both documents promise that Hong Kong will have its own currency, and that it will be convertible. That promise does not rule out the possibility that in future the Hong Kong dollar will be pegged to the Yuan. It could be argued that Scots have their own currency because their commercial banks issue Scottish pound notes, which, coincidentally, are the same as those issued by the Bank of England. A similar situation could occur in Hong Kong, where three commercial banks issue Hong Kong currency notes.

Convertibility, however, is the key. Hong Kong as an international commercial center could not exist in anything like its present form without a convertible currency. Any suggestion of an end to convertibility would create financial panic. Technically, it is possible to imagine a situation in which foreign currency–based operations in Hong Kong remained free while domestic, Hong Kong dollar–based operations did not. Singapore, for instance, while always keeping a convertible currency, has, for monetary control purposes, endeavored to limit foreign access to Singapore dollars. Hong Kong would be coming from a different direction, however.

It is possible that at some point the Hong Kong currency will be pegged to the Yuan, but will remain convertible and capital can still be moved freely. There is, of course, the possibility that the Yuan itself will become freely convertible, which is the government's goal. However, it seems unlikely that China will go so far as to abolish all controls on capital flows. If this does happen, the Hong Kong dollar will be marginalized.

In theory it is possible to imagine two convertible currencies existing side by side, with the exchange-rate movements reflecting different economic conditions and goals. For instance, since the 1973 separation of the Malaysian and Singapore currencies, both have gone their own ways gradually while remaining freely exchangeable. However, the expectation in Hong Kong is that the current peg to the U.S. dollar, which has survived for twelve years, will be maintained well into the twenty-first century.

The history of Hong Kong's currency shows that international financial events, the politics of the relationship with China, and local monetary and banking management have all played roles in changing the currency's basis and value. There is also a clear link between monetary developments and the asset bubbles (and busts) that Hong Kong has experienced.

Both at the time the 7.80 peg was established and subsequently, suggestions were made that the peg should have been, or should have been changed to, a basket of currencies or special drawing rights (SDR). However, it was counterargued that the dollar peg was more easily understood by the public, and therefore more easily administered. As the years went by, the authorities became more and more wedded to the importance not only of a peg, but also of the 7.80 level.

The theory of the peg – or "link," as the authorities prefer to call it – is simple enough. The note issue is backed by foreign currency deposited by the three note-issuing banks with the Exchange Fund. Thus, if the actual rate in the marketplace deviates significantly from 7.80, any bank (but not an individual) will be able to make a profit by going to the Exchange Fund and demanding foreign currency in return for its Hong Kong dollar notes, or vice versa. This process will have the effect of expanding or contracting the monetary base. Thus if the pressure on the Hong Kong currency is downward, the money supply will shrink, and interest rates will rise to the point where exchange-rate equilibrium is reestablished.

In practice, things work somewhat differently: Interest rates respond automatically to the supply-and-demand situation in the market regardless of the cumbersome question of note issue. However, in extremis, the theoretical process does become important. While holders of Hong Kong dollars may be comforted by the fact that the current note issue is fully backed by foreign currency, the fact remains that the note issue represents only 5 percent of Hong Kong dollar money supply.

Therefore, any wholesale flight from the Hong Kong dollar has to be met by a combination of interest rates and intervention. Longer-term, it means that economic policy validates the 7.80 level.

A case might be made that the Hong Kong dollar is now overvalued as a result of several years of high inflation and, more recently, the recovery of the U.S. dollar against the yen. However, it would be hard to argue that the exchange rate is so out of line as to precipitate a run on the currency. Nor is there any reason to believe that the economy cannot adjust downward.

If there are to be problems, they lie with the capital account, which is primarily a function of political sentiment, and with asset values. Capital outflow could come in several forms: sales of assets by residents uncertain of the future and anxious to cash in on the gains of the past few years; a precautionary shift of financial assets from Hong Kong dollars to other currencies; an exodus of private mainland capital to less accessible locations.

Capital outflow in itself should not in theory lead to a rise in interest rates. So long as the interbank market believes that the peg will be maintained, U.S. dollars will flow in to replace those leaving. However, some additional interest premium could be expected to develop. Indeed, it is perhaps curious that while the Hong Kong premium over one year is only 50 to 60 basis points, the premium for the Thai baht, which has a better history of stability than the Hong Kong dollar and no fundamental political problems, is around 350 basis points.

Hong Kong's equilibrium owes something to good management by the Hong Kong Monetary Authority (HKMA). When the peg was introduced, the government had only the crudest weapons of intervention in the money market. Now, however, through the liquidity adjustment facility and open market operations in the bills and notes that it issues, the HKMA has been able to maintain stable rates. It has created a well-padded buffer between the money market – still largely convinced of the stability of the peg, and of Hong Kong in general – and the wider world, where doubts about the future are more widespread.

In the final analysis, only a combination of two forces – interest rates and intervention – can guard the Hong Kong dollar against a run. The HKMA has expressed confidence in its ability to deter speculators, such as those who made a small foray against the currency in the wake of the Mexico crisis. As a result of meetings initiated by the HKMA following that episode, regional central

banks have agreed among themselves on a plan for joint action against speculators. China has also indicated its readiness to defend the peg. Hong Kong's
more serious problem lies not so much with the speculator battalions as with its
own population of small savers who can so easily move their money if their
confidence either in the currency, specifically, or in Hong Kong, generally, is
undermined.

So much political capital has been invested by the Hong Kong authorities in
maintaining the peg at 7.80 that no one should doubt the lengths to which they
may go to defend it. Under normal circumstances, probably some intervention
and an increase in interest rates would be sufficient. However, a prolonged period of high interest rates could place intolerable strains on parts of the banking
system as a result of its exposure to interest-rate-sensitive property loans.
While the global outlook is for continuation of low inflation and interest for the
foreseeable future, potential vulnerability to exogenous shocks must be considered.

Almost all Hong Kong's most influential businessmen are property developers in whole or part. They have prospered not only because of Hong Kong's natural land shortage but also because of their relationships with leading banks
and the low real costs of money. In any currency crisis there comes a point
where governments must decide which is more important: a strong currency, or
the damage done in defending it.

Before Hong Kong reaches that turning point, however, it does have a formidable ability to intervene with cash rather than simply interest rates. At the
end of 1995, the HKMA had foreign currency reserves of some US$65 billion.
In addition to backing for the note issue, this consisted partly of fiscal reserves
of the Hong Kong government and partly of the HKMA's own accumulated
profits.

Massive use of reserves to defend the Hong Kong dollar will likely be effective so long as this action does not cause the people of Hong Kong to lose confidence in their currency. The Hong Kong dollar is not so widely held as to be
vulnerable to foreign flight. In short, Hong Kong's foreign-exchange reserves
make a very strong line of defense. The interest rate defense, however, is much
less certain and could expose the wider economic consequences of Hong
Kong's high-priced assets.

Also uncertain is the extent to which China is prepared to allow Hong Kong's
foreign-exchange reserves to be spent in defending a peg to the U.S. dollar.
Although reserve management is officially none of China's business, in practice China's perceived national interest is unlikely to be sacrificed to Hong

19

Kong's perceived interests. For the time being, defense of the status quo of the Hong Kong dollar would appear to be in China's larger national interest. However, the future is less certain.

In the past, one banker close to China, David Li of the Bank of East Asia, publicly criticized the peg and suggested shifting from the U.S. dollar to a basket of currencies. A shift to a basket remains a theoretical possibility. If undertaken a few years ago, this shift might have given Hong Kong a peg that reflected its trade position but was not as politically sensitive as the U.S. dollar. It is now probably too late to make such a change without sparking instability. If change does come, it is now likely to consist of abandoning 7.80 and moving to a floating rate or to a peg to the Yuan. In the past, the anchorless floating rate proved destabilizing. Now, however, a floating rate in the context of monetary goals is probably possible, given the development of the HKMA. A peg to the Yuan would have seemed impossible only three years ago; however, China's achievement of currency stability since the major devaluation in January 1995, along with its abolition of a two-tier exchange system for the Yuan, makes a direct relationship between the Hong Kong dollar and the Yuan more feasible for the medium term.

For the short term, there is little doubt that China is content with the status quo of the Hong Kong dollar and will want to maintain it through the handover and immediately afterward. China's ultimate goals remain unclear, however. Its reaction to a Hong Kong currency crisis would also be hard to predict. China has said it would help defend the Hong Kong currency against speculative attack, and now it has huge foreign-exchange reserves of its own to add to those of the HKMA to mount a defense. However, any threats to the peg are far more likely to stem from political events in China than from economic events in Hong Kong. So many other aspects of Hong Kong are attached to its currency and banking systems that it is difficult to visualize the territory were there to be a major change. Almost all aspects of commercial life would be affected, though not fatally.

Although Hong Kong's role as a center for China trade is closely tied to its banking system, the city's physical attributes are just as important. In relative terms, Hong Kong's economic growth seems destined to decline, but absolute growth should continue. The time is now long gone when China deliberately kept foreigners and their trade concentrated in the remote south. The time has also passed when Guangdong was the growth center for all China, attracting most of the investment by Hong Kong and Taiwan firms in light export industry. Now the focus of trade and investment growth has shifted to the central and northern coasts: to Shanghai, Shandong, and Dalian. Port developments are attracting industries, and cargo volumes are attracting shipping services to such locations. Guangdong's economy is now growing no faster than the national average.

Assuming that China's total trade continues to grow at 8 to 10 percent per year, some growth for Hong Kong itself can still be expected. Such an overall rate of trade growth would be much lower than that in the recent past. However, China's foreign trade is now so big that henceforward, it will probably expand only a little faster than global trade, which has been growing at 6 to 8 percent per year.

Some shadows exist in Hong Kong's economic future. One is the likelihood of direct trade, sooner or later, between the mainland and Taiwan. This would not only reduce Hong Kong's role as an intermediary in trade between those two parties but also enable Kaohsiung to compete directly with Hong Kong for transshipment business. This southern Taiwanese port once had a bigger output than Hong Kong, a status it lost because of lack of direct trade with a booming China. Kaohsiung is geographically superbly positioned. Subic Bay in the Philippines is also developing as a lesser transshipment hub.

The future of port development in Hong Kong is also uncertain. Although there are plans for several new container terminals, some argue that land and labor costs are too high, and the environment too crowded and polluted, to make Hong Kong suitable for such a low value-added industry. It is possible that future port development will be concentrated in nearby locations outside the territory. For instance, Yantian, to the northeast of the territory, is close enough to be accessible.

Despite these obstacles to increasing its physical trade output, Hong Kong should remain the place from which trade and much export manufacturing from southern and central China is organized. In time, Shanghai may compete for some of this business, but the quality of Hong Kong's infrastructure and service industries will ensure that neither the south China coast nor Taiwan can rival Hong Kong as a base for conducting China trade. Hong Kong is not simply a physical conduit: The majority of southern China's manufactured exports are produced by outward processing industries organized from Hong Kong by Hong Kong–based buyers and merchandisers, both local and foreign.

China does not earn foreign currency directly from Hong Kong to the degree that it once did. As China's foreign trade has bloomed, Hong Kong's relative importance has declined. Hong Kong is a place *through* which rather than *from* which China earns foreign exchange. Hong Kong is also now more of a conduit for foreign investment than a source. Hong Kong money's relative importance has declined as foreign investors have arrived in droves from elsewhere. However, the city remains the pivot point for a very large part of China's overall trade, and that position will decline only gradually.

Still less certain is Hong Kong's position as a base for foreign companies with China operations. In the past, because of its ease of access, commercial infrastructure, and quality of life, Hong Kong has been the base for many – perhaps the majority – of foreign companies investing in, or selling goods to, China. Although some form of presence in Beijing has in many cases been necessary for liaison with ministries, and a presence in Shanghai has been important for organizing sales or joint ventures, most foreign companies prefer to be based in Hong Kong, if possible – particularly companies that can run their other Asian operations from there, too.

Recently, however, foreign companies have been making greater efforts to develop networks in China and to set up joint ventures with state-owned enterprises, with the result that many of these companies now feel the need to expand their presence in Shanghai or Beijing. In the case of Shanghai, rapid improvement in living conditions for foreigners, development of quality offices and apartments, and the creation of international schools and a service network which makes foreigners feel at home have all enhanced the city's attractiveness as a place for foreigners to be based. Tax incentives to move to Pudong are an additional factor. In time, development of Shanghai's new airport and other infrastructure such as an underground railway will add to its attractions. Shanghai makes no secret of its determination to become once again – as it was before the Japanese invasion – the leading commercial city of China and the focus of its foreign trade. It is on the way to achieving critical mass as a commercial center that can compete with Hong Kong. Shanghai has few of the nationalistic hang-ups found elsewhere in China, and is proud of its past. Huge numbers have been learning English as a step toward their own, and the city's, advancement. In addition, the overbuilding of offices and luxury apartments will create price competition with Hong Kong for years to come so that, even if headquarters stay in Hong Kong, many firms will opt to transfer some of their office work to Shanghai.

As a regional operations center, Hong Kong has always faced competition from Singapore. Over the years, companies have moved back and forth between the two cities, depending on cost levels, tax issues, and whether the main focus of business is Northeast Asia or Southeast Asia. While Singapore has offered specific tax concessions for regional operations, Hong Kong has maintained a lower base rate (the same for all industries and activities); also, its personal tax code is less complex than Singapore's. In recent years, huge increases in office and rental costs have been to Hong Kong's disadvantage, although these increases were partly offset by the strength of the Singapore dollar against the U.S.-linked Hong Kong currency.

Competition from other centers is increasing, however. Bangkok may have appalling infrastructure problems, but it offers a central location and relative ease of access for foreigners. Tokyo's once prohibitive costs have declined relatively, with the slump first in property prices and now the yen. Sydney is far away but inexpensive and hospitable. The Philippines' recovery has progressed sufficiently to make it an option for manufacturers requiring low-cost, English-speaking workers. Kuala Lumpur is bidding for a few services, and the quality of life there is favorable for expatriates. Taiwan is attempting to develop itself as a regional operations center; however, these efforts are unlikely to succeed without direct links to the mainland and before liberalization of banking and financial services progresses much further. Lack of English language skills is another drawback. However, Taiwan has other drawing points: workers with industrial skills, geographical location, a strong currency, and an already huge role in global shipping.

Hong Kong faces multiple challenges. Its biggest challenge may be to retain its own openness and accessibility. For example, its freedom of the press and lack of politically driven constraints on social behavior have given it an advantage over Singapore. Official corruption may be more prevalent than in Singapore, but it is less pervasive than elsewhere in the region. The colonial regime has, by nature, also been instinctively responsive to the perceived needs of foreigners. In particular, foreigners have always found it easy to obtain work permits (Britons do not need them at all). A local or self-consciously Chinese administration may want to change that. A crackdown on easy access for foreigners to jobs in Hong Kong would be understandable but not necessarily to Hong Kong's advantage. As of now, even those foreigners who hold Hong Kong permanent identity cards, which give them right of abode, do not know whether they will retain their right to work.

Another potential threat to Hong Kong comes from the opposite direction. Most foreign countries have yet to agree to provide visa-free access to holders of People's Republic of China passports issued by the Hong Kong SAR government. Although many people in Hong Kong will continue to hold British travel documents after the handover, Hong Kong's ability to act as a regional center will be impaired if most of its citizens need visas to travel to most foreign destinations. At present, only Great Britain, Singapore, and Western Samoa have agreed to grant visa-free access to those holding SAR passports.

A number of political controversies arising from the change of sovereignty will have an impact on Hong Kong's role as both a regional and international center. From an employment perspective, the most sensitive area involves professionals – specifically, lawyers. The current dominant use of the English language in the courts is viewed as vital in the civil courts with which foreign business is concerned. A large number of foreign lawyers operate in Hong Kong, primarily but not exclusively serving international businesses – corporations which, in turn, are prepared to use Hong Kong courts for some of their litigation purposes. Arbitration is also active. Any rapidly enforced localization of the legal profession which would limit choice would affect not only Hong Kong's role as a legal center but, ultimately, its attraction to international business. The same controversy applies – though less critically – to other professionals such as accountants and physicians. Though the number of highly competent local professionals is huge – and more may come from China after 1997 – freedom of foreign access is important to other foreigners such as bankers and fund managers.

Hong Kong's current position as the region's premier international financial center is undoubted. Singapore does more foreign-exchange trading than Hong Kong, but lags far behind in number of foreign institutions, offshore lending, and regional corporate finance. Hong Kong surpasses Singapore because it is able to combine a wide range of services with a large trade finance base, proximity to China, and a light regulatory touch. The Hong Kong–U.S. dollar peg has also been of benefit by encouraging foreign banks with negligible Hong Kong dollar deposit bases to become active players in the local market.

Threats to this position are mainly theoretical at present. However, over the longer term they include the development of Shanghai as an intermediary for capital flows into China. If foreign banks were to have the ability to make Yuan-denominated loans, they might be tempted to move their international China business to Shanghai at Hong Kong's expense. Full convertibility of the Yuan would also help Shanghai and make the Hong Kong dollar increasingly irrelevant, whether or not the U.S.-dollar peg were maintained.

Competition for other financial services is close at hand. Hong Kong is far in the lead when it comes to fund management in Asia. Some US$80 billion is currently managed out of Hong Kong, along with large sums from British- and

American-based institutions which use Hong Kong–based international brokers to conduct regional securities trading. Fund managers and brokers are attracted to Hong Kong because of its cordial Anglo-Saxon atmosphere, because of the range of English-language services available, and especially because they can operate on a level playing field in the stock and futures markets rather than having to enter joint ventures or share commissions with local brokers. The dollar peg has helped, too, tying Hong Kong to U.S. interest rates and leading many fund managers to regard Hong Kong as a proxy for Wall Street. Foreign institutions now account for approximately two-thirds of turnover in Hong Kong–listed stocks and are even more dominant in the futures and warrants markets.

The huge foreign portfolio presence in Hong Kong's stock market has been a major benefit. The large inflow over the past three years has helped the Hang Seng index to combat nervousness concerning both the events of 1997 and the extremely high property prices, which, via property companies and banks, are key to the stock market.

However, there could well be potential problems. The market has grown very large relative to the size of the economy – market capitalization is some US$400 billion, while gross domestic product (GDP) is approximately US$150 billion. This ratio is about the highest in the world. The market could be in serious trouble if the foreigners who have pumped it up lose faith.

However uncertain Hong Kong's future may be, it has established itself as a present-day success in several areas. Because of its openness and liquidity, and the presence of foreign brokers and fund managers, Hong Kong has succeeded in attracting roughly one-third of the portfolio capital flowing into Asia, excluding Japan, and has been the conduit for another third. Hong Kong has also proved to be the most successful place for Chinese firms to raise foreign capital. Listings of mainland companies have not been a great success anywhere. However, the track record of the Hong Kong–listed "H shares" has exceeded that of both the B shares (reserved for foreigners) traded in Shanghai and Shenzhen, and mainland listings in New York and elsewhere.

Although Hong Kong has proved its worth to China as a capital market, other markets threaten to usurp its position. In the long term, Shanghai, which has an active A (domestic) share market, will make a stronger pitch for foreign business. Some of the fund management business now in Hong Kong may be tempted to move elsewhere. Singapore, in particular, is using the prospect of managing a small part of its huge household savings pool as a carrot for fund managers, along with tax incentives. Malaysia is doing the same. In future, fund management may become more decentralized as managers increase weightings in larger economies with hitherto less open markets such as Korea.

Hong Kong, neverthless, remains important as a safe haven for flight capital from Southeast Asia, as it has always been, as well as – once again – from China. However, this function has probably diminished over the years as political stability has improved and the regional rich have become more confident in currencies such as the Thai baht. Alternative havens for money have become easier to access. In particular, holders of ill-gotten mainland money may eventually decide that a Swiss bank account is safer than one located in Hong Kong. However, Hong Kong's banks, currency, supervisory system, and political stability continue to give the territory an edge over most countries in the region (with the obvious exception of Singapore).

Another important industry in Hong Kong is more directly threatened: the media, which encompasses advertising, television, book publishing, news agencies, trade magazines, and newspapers. Most of this material is apolitical. Nonetheless, linkages do exist between the politics and the media – whether editorial or commercial. Foreign media located in Hong Kong will not be able to ignore China (or Taiwan, for that matter). Singapore may be able to subdue the foreign media with sticks, carrots, and its relative insignificance as a news source. However, China, and its relations with its neighbors and the West, must be covered.

Although in theory media freedom is guaranteed by the Joint Declaration and Basic Law, Chinese officials have indicated that it will be subject to as yet undefined laws which could make it very difficult to publish discussion of important issues of international concern – such as the status of Taiwan, Diaoyu, Tibet, and the Spratlys – or to question the legitimacy of communist rule. It is expected (though not confirmed) that foreign media will be the province not of the Hong Kong authorities but of the Foreign Ministry, requiring accreditation as well as work permits. Hong Kong–based regional media may be treated differently but may be subject to severe constraints on the way they report regional as well as local and Chinese issues. Reporting for foreign media is one thing; reporting for China-based media is quite another.

The year 1997 itself is currently a news attraction for foreign media, and Hong Kong remains the preferred base for regional media operations – despite lack of satellite transmission for television owing to Beijing's opposition. However, in time it seems likely that many news organizations will move at least some of their activities to more liberal locations, and that advertising, printing, and related services will move in their wake. For China, this would be a small commercial price to pay for keeping the threat of liberal and unpatriotic viruses to a minimum.

The prospects for the tourism and air transport industries in Hong Kong are rather brighter. It is hard to predict whether the change in sovereignty will have a significant impact on Hong Kong's attraction as a tourist destination for foreigners after 1997 itself, which will likely be a landmark year for foreign visitors. Tourism into China using Hong Kong as a gateway should keep growing. A rise in the number of visitors to the mainland is also expected, based on the assumption that controls will be less tight. However, such an increase could be offset by a decline in the number of wealthy Taiwanese visitors if direct transport links between Taiwan and the mainland follow the handover.

The opening of the new airport in 1998 will greatly improve airline access to Hong Kong. Foreign airlines have long complained that landing slot limits at the existing Kai Tak Airport have been used by Hong Kong's airline, Cathay Pacific, to limit competition. More capacity and pressure from foreign governments for Fifth Freedom rights should help improve access. It is possible, too, that mainland carriers will be able to fly through Hong Kong (which will then be a domestic destination) to foreign cities. Air service agreements with many countries have already been signed, straddling 1997. However, because such agreements fall under the authority of the sovereign power, it remains to be seen how Beijing will honor them in the future.

The outlook for Hong Kong as a regional airport hub is, however, very positive. The new Chek Lap Kok Airport will begin operation at a time when most airports in the region are overcrowded. Looking beyond 2000, the prospects are less certain. Hong Kong will be the first of the new generation, but plenty of international hub competition lies ahead. Shanghai, Seoul, Bangkok, and Kuala Lumpur all have huge new airport projects which are moving off the drawing board into the construction stage. Domestic China routes will also face competition from smaller airports, with lower landing fees, in Macao, Shenzhen, and Guangzhou.

Hong Kong's attraction as a low-tax location is unlikely to change. The maximum rate of direct tax on profits and incomes is 15 percent, which applies only to profits earned in, or derived from, the territory. This means that wholly offshore income is not taxed, and the low rate is attractive to firms which need to pay tax somewhere and therefore may route profits through Hong Kong. It is possible that after 1997, Chinese authorities will take a firmer line against mainland companies intermediating through Hong Kong to enjoy the lower tax rate. In the past, Hong Kong has avoided double taxation treaties with other countries, but the mainland may become a special case.

In the medium term, Hong Kong is likely to be shielded from the need to increase tax rates. When the handover occurs, the government will no longer have to pay – as has been the case since the Joint Declaration – 50 percent of its land sales revenue into the SAR Land Fund, a reserve fund which the new government will inherit. Payments into the Land Fund are now running at US$30 billion a year. Also, government infrastructure spending is likely to plateau as projects related to the new airport are completed. However, Hong Kong does have some concerns that the SAR Land Fund and perhaps some of its fiscal reserves will be used for "patriotic" purposes such as financing low-yield projects in the poorer provinces of central and western China. There are numerous ways to tax Hong Kong effectively without imposing specific taxes.

Similarly, commercial practices in the territory can be altered to benefit mainland firms. The parent companies of Cathay Pacific (Swire Group) and HK Telecom (Cable and Wireless) have seen how Beijing ministries have used their political clout to the disadvantage of existing owners. These examples may prove exceptional: both are in franchised industries subject to international and domestic regulation, and both are British-dominated. However, it is reasonable to expect mainland firms – particularly those which are direct offshoots of central ministries – to try to use their muscle for commercial advantage. For example, there are many who wonder whether the British-based Hong Kong Bank group, which controls the Hang Seng as well as Hong Kong and Shanghai Bank, will be allowed to remain the premier banking institution in the territory after 1997. It was once the leading bank in Singapore and Malaysia, but after independence, its growth was curtailed in order to make way for locally owned banks. Mainland firms may also want a bigger stake in property development; the current entry cost into this cartelized business is far too high. It remains to be seen whether the Hong Kong SAR government will be able to protect existing commercial interests from mainland intrusion, and whether Beijing's representatives in the SAR will be able to keep the ambitions of central ministries and corporations under control.

Economically, through trade and investment as well as language, Hong Kong is closely integrated with Guangdong, but politically it will remain separate. China has assured that power linkages will be direct between Hong Kong and the highest administrative levels in China. The Chief Executive of the SAR is unlikely to have much independence. The chosen first incumbent, shipping magnate Tung Chee-hwa, has strong connections abroad; however, he has no political or government administrative experience. Also, prior to being anointed as the front-running candidate, he was little known in Hong Kong – he is from Shanghai, and most of his business is offshore. Beijing clearly trusts him, but he will have three powerful central representatives looking over his shoulder: the head of the Foreign Ministry office in Hong Kong – a vice-minister; the head of the People's Liberation Army – a lieutenant general; and the local head of the Communist Party – currently, Zhou Nan, soon-to-retire local head of Xinhua.

This direct Hong Kong–Beijing political link may work for or against Hong Kong, depending on the unpredictable evolution of politics at the center. On the one hand, this link will make it very difficult for Hong Kong to go its own way and may indeed mean that Beijing watches such "undesirable" features as media freedom almost as closely as it would watch the media in Guangzhou. At some point, the link might also mean pressure for Hong Kong to "invest" significant parts of its reserves in huge, long-gestation national projects such as the Three Gorges Dam. Hong Kong may be hard pressed to avoid cash calls issued in the name of patriotism. There is a very narrow line between forced saving and taxation, between patriotic contributions and forced investment.

On the other hand, the direct Beijing link should help preserve Hong Kong's separate existence. Hong Kong could maintain a sufficient barrier between itself and the Shenzhen special economic zone (SEZ) and Guangdong Province to prevent it from being flooded with migrants. Beijing may also wish to protect Hong Kong from being obviously tarnished by the crime that plagues Guangdong – not only for practical purposes, but also to maintain appearances.

China indubitably wants to make Hong Kong work. The risks to Hong Kong are twofold: First, political change in China toward either a more leftist or a more nationalist regime could mean that foreign relations will become less of a priority. Indeed, fanning the flames of anti-foreign sentiment has been a recurring theme of Chinese politics off and on for the past 150 years, surfacing in the Diaoyu saga and the popular anti-American book *China Can Say No*.

The second risk to Hong Kong is that Beijing does not properly understand the interconnections and the ethos that make Hong Kong work as an international city. Hong Kong typically presents itself to outsiders as the triumph of unfettered market economy capitalism in an apolitical environment. That is easy enough for Beijing to understand. Yet Hong Kong's domestic politics – whatever may have been promised in the Joint Declaration about freedom and representative government – can be claimed to be irrelevant.

Beijing needs to understand, and shape policy to ensure that the interconnections do not break down. It needs to ensure that standards for a multitude of professions – from accountancy to medicine – are maintained and not diluted by nationalist demands that mediocre mainland qualifications apply to Hong Kong. It needs to ensure that the legal system – imperfect though it may be – is not influenced by Chinese practices, and that the arbitrariness of the mainland justice system is not imported. It needs to ensure ease of entry for foreigners, trust in banking secrecy, and a civil service based on meritocracy, not *guanxi* (personal connections) or freedom of access to information. Individually, these policies are not critical; collectively, however, they form a critical mass.

Hong Kong is a reminder that city-states and trading and international cities can be immensely successful. However, they are highly vulnerable to political upheavals which have no direct connection with them. They can be sunk by storms that larger states can easily weather. Examples include Beirut, Trieste, Tangier, and especially pre-Communist (and pre-Japanese) Shanghai, described even in the late 1940s as "Queen of the Pacific" but also as an "unreal, fantastic creation." Hong Kong, for all its success, remains "a peculiar institution."

Hong Kong is now too important to international capitalists and to Chinese Communists to be allowed to fail abruptly. Its best fate is to remain as it is, except for a change of flag. This is its own vision of the future. Its worst fate is to become simply another big city on the China coast – to become "Guangzhou-on-the-sea." Either fate depends upon whether Beijing allows it to maintain its international critical mass – to compete successfully with Tokyo, New York, and London – or whether Beijing decides that reintegration into the rest of China is the goal once the formal change of sovereignty has occurred.

2

Cooking the Rice without Cooking the Goose

The Rule of Law, the Battle over Business, and the Quest for Prosperity in Hong Kong after 1997

JACQUES DELISLE AND KEVIN P. LANE[1]

IN the long and contentious process of crafting arrangements for Hong Kong's return to Chinese rule, there has been a consensus on the importance of preserving Hong Kong's prosperity and the distinctly capitalist system that has produced it. All the major players – the People's Republic of China (PRC), the United Kingdom, the colonial government, and Hong Kong groups ranging from PRC surrogates to business interests to democracy activists – have agreed that the transition from British colony to Chinese Special Administrative Region (SAR) must not, in the popular phrase, "kill the goose that lays the golden eggs." They have also unanimously declared that preserving prosperity requires maintaining the "rule of law" in the territory after July 1, 1997.

Beneath this common ground, however, lie serious fault lines. Participants in the wrangling over the territory's future order have differed fundamentally over what the "rule of law" means, how it is linked to prosperity, and what maintaining it will require. How uncompromising and substantively broad must legality be in order to secure the territory's material success? Is narrowly economic legality possible without a rule of law that extends to more "political" matters? What mix of SAR autonomy and continuity with the past colonial order will provide for a rule of law that will sustain Hong Kong's prosperity?

The answers to these questions from Beijing, London, and Hong Kong suggest three paradigms of a "rule of law" for the territory. Loosely captured by the labels "China," "Singapore," and "Augmented Hong Kong," these models range along a continuum. At one end is an economic legal order that is over-

[1] The authors thank the University of Pennsylvania Research Foundation for financial support and Beatrice Mohini Schaffrath for research assistance.

shadowed by extralegal and illegal norms, lacking a grounding in autonomous or accountable Hong Kong institutions; at the other end is a system that is much more robust in practice, sweepingly political and economic in focus, and rooted in reliably independent judicial institutions and substantially democratized governmental ones.

The conflict over which of these models can, should, or must be established in post-1997 Hong Kong has been waged primarily between two coherent yet internally diverse (and sometimes discordant) political camps that have engaged in a larger clash over the nature and basis of governmental and legal authority for the territory. One camp includes Chinese authorities and Hong Kong's most ardently pro-PRC forces; the other consists of London, the Hong Kong government, and liberal and pro-democracy elements in Hong Kong. Their conflict over the rule of law has accorded a central position to a fractious collection of business elites who have stood primarily on the sidelines or in the shadows of the broader political battle.

It is not surprising that leaders of Hong Kong's local and foreign business communities have emerged as key objects of prediction, persuasion, and pandering in the debate over an acceptable and adequate "rule of law" for the territory. Their actions will do much to determine whether economic prosperity proves compatible with any "rule of law" arrangement that results from the political tussles over the Joint Declaration, the Basic Law, and a host of transitional issues. Yet, most of these vital elites have preferred to stay out of the immediate fray, relying instead on low-profile mechanisms to ensure that their concerns are accommodated. Avoiding any unequivocal casting of their lots in an era of uncertainty, they have come to occupy a curious position in transitional Hong Kong – their impact potentially determinative, yet not clearly determined.

Thus, especially in the final years before 1997, the political battle over the rule of law has centered on what notion of legality Hong Kong's principal business communities do, should, or must believe is adequate to maintain prosperity. As all sides recognize, a political victory by proponents of any model of legality will be economically pyrrhic if the business community cannot accept the result.

The link between the debate over the rule of law and a broader and more fundamental political conflict about Hong Kong's future is perhaps less obvious. This more sweeping clash is framed by two conflicting conceptions of sovereignty at the international and domestic levels that have collided repeatedly throughout the process of establishing the framework for Hong Kong's return to China and its operation as an SAR. That conflict has defined the environment in which political struggles over the rule of law occur, and in which Hong Kong's business leaders must assess what kind of legality they want or need. It centers on questions that are, from the perspectives of the principal political players, even more critical than prosperity.

Lu Ping, director of the Chinese State Council's Hong Kong and Macau Affairs Office, and Chinese Vice-Premier Qian Qichen have provided a colorful metaphor that suggests the primacy of non-economic concerns. Referring to the irrevocability of a decision to dissolve Hong Kong's last colonial legislature, but evoking the sense that some legal and institutional questions are non-negotiable, they have said that "the rice is cooked."

In the quest for a formula to preserve the rule of law, Hong Kong's business communities therefore find themselves at the center of a struggle that is only partly about prosperity. At the same time, Hong Kong's once and future rulers and its emergent politicians are engaged in a political clash that is necessarily partly a battle over Hong Kong's business communities. For all parties, the question is whether the outcome will be a rule of law regime that is politically acceptable and economically adequate: Can they manage to "cook the rice" without "cooking the goose"?

THE RULE OF LAW: THREE MODELS AND THE BASIC DEBATE

Assuring Hong Kong's stability and prosperity has been the touchstone of Sino-British negotiations over the territory since they began in 1982. It was the only explicitly agreed-upon condition of the talks on Hong Kong's future that led to the 1984 Sino-British Joint Declaration. Up to the eve of the transition, these goals have remained preeminent, restated like a mantra at every opportunity. Both sides have repeatedly invoked the demands of stability and prosperity in criticizing and justifying proposed arrangements for Hong Kong's future – ranging from Governor Chris Patten's proposals to expand the electorate, to issues surrounding the creation of a Court of Final Appeal, to questions of government spending commitments straddling 1997, to matters of emigration.

The principal legal documents addressing Hong Kong's transition – the Joint Declaration and the Basic Law of the Hong Kong SAR – set forth a framework for pursuing the shared goals of stability and prosperity. They provide that Hong Kong's capitalist economic system and common law legal system will remain unchanged for fifty years and that the SAR will enjoy a "high degree" of legal and political autonomy, including authority to enact its own laws, adjudicate its own cases, and conclude its own international economic agreements. Taken together, such provisions appear to reflect a welcome understanding by Beijing that maintaining the vitality of Hong Kong's economy and the confidence of key business sectors requires a judicious mix of assuring continuity in Hong Kong's established non-socialist ways, a substantial degree of flexibility, and a commitment to the rule of law. But this shared framework masks divergent notions of what kind of rule of law can maintain Hong Kong's prosperity and satisfy the demands of sovereignty that opposing sides have articulated.

Participants in the dispute over Hong Kong's future have pointed to (if not always articulated) three distinct models of a rule of law for a prosperous, capitalist Hong Kong. The models vary in the importance attached to a robust "rule of law" of any scope, the perceived tightness of the link between the rule of law in the "economic" and "political" spheres, and the sense of what degrees and dimensions of continuity and autonomy are necessary in the transition from colony to SAR.

China Model

The first model posits a quite weak form of legality. It concedes that a rule of law framework for structuring voluntary, market-oriented activity requires some fairly substantial and sophisticated laws, some capacity to adapt those laws to changing circumstances, and some mechanisms for making the norms embodied in laws relevant in practice. Absent these qualities, a nominal legal order will fail to provide economic actors with adequate security of expectations, to facilitate their predictions about others' economic behavior, and generally to reduce the transaction costs they face below potentially prohibitive levels. A prosperity-sustaining rule of law requires no less. This model is severely limited in its scope and modest in its demands, however. A legal order for Hong Kong that is acceptable under this model could have major substantive gaps and uneven implementation, fail to guarantee civil liberties or democratic political participation, and accord SAR institutions little in the way of meaningful, reliable autonomy.

This is, roughly, a "China Model." Its main referents are the booming areas of the reform-era PRC, where the economy has thrived despite a limited vision, and even weaker realization, of the rule of law. It also fits some critical readings of Hong Kong before 1974, when the government established the Independent Commission Against Corruption and began an aggressive campaign to attack bribery, kickbacks, and the like. It assumes or accepts extensive use of *guanxi* (personal connections) among business leaders and officials, timely (often corrupt) interventions by government authorities in business affairs, and reliance on a variety of informal norms and sanctions to supplement a less-than-perfect legal system. It sees weak legal protection for civil and political liberties – striking in reform-era PRC practice but hardly uncharacteristic of Hong Kong's colonial laws on the books – as posing no barrier to rapid economic growth or high levels of foreign investment. Finally, this model claims that economic actors can continue – to some adequate degree, and perhaps with informal supplements – to be guided by and to rely on norms set forth in laws when structuring their business activities despite the risk of market-perverting political intervention and the absence of reliable judicial enforcement. Considerable discontinuity – in the form of backsliding from the ethos and practices of late colonial era legality in Hong Kong – would be unproblematic under this model.

The view that this form of the rule of law will work for Hong Kong is nicely summed up by a business consultant, who argues that if Hong Kong becomes "just another Chinese city," then "the risk of investing in Hong Kong is no greater than in investing in China. And there are so many reasons for investing in China."[2]

Singapore Model

A second model places far greater emphasis on a robust system of legality for economic affairs. It requires elaborate and comprehensive market-supporting and market-regulating laws, together with reliable mechanisms for amending and adapting them to changing business environments and practices. Competent, honest officials must interpret and apply those laws in a fair and neutral manner, assuring the general reliability of market information, resolving disputes, and deterring market-subverting violations. While this implies some autonomy for legal and even legislative institutions, it demands a minimal regime beyond business law, and sees little need for legal protection of political and civil liberties or rights to participate in the institutions of government.

This is, broadly, a "Singapore Model" of the rule of law. It emphasizes the features that have made Singapore the envy of some countries and the target of

[2] Maggie Farley, "Ditching the Colonial Past," *Sunday Times*, Feb. 6, 1994 (quoting Henry Wu).

criticism from others: scrupulous enforcement of a broad and sophisticated set of laws to achieve economic prosperity, but tight restrictions on dissent, pressure for political reform, and actions threatening social order. This model also offers a plausible characterization of Hong Kong's legal order under what has sometimes been called the "benevolent dictatorship" of colonial rule, especially prior to the 1990 enactment of the Bill of Rights Ordinance and the recent implementation of modestly democratizing electoral reforms. The model thus mandates continuity with what Hong Kong has had in the past: prosperity through an institutionally strong, but narrowly economic, liberal rule of law.

The model's relevance in the debate over Hong Kong's future rule of law is suggested by a pair of cautions from prominent sources: Lu Ping has warned that "Hong Kong has been an economic city, never a political city," and should remain that way lest it become of "negative value" to China; Lee Kuan Yew, father of the Singapore Model and critic of Western liberal "rights-focused" legal orders, has admonished China that Hong Kong's legal system is "its most important advantage" – a "vital economic asset" that is "most valuable but most difficult to establish."[3]

"Augmented Hong Kong" Model

A third, "Augmented Hong Kong" Model is much more expansive in its notion of what the rule of law entails. It accepts the Singapore Model's notion of a rule of law to guarantee a liberal order and a "level playing field" in economic affairs, but it insists that laws must protect civil liberties and political rights as well. Otherwise, the rule of law even for narrowly economic affairs will be undermined by, among other things, a governmental culture of lawlessness and a societal sense of personal insecurity. In addition, autonomy must extend beyond economic bureaucrats and commercial courts to governmental institutions – by some lights, necessarily democratic ones – that will assure the public accountability that guarantees fair and impartial administration of the laws. Only truly accountable institutions will enact and apply laws that are just and acceptable in the eyes of the public, and thus warrant the public confidence in the legal and political structure that ultimately undergirds prosperity.

[3] Louise do Rosario, "Future Shock," *Far Eastern Economic Review* [hereafter, "*FEER*"], May 19, 1994, p. 24 (quoting Lu Ping); Diane Stormont, "China Envoy Paints Rosy Picture of Post-97 HK," Reuters, Apr. 12, 1996 (quoting Xinhua Hong Kong Director Zhou Nan, affirming Lu Ping's point); "No Appeal: China Rules Against Hong Kong," *FEER*, Dec. 22, 1994, p. 5 (quoting Lee Kuan Yew).

Cooking the Rice without Cooking the Goose

Seeking to build upon the trends toward stronger legal protection of civil liberties and expanded democracy that have marked Hong Kong's recent political development, this model draws on the ideals of Western liberal democracies, primarily the United States and Great Britain. It adopts a vision of an inseparable rule of law for political and economic affairs, its elements mutually supportive and necessarily grounded in liberal-democratic values and accountable institutions. Applied to Hong Kong, it demands a level and breadth of political autonomy that the territory has hitherto not enjoyed – in part because, in the circumstances of post-reversion Hong Kong, nothing less will sustain the continuity of a legal system conducive to preserving economic prosperity.

The conviction that only this model, in relatively pure form, will work for Hong Kong has pervaded the most ardent calls for political change during Hong Kong's last days as a colony. A typical passage by a leading democratic politician illustrates the position:

> [O]ur legal system has functioned solely because . . . a democratically
> elected British parliament has guaranteed our rule of law. . . . The rule
> of law continues to be vital to Hong Kong not only because it protects
> individual rights, but because it safeguards Hong Kong's free market
> system by guaranteeing the protection . . . necessary to continue our
> economic success. That is why we make the introduction of democratic
> and accountable government our highest priority.[4]

As they have struggled to assess the requirements and secure the acceptance of the territory's vital business elites, and especially as the endgame of Hong Kong's transition has drawn near, the main participants in the political battle over Hong Kong's future rule of law have divided along lines that separate these models. Hong Kong's most prominent pro-democracy politicians, Governor Chris Patten, colonial government officials, and London – with declining alacrity, constancy, and audibility as one moves down the list – have pressed for the Augmented Hong Kong Model. This group has been more uniform in its expressed rejection of the China Model. On the other side, Chinese officials and China's supporters in Hong Kong – also to varying degrees and with fluctuating zeal – have rejected key elements of the Augmented Hong Kong Model while promising something more than a China Model, even as many of their statements and actions have suggested that a China Model is what some on the

[4] Martin Lee, "Need for 'Rule of Law,'" *South China Morning Post* [hereafter, "*SCMP*"], Aug. 1, 1993, p. 11.

PRC side ultimately have in mind. The Singapore Model – seemingly a potential compromise solution – has received relatively little explicit support, an odd circumstance that reflects the deeper political forces at work in a struggle that is only partly about prosperity.

BATTLING OVER BUSINESS: PREDICTION AND PERSUASION

The principal participants in the political struggle over Hong Kong's future have, from the beginning, recognized the importance of crafting legal arrangements that could accommodate the needs and preferences of Hong Kong's leading indigenous business interests and its foreign business community. This general battle for the allegiance – or mere acquiescence – of business elites has taken place in both the highly public and shadowy, informal arenas in the contentious process of defining the terms of Hong Kong's return to Chinese control.

The worries of major business interests led the British government to place Hong Kong's future status on the agenda. By the late 1970s, the approaching expiration of the New Territories' ninety-nine-year lease was generating anxiety. The colonial government, owner of nearly all Hong Kong's land, was unwilling to grant developers leases extending beyond 1997 for any of the three components of the colony (which the government was committed to treating as an integrated whole). As a result, business interests grew nervous about making investments that would require more than fifteen years to recoup.

Moreover, quasi-corporatist colonial rule in Hong Kong has long granted business a special place, including substantial representation in the Executive Council (Exco) and Legislative Council (Legco), two key institutions that until 1991 were composed entirely of appointed members. Many "unofficial" (non–civil servant) members of Exco and Legco came from Hong Kong's biggest and most internationally engaged companies. More than half of the unofficial Legco members in 1984 were company directors, senior business executives, or bankers. "Official members" were drawn from the ranks of a civil service whose unabashedly pro-capitalist, pro–free trade, and pro-business orientation was meant to appeal to both international investors and the colony's own business interests. Even after the electoral reforms of the 1990s brought non-business members into Legco's popularly elected seats, the business presence in government remained strong. In the 1991 elections, seven of the "elected" Legco seats were for functional constituencies representing business interests, a few of them chosen by tiny electorates composed of leading Hong Kong firms. The appointed seats, still nearly a third of the total, remained largely the province of business leaders and like-minded professionals. Liberals and democrats remained excluded from the fully appointive Exco. After the reform-minded Governor Patten introduced laws to broaden the electorate, business representation in Legco fell somewhat. Still, the Liberal Party – Hong Kong's leading pro-business party – emerged as the second largest party in the Legco selected in 1995, while the weakening of business influence in Exco has been less pronounced.[5]

The PRC has also paid special attention to Hong Kong's business interests. When Britain first raised the Hong Kong issue in 1979, the only element of Deng Xiaoping's response that was made public was his appeal to Hong Kong's businesspeople to "put their hearts at ease." During the negotiations that led to the Joint Declaration, business leaders from the territory made a series of pilgrimages to Beijing, where Chinese leaders consulted, cajoled, and reassured them about China's plans for the territory. Such contacts took on a formal structure during the middle 1980s, when the PRC appointed several of Hong Kong's most influential businessmen, including Y. K. Pao, An Tse Kai, and Cha Chi-Ming, to the Basic Law Drafting Committee (BLDC).[6] This special concern for business interests has continued through the transition. In the early 1990s, Beijing appointed several dozen official "advisers," including Li Ka-shing, Peter Woo, Robert Kuok, and others from the territory's business notables, as well as Legco member Allen Lee and other politicians from the Liberal Party.[7] More than half of the Hong Kong slots on the Preparatory Committee, established in 1996 to handle critical transition-related tasks, went to business leaders, many drawn from the ranks of Beijing's previously appointed advisers. The Hong Kong committees that Beijing appointed to nominate and elect the SAR's first chief executive also had half of their seats reserved for business and the professions.[8] Likewise, major foreign businesses with interests in Hong Kong have

---

[5] See Norman Miners, *The Government and Politics of Hong Kong* (Hong Kong: Oxford University Press, 5th ed., 1995), pp. 115–20; Ian Scott, *Political Change and the Crisis of Legitimacy in Hong Kong* (London: Hurst & Co., 1987), pp. 59–60, 248–49; Stacy Mosher, "Selective Suffrage," *FEER*, Aug. 29, 1991, p. 16; Stacy Mosher, "The Governor's Men," *FEER*, Oct. 3, 1991, p. 11; Stacy Mosher, "Out of the Club," *FEER*, Nov. 7, 1991, p. 12; Louise do Rosario, "Stand Up and Be Counted," *FEER*, Sept. 28, 1995, p. 16.

[6] Katsu Hiizumi, "Hong Kong Ponders Its Future after 1997," *The Daily Yomiyuri*, Mar. 17, 1996, p. 3.

[7] Carson Wen Ka-shuen, "No Flaw in Beijing's Choice of Adviser," *SCMP*, Apr. 25, 1993, p. 11.

[8] Bruce Gilley, "Down to Brass Tacks," *FEER*, Jan. 25, 1996, p. 14; "Chinese Statement on the Breakdown of Sino-British Talks on Hong Kong," BBC Monitoring Service: Far East, Mar. 2, 1994.

had substantial informal input with Beijing, not least because many of them are big investors in the PRC as well – key contributors to the economic revolution that the policy of "opening to the outside world" has brought to the mainland.

Especially since the adoption of the Basic Law in 1990, efforts by China, Hong Kong–British authorities, and emergent Hong Kong political elites to canvas, convince, and even coerce business have included a subtle and complex battle over where the territory's key foreign and domestic businesses would stand on fundamental "rule of law" questions. That battle has been fought in the context of empirical claims, articulated by prominent political actors, that reflect conflicting views about what model of a rule of law is adequate to sustain Hong Kong's prosperity.

Hong Kong Liberals and Democrats, Colonial Authorities, and the Augmented Hong Kong Model

Especially following the Tiananmen massacre of 1989, liberal and democratic politicians in Hong Kong and, at times, the colonial authorities have engaged in the battle over business by asserting that only an Augmented Hong Kong Model will safeguard prosperity. That general claim has rested on three specific arguments: claiming business support, persuading business, and claiming to be right about business' true needs.

Claiming Business Support. Legco member and Democratic Party leader Martin Lee, Governor Patten, and others sharing a broadly similar outlook have claimed that Hong Kong's elite business class (or at least a large segment of it) and the foreign business community with interests in the territory do embrace the Augmented Hong Kong Model of the rule of law, in large part because they ultimately believe that nothing less will suffice to serve their interests. As Patten has put it:

> There is hardly a well-off businessman in Hong Kong who doesn't
> want, for himself, the insurance of being able to live in a free society.
> So I can't believe that those businessmen don't understand the relation-
> ship between the rule of law, between the values of pluralism and being
> able to live a decent life.[9]

---

[9] Graham Hutchings, " 'Tango Dancer' Patten Stamps on China's Toes," *The Daily Telegraph*, Feb. 8, 1996, p. 10.

In Martin Lee's formulation, press freedom and freedom of information "are things that the business community knows they need" – and things that ultimately depend on democratically accountable institutions.[10]

Business leaders in Hong Kong have articulated positions that support these claims. Some – especially expatriate executives from the territory's most venerable institutions – declared that a degree of electorally accountable government was necessary to support the rule of law and maintain Hong Kong's prosperity when they backed Governor Patten's moves to reform electoral procedures in 1992. Patten's modest but controversial changes broadened the franchise by lowering the voting age, expanding rights to vote for Legco's "functional constituency" seats, and making ten Legco seats subject to indirect election by a committee consisting of directly elected local officials. While the resulting Legco remained more government watchdog than true legislature, its more democratic pedigree was desirable, even vital. As one prominent businessman and politician put it, "[T]he mainspring of our prosperity and stability remains rooted in the rule of law . . . and a legislature safeguarded by its accountability to the population."[11]

Much of the Hong Kong business leadership – particularly its Hong Kong Chinese element – was less enthusiastic about Patten's reforms, especially as stalemated talks with China over political reform held up progress on the new airport project and other issues of more immediate concern to business. Still, there is evidence of some support – intermittent and perhaps reluctant – for a degree of democratization, albeit more limited than the notions advanced by the reformist politicians who set the agenda. In the midst of popular pressures for reform that the Tiananmen massacre spawned in Hong Kong, some prominent business and pro-business voices endorsed the idea of "democratizing" Legco. With Y. K. Pao, Li Ka-shing, Henry Fok, David Li, and other leading business figures having expressed support for the students in Beijing, established Legco and Exco conservatives joined with pro-business organizations to

---

[10] "For Many Corporate Chiefs, 1997 Cannot Come Soon Enough," *Asiaweek*, Dec. 7, 1994, p. 23.

[11] Huang Chen-ya, "Jardines Salvo Is HK Wake-Up Call," *SCMP*, Dec. 20, 1992 (quoting GCC Chairman Jimmy McGregor); Catherine Ong, "Singapore: No Slowing Down for This Tough 'Last Taipan' – Simon Murray," *Business Times*, July 1, 1994, p. 17 (quoting outgoing Hutchison Whampoa Chief Simon Murray as believing that Patten is right and that democratic reform is necessary to preserving the rule of law, and thus the difference between Hong Kong and Guangdong); Doreen Cheung, "Purves Calls for Open and Fair Polls," *SCMP*, Oct. 5, 1993, p. 2 (quoting Hong Kong and Shanghai Bank chief).

support proposals to make a substantial portion of Legco's seats directly elected by 1997.[12] Later, after the Patten reforms were introduced, the conservative
and pro-business Cooperative Resources Center – joined at the eleventh hour
by the Liberal Party – endorsed a Legco reform plan that called for a modest
expansion of the franchise.[13]

Major business leaders and pro-business Legco members also organized to
contest elections, backing the newly formed Liberal Democratic Federation
(LDF) for the 1991 Legco vote and, later, the Liberal Party and other organi-
zations (including the Hong Kong Progressive Alliance), for the 1994 District
Board and 1995 Legco balloting. The LDF – whose top members later led the
Liberal Party – ran on a platform that supported limited and gradual democratization, the rule of law, and protection of human rights and freedoms.[14] James
Tien, a politician-businessman who has served in Legco and on the General
Committee of the Hong Kong General Chamber of Commerce, summed up
this perspective, saying that Patten "quite rightly feels that a mandate should
come from some form of representation . . . and that members of the business
community should run for elections" if they "want to make [their] views
known."[15]

More broadly, Hong Kong business elites have voiced some acceptance of
the linkage between legal protection for political and civil liberties and a rule
of law for economic matters. In the aftermath of Tiananmen, business and professional members of the Basic Law Consultative Committee proposed reforms
to the Basic Law to restrict Beijing's authority to declare a state of emergency
in Hong Kong, to clarify the scope of acts of state, to entrench international
human rights in the Basic Law, to give Basic Law provisions status equal to
PRC constitutional provisions, and to enhance protection of SAR legislative
autonomy.[16]

[12] Emily Lau, "Voice of the People," *FEER*, June 8, 1989, p. 18; Emily Lau, "Red Herring," *FEER*,
Sept. 14, 1989, p. 26.
[13] Teresa Poole, "Patten Faces Pro-China Alliance," *The Independent*, Jan. 20, 1993, p. 11; Louise
do Rosario, "Patten's Progress," *FEER*, July 14, 1994, p. 20.
[14] Bellette Lee, "Political Flag for Business," *SCMP*, Oct. 23, 1990; Emily Lau, "Peking's Tune,"
FEER, Aug. 23, 1990, p. 22 (describing LDF founding).
[15] James Tien, "HK Can Survive Under One Country, One System," *SCMP*, May 2, 1993, p. 11;
see also Emily Lau, "Political Shell Game," *FEER*, Apr. 5, 1990 (Li Ka-shing statement that
businessmen must take part in politics).
[16] "Hong Kong: Group's Plan Tackles Flaws in Basic Law," *SCMP*, Sept. 6, 1989.

Hong Kong business leaders also expressed concern that China's intransigence on a Court of Final Appeal would jeopardize prosperity. In 1991, Allen Lee and other pro-business Legco members were sufficiently troubled by the prospect of a Court of Final Appeal that limited to one the number of foreign judges (who were seen as key bearers and defenders of the common-law tradition for post-1997 Hong Kong) that they joined liberal Legco members in voting to reject a bill implementing the Sino-British deal on the issue.[17] Leading banker David Li, a member of Legco and the BLDC, cautioned that the difficulty in reaching an early and satisfactory resolution to the Court of Final Appeal question portended a threat to "[t]he judiciary's independence" which "is vital to Hong Kong's continued prosperity."[18] Foreign business interests have generally shared this view.[19]

At the very least, failure to resolve the issue in a timely way, many business sources admonished, meant a level of uncertainty inimical to local and international business confidence in the territory.[20] When business voices generally praised the Court bill that passed Legco in 1995 (despite its closely tracking the 1991 proposal), opponents of the bill questioned their sincerity.[21] As Martin Lee asked rhetorically, "How many companies which left [shifted domiciles from Hong Kong] are coming back now that we have such a good Court of Final Appeal agreement?"[22]

However apparently weak their support for the Augmented Hong Kong Model, Hong Kong's business communities are at least deeply anxious over the prospect of a rule of law no more robust and expansive than a China Model. Fearing that it could open a wide window for PRC intervention in Hong Kong courts, some business sources worried about a provision in the Court of Final Appeal accord (tracking Article 19 of the Basic Law) denying jurisdiction over "acts of state *such as* defense and foreign affairs [emphasis added]." As some liberals pointed out, the provision might be used to preclude judicial relief in

---

[17] Stacy Mosher, "Court of Contention," *FEER*, Dec. 19, 1991, p. 10.

[18] Nigel Page, "Hong Kong's Alternative Voice," *International Financial Law Review*, May 1994, p. 48.

[19] See, e.g., "A Rosy Future for Hong Kong's Legal System?" *Lloyds List*, Dec. 11, 1992.

[20] See, e.g., Mary Kwang, "HK Govt Faces Tough Fight on Appeal Court Bill," *The Straits Times* (Singapore), June 10, 1995, p. 17; Chris Yeung & Linda Choy, "Issue 'Back to Square One,'" *SCMP*, May 4, 1995; Louise do Rosario, "A Court Too Far," *FEER*, June 22, 1995, p. 20.

[21] Chris Yeung & No Kwai-yan, "Governor Survives Vote," *SCMP*, July 13, 1995, p. 1.

[22] Michael Steinberger, "Pact on HK's Legal System Has Not Put Fears to Rest," *Business Times*, Aug. 9, 1995, p. 8.

the event of business-affecting actions by SAR officials and breaches of contract by Chinese state-owned corporations – and not solely in national security or other "political" cases.

Business sources have also expressed concern that some of the quintessential features of the China Model of legality would spread to Hong Kong and undermine the special features of Hong Kong's prosperity-providing rule of law. Business and pro-business voices have frequently noted the danger to Hong Kong of corruption and *guanxi* spilling across the border and displacing the role of law in the territory's business environment. Beijing's reported 1995 order to major PRC state-owned enterprises to increase investments in Hong Kong "to make a contribution to a smooth transition" reinforced business fears that the PRC would extend to Hong Kong its domestic practice of directing business enterprises to serve policy ends.[23]

Similar concerns appeared to underlie positions taken within the business community during the controversy over selection of the SAR's first chief executive. Prior to Beijing's anointment of shipping magnate Tung Chee-hwa for the post, business interests were strikingly ambivalent about having a businessperson fill the job. There appeared to be significant support for candidates drawn from institutions closely associated with the territory's special rule of law traditions – the civil service or the judiciary. And leading business figures such as Li Ka-shing were regarded as troubling because their selection raised the prospect of a conflict-of-interest–generating merger of political and vast economic power, redolent of the reform-era PRC. Tellingly, Tung Chee-hwa had been controversial because of both his ties to Li Ka-shing and the sense that he was overly beholden to the PRC, which had engineered a bailout of his troubled company during the 1980s.[24]

A number of recent PRC threats and acts have revealed to Hong Kong's business community an approach to law and business that has aroused fears about what China has in store for the territory's rule of law. Most notoriously, China expressed its opposition to Patten's political reforms by stalling progress on the new airport and port facilities – a vast infrastructure project that not only

---

[23] "Sticky Chinese Fingers Close to the Honey Pot," *Independent*, July 1, 1995; Bruce Gilley, "Great Leap Southward," *FEER*, Nov. 23, 1995; Bruce Gilley, "Here Come the Jitters," *FEER*, Apr. 25, 1996, p. 54.

[24] Angela Li, "Businessman Expresses Doubts over British Links," *SCMP*, Nov. 9, 1996, p. 6; "Wanted: The Right Man, Whatever His Job," *SCMP*, Sept. 13, 1996, p. 23; Bruce Gilley, "Henry ... Who? Tung Will Need to Ignore Old Friends and Business Interests," *FEER*, Jan. 9, 1997, p. 82.

involves lucrative construction contracts for some of Hong Kong's leading firms, but also will provide vital benefits to all internationalized business interests operating in the territory.[25] In the same vein, China delayed progress on construction of a new container terminal because it objected to the participation of Jardine Matheson – the venerable *hong* that had openly supported Patten's political reforms. The PRC's warning that all government contracts straddling 1997 would need to secure China's approval provided further cause for concern about the politicization of business and the weakening rule of law.[26] A wave of kidnappings of Hong Kong entrepreneurs and executives – at the behest of disappointed PRC business partners, or with the connivance of local PRC authorities – suggests to some that the picture for business could become bleak indeed under the rule of law that China seems willing or able to impose on post-1997 Hong Kong.[27]

Those claiming that business demands a robust rule of law can, and do, point to several practices adopted by Hong Kong's key business leaders that suggest a lack of confidence in the territory's legal future if that future promises nothing more than a China Model of the rule of law. As 1997 draws near, more businesses in the territory have been insisting that international business contracts specify British or some other non–Hong Kong law.[28] By 1995, more than half of the companies listed on the Hong Kong stock exchange had moved their corporate domiciles from Hong Kong, often to Singapore, Bermuda, or the Cayman Islands (which offered the virtue, heretofore provided in Hong Kong, of final judicial appeal to the Privy Council in London).[29] Jardine Matheson, whose roots in the colony date to the opium trade, was the most prominent (and one of the earliest) to leave in quest of "freedom from politically influenced

---

[25] Emily Lau, "Terminal Delay," *FEER,* Mar. 21, 1991, p. 11; Stacy Mosher, "Creeping Intervention," *FEER,* July 18, 1991, p. 10; "China and Britain Should Still Cooperate on Other Issues," *Wen Wei Po,* May 14, 1994, p. A3.

[26] Tai Ming Cheung, "Push Came to Shove," *FEER,* Dec. 10, 1992, p. 8; Tai Ming Cheung, "Silent Night," *FEER,* Jan. 7, 1993, pp. 8–9; "China Accused of Threatening Rule of Law," Reuters, Dec. 23, 1992; Chen Chien-ping, "Quoting Out of Context and Misleading the Public," *Wen Wei Po,* Dec. 7, 1992, p. 2; Liu Shih-hsin, "Lu Ping Talks with Visiting Textile Delegation from Hong Kong," *Wen Wei Po,* Dec. 1, 1992, p. 2 (contracts extending beyond 1997 must be "discussed" with the PRC or else parties will lack "legal protection").

[27] "HK Kept in Dark on Business Disputes – Plea to China over Detainees," *SCMP,* July 7, 1994, p. 7; Louise do Rosario, "Justice Under Siege," *FEER,* Jan. 26, 1995, p. 18; Louise do Rosario, "Risky Business," *FEER,* Jan. 26, 1996, p. 20.

[28] Michael Steinberger, "Companies Ring-Fence Assets in Hong Kong Twilight Raid," *The Times* (London) Aug. 4, 1995.

[29] Michael Steinberger, "Pact on HK's Legal System," op. cit., p. 8.

regulation."[30] Some companies have taken less dramatic measures reflecting the same concerns. Some multinational banks have shifted their accounting and legal operations to Singapore; other foreign lenders and investors have begun treating Hong Kong risks as China risks, therefore demanding a higher rate of return. Many Hong Kong companies have moved some of their assets outside the territory.[31]

The anxiety driving these moves is reflected in a 1996 poll of expatriate and local executives, nearly half of whom indicated that they had little confidence in the territory's future.[32] Hong Kong's volatile Hang Seng index has provided another barometer, plummeting in response to PRC announcements that, among other things, suggested trouble for a robust rule of law. The index fell by more than 20 percent in December 1992 amid the initial confrontation over Patten's proposed reforms (reportedly in large part due to sell-offs by U.K. and U.S. funds), and nearly 10 percent in March 1993, when Patten gazetted his reform bill and drew a predictably harsh Chinese response.[33]

Prominent members of Hong Kong's business community have also adopted what liberals and democrats can plausibly interpret as a reluctant strategy of "If you can't beat 'em, join 'em." The Swire Group, another of Hong Kong's great *hongs*, sold a substantial stake in its highly profitable airline, Cathay Pacific, to Chinese state interests in a move that was widely interpreted as an attempt to buy protection and influence that might become useful under a weakened rule of law. By 1996, the apparent failure of that political risk insurance policy to pay off – Beijing threatened to end Cathay's dominance and hand a large share of the traffic in one of China's prime destinations to an airline "run mainly by Chinese people, not foreigners" – seemed tailor-made to

---

[30] Carol Kennedy, "Can Two Hongs Get It Right?" *Director*, Feb. 1996, pp. 34–40 (quoting managing director Nigel Rich). Fearing how Hong Kong takeover and merger laws might be used against it after 1997, Jardine's de-listed on the Hong Kong Stock Exchange after its request for a formal exemption was denied. Ian K. Perkin, "Primary Listing Is Now London, Says Jardines," *SCMP*, June 8, 1991; "Hong Kong: Business Community Maintaining Optimism Despite Uncertainty About Its Future Post 1997," *Euromoney Supplement*, July 16, 1991 (describing Hong Kong and Shanghai Bank's restructuring under a U.K. holding company in 1991).

[31] Gary Silverman, "The Price of Success," *FEER*, July 6, 1995, p. 54; Henry Sender, "Politics, Not Profits," *FEER*, Dec. 17, 1992, p. 20.

[32] Bruce Gilley, "Here Come the Jitters," op. cit., p. 54.

[33] Alex Brummer, "Harvesting Plums in the Claw of the Dragon," *The Guardian*, Jan. 16, 1993, p. 40; Tai Ming Cheung, "Silent Night," op. cit., p. 8; Jonathan Karp, "Through Train Slows Down," *FEER*, Mar. 25, 1993, p. 12.

underscore the dangers of a weakened rule of law.[34] Business interests took the double-edged point, with many seeking to succeed where Swire had apparently failed. Some rushed to join (and others, to criticize) T. T. Tsui's New China Hong Kong Group, whose investors – in quest of China and Hong Kong opportunities – included Li Ka-shing, other Hong Kong tycoons, Goldman Sachs, and over a dozen PRC companies, many of them under direct State Council, ministerial, or provincial control.[35] Many more engaged in lower-profile versions of the same strategy of developing closer ties to politically well-connected Chinese entities.

For proponents of the view that Hong Kong business interests actually favor a rule of law consistent with the Augmented Hong Kong Model, such moves are the result of fear and (shortsighted) pragmatism. The problem, on this view, is not that the territory's leading businesses reject the gist of the Augmented Hong Kong Model, but that they refuse to push publicly (sometimes even privately) for rule of law–supporting proposals because they fear a chilly reception from Hong Kong's future masters (who are already its largest economic partners).[36]

This misleading silence, on the view of liberals and democrats, has been compounded by the success of PRC "united front" tactics in capturing some of the traditional voices of business opinion in the colony, thus drowning out those who are more sympathetic to an Augmented Hong Kong Model. Perhaps the most notable example of such moves was the expansion of the membership in the General Chamber of Commerce (GCC) to include a larger number of pro-China elements. When they in turn helped vote out long-time liberal GCC leader and Legco member Jimmy McGregor, it consolidated the hold of pro-China forces on the four business functional constituencies in the pre-1995 Legco.[37]

---

[34] Carol Kennedy, "Two Hongs," op. cit., pp. 34–40; Garth Alexander, "Hong Kong's Top Taipans Get Ready for Takeover," *Sunday Times* (London), Oct. 3, 1993; Bruce Gilley, "Here Come the Jitters," op. cit., p. 54 (quoting Ma Xiaowen of CAAC).

[35] Jonathan Karp, "The New Insiders," *FEER*, May 27, 1993, p. 62.

[36] "Corporate Chiefs," *Asiaweek*, op. cit., p. 22 (quoting Martin Lee).

[37] Mary Kwang, "Pro-China Lobby Out of the Backseat," *The Straits Times* (Singapore), May 9, 1993, p. 14; Fung Wai-kong & Linda Choy, "Chamber Spurns McGregor in Poll for Committee," *SCMP*, Apr. 27, 1994, p. 1; Simon Holberton, "China Tries to Win Control of HK Chamber," *Financial Times*, Apr. 2, 1993, p. 3; "Bitter Battle for the Business Seat," *SCMP*, June 12, 1991; Timothy Charlton, "Legco Reforms Create Problems," *SCMP*, July 4, 1994, p. 1.

Persuading Business. Those in Hong Kong who favor the Augmented Hong Kong Model argue that while business' apparent lack of zeal for that paradigm is real, business elites can – and must – be convinced that a robust rule of law is indispensable. Proponents of this view have sought to persuade business with arguments addressed directly to their self-interests. For instance, Hong Kong Chief Secretary Anson Chan assured business that the Patten electoral reforms would "in no way weaken our commitment to maintaining Hong Kong's attraction as the premier business location in this region. Indeed, by strengthening our representative institutions, they can only enhance investors' confidence."[38] As Patten put it, in a statement surely meant to persuade and not simply to predict, "What business needs above all, in the long term, is the certainty of the rule of law – of laws democratically enacted and rooted in the community."[39] If Hong Kong does not have "fair" and "credible" elections, Patten warned, it will be impossible to "maintain the rule of law," fight corruption, and maintain Hong Kong's "lifestyle."[40] Similarly, Martin Lee explained that he and his colleagues make democratic and accountable government their top priority precisely because it undergirds the rule of law, which is "vital to Hong Kong not only because it protects individual rights, but because it safeguards Hong Kong's free-market system by guaranteeing the protection of contracts and property necessary to continue our economic success."[41]

Other efforts at persuasion have played more on business fears. Patten has warned that "billionaires whose principal concern is that they should go on being billionaires" risk, in their role as China's principal advisers on Hong Kong, exacerbating Chinese officials' dangerous "lack of understanding about what makes Hong Kong tick."[42] The governor has urged business to "give Hong Kong a lead in defending the rule of law, [and] open and accountable government," stressing that "[t]he rule of law is not an optional extra," but, rather, "what makes Hong Kong successful."[43] Patten also cautioned that China's efforts to hand-pick a legislature and other such moves could give Hong Kong "the reputation that the rule of law was under threat," which would mean that

[38] "Chan Says Companies Should Not Fear Legco Bill," *SCMP*, Mar. 11, 1994, p. 2.
[39] "Interview – Chris Patten," *FEER*, Oct. 22, 1992, p. 22.
[40] "Comment on Chris Patten's 'Theory of the Infiltration of Corruption,'" *Ta Kung Pao*, Oct. 27, 1993, p. 2.
[41] Martin Lee, "Rule of Law," op. cit., p. 11.
[42] Graham Hutchings, "'Tango Dancer' Patten," op. cit., p. 10.
[43] Chris Yeung & Genevieve Ku, "Patten Tells Businessmen to Stand Up for Autonomy," *SCMP*, Oct. 11, 1996, p. 1.

"the international business community would move its cash elsewhere, and it would not take very long to do it."[44] Martin Lee stoked business fears about the advent of Chinese-style legality, conjuring the specter of a world in which "the success of a Hong Kong businessman would no longer be determined by his ability or industry but rather his *guanxi* . . . with Chinese officials" and in which disputes between Hong Kong and Chinese companies would be heard by SAR judges "subject to constant pressure exerted by . . . the Chinese Government" or the Communist Party.[45] Similarly, pro-democracy Legco members warned that China's plan to replace Legco with a provisional legislature in 1997 would undermine the territory's "business environment" and the rule of law, which is "the bedrock of Hong Kong's success."[46]

A more subtle element of the strategy to convince the business community is the assertion that ordinary Hong Kong citizens – the work force on which business depends and which contributes to the creation of the political milieu in which business must operate – have come to believe in representative democracy, a bill of rights, and the like. As Martin Lee put it, "Hong Kong's six million citizens cherish our civil liberties and freedoms," and they recognize "that a difference in approach to human rights and democracy – in combination with a fundamental misunderstanding of the values and practices of a free society – will pose the greatest threat to Hong Kong" under Chinese rule.[47] In defense of his electoral reform plans, Patten asked rhetorically, "[I]s it more destabilising to try to accommodate, in a modest way, people's political and democratic aspirations or to block them off? I think the business community needs to consider those issues. . . ."[48]

On this argument, Hong Kong residents prefer – and will demand – a rule of law consistent with the Augmented Hong Kong Model. Failure to deliver such a rule of law will threaten the SAR's stability and thereby harm the interests of big business, both indigenous and transnational. The resounding victories of

[44] Maggie Farley, "Ditching the Colonial Past" (quoting Patten's statement to the House of Commons Foreign Affairs Committee), op. cit.
[45] Martin Lee, "Hong Kong: One Country, No System?" *SCMP*, Dec. 14, 1989; Martin Lee, "Rule of Law," op. cit., p. 11.
[46] Angela Li & Vivian Lee, "Business Lobby Under Fire for Patten Letter," *SCMP*, May 23, 1996, p. 6.
[47] Martin Lee, "From Tiananmen to Hong Kong," *Washington Post*, June 22, 1994, p. A21; Martin Lee, "Beijing's Tiananmen Mentality Augurs Most Ill for Hong Kong," *International Herald Tribune*, June 23, 1994; Martin Lee, "The Sell-Out that Has to Stop," *SCMP*, July 1, 1995, p. 19.
[48] "Interview – Chris Patten," op. cit., p. 22.

thinly financed pro-democracy parties in the contests for Legco's directly elected seats and for representation in lower-level bodies make the point tangible to business. So do polls indicating that roughly half of Hong Kong's residents think it will be impossible to sue the government or a PRC company successfully after 1997, that nearly three-quarters lack confidence in the PRC's transitional institutions for Hong Kong, and that the same percentage object to the PRC's stance on disbanding the representative bodies elected as a result of the Patten reforms.[49]

The effort to persuade business to demand a stronger and more expansive rule of law has included warnings that failure to do so would be to betray Hong Kong. This appeal – whether to a sense of shame or to the fear of being labeled "anti–Hong Kong" – has come in a variety of forms. Patten has spoken of tycoons' "social responsibility" to stand up for Hong Kong, and the need to "get business to understand it would not be in Hong Kong's interest to sell out the Joint Declaration as a way of securing a quiet life."[50] Martin Lee has charged that, for a businessman to oppose Patten's reforms "is to display an appalling lack of faith in the people of Hongkong who have made their success possible."[51] And the *South China Morning Post* cautioned that "the rule of law itself" – which few dare dispute is a key part of what makes Hong Kong special – "will be put at risk if businessmen make a habit of going to Beijing" to seek regulatory and other favors.[52]

Claiming to Be Right. Recognizing the difficulty of bringing the business community around to their notion of the rule of law, proponents of the Augmented Hong Kong Model have also resorted to a third argument, one that is almost indifferent to what business elites actually believe, or can be made to believe in the near term. This argument claims simply that the rule of law can exist in the economic sphere only if it is supported by liberal values and democratically accountable institutions. On this view, although the foreign business community and Hong Kong's internationalized business elites may be too benighted to recognize it, nothing less than such sweeping legality (including sound democratic constitutional underpinnings) will preserve Hong Kong's

[49] Jacqueline Leong, "A Few Points of Law for Hong Kong," *SCMP*, Aug. 8, 1993, p. 11; prepared testimony of Andrew Y. Au before the Senate Foreign Relations Committee, Federal News Service, July 18, 1996.
[50] Bruce Gilley, "Standing Pat," *FEER*, May 30, 1996, p. 16; Simon Holberton, "Hong Kong Reforms Upset Business Community," *Financial Times*, July 2, 1994.
[51] Martin Lee, "Tide of Democracy," *FEER*, Nov. 26, 1992, p. 31.
[52] "HK Must Keep Its Business Autonomy Intact," *SCMP*, July 7, 1996, p. 10.

tradition of the rule of law and the resulting thriving economy. Together with other pro-democracy voices, Martin Lee has lamented that Hong Kong businessmen take the shortsighted and mistaken view that "so long as they can establish good connections with Chinese officials, their profits are guaranteed."[53] Governor Patten has made the same point in a more understated way:

I think people should recognize perhaps more sharply the relationship between a credible legislature, a free press, and the rule of law and Hong Kong's prosperity. . . . I think there are some people in the business community who should know better . . . [who] underestimate the importance of the rule of law to Hong Kong."[54]

Proponents of such views are not optimistic that those who should "know better" will learn the lesson before 1997. Nevertheless, they continue to engage in the battle over Hong Kong's future, believing that this battle will continue beyond 1997, and remaining convinced that only the ambitious program they propose can prevent a devastating erosion of the rule of law, and thus save the business community in spite of itself.

China, Hong Kong's "Pro-China" Elements, and the China Model

China and its allies in the territory have starkly opposed Hong Kong's liberal and pro-democracy elements in their approach to the business community. Rejecting elements of the Augmented Hong Kong paradigm as unacceptable and irrelevant, Beijing and its supporters have made arguments to – and about – business that advance a narrower conception of legality, one perhaps no broader than a China Model.

Claiming Business Support. This view assumes first that Hong Kong's business community would prefer not to press for anything closely approaching an Augmented Hong Kong Model of the rule of law. Although Beijing has had little reason to state its position publicly, its stance can be deduced from its actions. For example, China has summarily dismissed suggestions that business confidence would plummet in the event of a "legal vacuum" caused by a failure to complete the work of establishing SAR institutions and harmonizing local legislation with the Basic Law before the transition takes place.[55] The

---

[53] Martin Lee, "One Country, No System?" op. cit.

[54] H. D. S. Greenway, "Borrowed Time," *Boston Globe Magazine*, June 20, 1993, p. 14.

[55] Linda Choy & Chris Yeung, "China Rejects Laws Talks," *SCMP*, Oct. 25, 1994, p. 1 (quoting Joint Liaison Group member Guo Fengmin).

PRC has also sharply contested nearly every effort by Hong Kong's colonial authorities and reformist politicians to adopt elements of an Augmented Hong Kong Model of legality, such as the Bill of Rights, and election law reform. Indeed, the PRC's allies in the territory have worried that the top leadership in Beijing has sometimes gone too far, underestimating business' demands for some substantial system of legality.[56]

Beijing's basic assumptions do appear to have some foundation in reality. The public statements of many among Hong Kong's business elite reveal a fairly explicit parting of company with the proponents of an Augmented Hong Kong Model of the rule of law. Indeed, Hong Kong's liberal and pro-democracy politicians and Governor Patten have railed against business for its apparent willingness to side with China on controversial issues of legal and political reform. Most of the business establishment criticized those business leaders who flirted briefly with endorsing the democratization proposals of Hong Kong liberals or the Patten reforms. By early 1990, the business lobby and sympathetic Exco and Legco members accepted the draft Basic Law provision that seemed to mandate a pace of democratization slower than the modest one the Office of the Members of the Executive and Legislative Councils (Omelco) had proposed, urging all sides to contest the 1991 elections under the framework that China had accepted.[57] Shortly after Patten proposed his reforms (and China made clear that it opposed them), many Hong Kong Chinese and expatriate executives began a sustained call for their withdrawal or rejection by Legco.[58] One bluntly urged Patten to "forget about democracy for the time being" and return the focus to Hong Kong's "fundamental law" of furthering the territory's economic prosperity.[59] As many business leaders saw it, whatever the theoretical merits of democratization, Patten's quixotic proposals had produced an unnecessarily destabilizing confrontation. In their view, Patten could best serve Hong Kong's interests by backing down. Business and Pro-

---

[56] Doreen Cheung, "Tsang Sees Clearly Drawn Role for PWC," *SCMP*, Sept. 3, 1993, p. 5; Bruce Gilley, "Old Game, New Strategy," *FEER*, May 23, 1996, p. 31 (describing David Chu's pledge to work to keep Martin Lee a potential candidate for the provisional legislature).

[57] Emily Lau, "Backroom Betrayal," *FEER*, Mar. 1, 1990, p. 14.

[58] Nick Rufford, "Patten Worries the Money Men," *Sunday Times* (London), July 3, 1994; "Xinhua's Zhou Nan Reaffirms Chinese Stance on Hong Kong," BBC Monitoring Service: Far East, Mar. 18, 1993 ("A few hundred influential organizations from the industrial and commercial circles . . . issues statements opposing the Hong Kong British authorities' political reform programme").

[59] "HK Must Speak with One Voice," *SCMP*, Nov. 1, 1992, p. 10 (quoting Gordon Macwhinnie, former chairman of the Hong Kong Jockey Club).

fessionals Federation Chairman Vincent Lo expressed this notion of priorities clearly: "Democracy is important, but it is not the only goal. A smooth transition is more important."[60] Bankers Trust Managing Director William Overholt warned that pressing the Patten proposal risked giving China a sense of "moral and legal right to destroy the rule of law, democracy and autonomy which we all want for Hong Kong."[61]

By the eve of Patten's final policy address, the GCC was warning the Governor to limit himself to "essential legislation for the immediate good government of Hong Kong and enhancing the transition process to Chinese sovereignty," and also to seek prior consultation with the SAR's Chief Executive designate.[62] The president of the American Chamber of Commerce in Hong Kong has said that the provisional legislature was acceptable to U.S. business interests in the territory, which were generally confident that China would not tamper with the key legal requisites of Hong Kong's thriving capitalist system.[63]

Business representatives in government and the pro-business organizations that emerged during Hong Kong's final years under British rule certainly expressed no love for Patten's version of democratic reform. Half of the non–civil service members of the government-appointed Exco – several of them business leaders – failed to defend the government's electoral reform package, and one – Federation of Hong Kong Industries Chairman Raymond Chien – called for its defeat.[64] Members of the Liberal Party banded together with other pro-business, as well as the pro-China, members of Legco to oppose the bill Patten had tabled, coming within one vote of a majority.[65] In a position

[60] Tai Ming Cheung, "Embattled Governor," *FEER*, Nov. 26, 1992, p. 10. A Pro-China Hong Kong newspaper praised the Business and Professionals Federation (which called for political development to follow the principle of a "smooth transition") and the Cooperative Resources Center (whose spokesman endorsed "convergence" of Hong Kong's and China's political systems) for their "pragmatic" rejection of the Patten proposals, indicative of "a profound understanding" of the requisites of Hong Kong's political stability. "The Strong Points of Business and Professional Circles Are the Weak Points of Chris Patten," *Wen Wei Po*, Nov. 11, 1992, p. 2.
[61] Louise do Rosario, "Democracy's Pros and Cons," *FEER*, Mar. 24, 1994, p. 24.
[62] Simon Pritchard, "Chamber's Nervousness a Worrisome Pointer," *SCMP*, Oct. 2, 1996, p. 12.
[63] Vivian Lee, "US Investors Shun Debate," *SCMP*, May 21, 1996, p. 6; "Hong Kong's Dwindling Hopes for Democracy," *Business Week*, May 11, 1992, p. 57.
[64] Andy Ho, "Why Patten's Exco Might Still Come to the Party," *SCMP*, July 21, 1994, p. 17.
[65] Mary Kwang, "What Victory?" *The Straits Times* (Singapore) July 2, 1994, p. 4; Chris Yeung & Fung Wai-kong, "Liberals Look to Take the Lead in Legco," *SCMP*, July 1, 1994, p. 25; Louise do Rosario, "Patten's Progress," op., cit., p. 20 (the Liberal Party's more modest democratic reforms, principally a much narrower constituency); Tai Ming Cheung, "Pressure Tactics,"

typical of pro-business politicians during the 1990s, businessman-politician
James Tien opposed Patten's efforts to "redefine all the grey areas" in the Basic
Law by expanding the voter base and undermining the accountability of func-
tional constituency representatives to their narrow electorates.[66]

This tepid attitude toward elements of an Augmented Hong Kong Model permeates other aspects of articulated business positions. Property developer
David Chu criticized the colonial government's moves to relax press censor-
ship and other reforms "done in the name of freedom and democracy" as having "side-effects" detrimental to stability.[67] When China has threatened to
rescind the Bill of Rights, or to reinstate laws that the colonial authorities have
amended to conform to it, business interests have been nearly silent, or, more
recently, have followed Tung Chee-hwa's lead in calling for an appropriate balance between individual rights and society's interest in order.[68] Swire drew the
ire of the Law Society for withdrawing permission to use its shopping center
for a public program to discuss the Bill of Rights and other legal questions,
allegedly because of the program's controversial content.[69]

In the controversy over the Court of Final Appeal, the predominant position
ultimately adopted by the Hong Kong business community was at least as san-
guine as the face-saving claims made by British authorities. Business leaders
declared acceptable a deal that limited the number of foreign judges on the five-
member bench to one, that failed to clarify the scope of non-justiciable acts of
state, and that did not establish the Court before the final transition. Leaders of
the GCC, the Hong Kong Federation of Industries, and the American Chamber
of Commerce, as well as key pro-business Legco members, welcomed such a
deal as providing the stability and certainty that business needed.[70] Anson Chan
echoed business views when defending the bill on the grounds that it "ensures
the continuity of the rule of law in Hong Kong through the transition and will

FEER, Nov. 5, 1992, p. 8 (early opposition to Patten reforms from appointive and business functional constituency Legco members).

[66] James Tien, "One Country, One System," op. cit., p. 11.

[67] "Corporate Chiefs," op. cit., p. 22.

[68] "Lu Ping Stresses Partial Abrogation of Ordinances Amended by British Hong Kong Government Is Intended to Maintain Hong Kong's Prosperity and Stability," *Wen Wei Po*, Jan. 26, 1997,
p. A11.

[69] Jeremy Lau & Lana Wong, "Swire Objects to Discussion of Rights Bill," *SCMP*, Mar. 11, 1992.

[70] Steve Vines, "Beijing, London Sign Agreement on HK Court of Final Appeal," *Business Times*,
June 10, 1995, p. 3; Louis Won & Lok Wong, "From Politicians: Outrage," *SCMP*, June 10,
1995, p. 3; "Hong Kong Court," *Financial Times*, June 12, 1995, p. 19; "Hong Kong: Politics of
a New Era," *Euromoney*, Sept. 30, 1995.

safeguard public and international confidence in Hong Kong."[71] Similarly, prominent members of Hong Kong's business community publicly accepted that Beijing would tightly control the choice of the SAR's first Chief Executive. Of those expressing a view, most asserted that, despite fears of conflicts of interest, a businessperson would make a better choice than a civil servant or a judge – suggesting that understanding business' interests is a more important qualification than experience in Hong Kong's law or government.[72]

China and its allies can also point to specific actions by Hong Kong's business communities that suggest support for China's rejection of an Augmented Hong Kong Model of the rule of law. For Hong Kong's big businesses and much of its foreign business community, "1997," as one of their number put it in 1994, has "already happened."[73] Reluctantly or not, businesses have adapted aggressively, playing their old games by the new rules imposed on the territory by its impending masters. The moves of the New China Hong Kong Group and of Swire – as well as burgeoning property and infrastructure projects undertaken in China by Li Ka-shing, Walter Kuok, Gordon Wu, and others – are merely the most prominent illustrations of a widespread phenomenon: building ties to Chinese entities and individuals well positioned to help in a world where informal connections matter more than legal formalities.[74] Proponents of the China Model have taken heart in the fact that accelerating integration of Hong Kong's economy with that of the Chinese mainland – where the rule of law is clearly weak – seems to have had little impact on business confidence in the territory. Despite occasional hiccups, the stock and property markets and overall economic health have remained strong.

The foreign business community has been harder for China and its allies to read, but it still provides cause for comfort. Mid-1990s surveys of U.S. businesspeople in the territory taken by Hong Kong's American Chamber of Commerce showed that an overwhelming majority of respondents had "favorable" or "very favorable" assessments of Hong Kong's business environment through

[71] Chris Yeung, Louis Won, & Catherine Ng, "Fight Not Over, Says Martin Lee," *SCMP*, July 27, 1995, p. 1; "Mathews Strikes at Opposition," *SCMP*, June 15, 1995, p. 6 (Attorney General's similar defense of bill).

[72] Bruce Gilley,"Playing Favourites," *FEER*, Feb. 8, 1996, p. 22 (quoting T. T. Tsui, David Chu, & Li Ka-shing).

[73] Robert Tyerman, "Hong Kong Awaits the Dragon," *Sunday Telegraph*, June 26, 1994, p. 6.

[74] "Early Birds," *Wall Street Journal*, Nov. 29, 1996, p. 1; Katsu Hiizumi, "Hong Kong Ponders," op. cit., p. 3; "Hong Kong's Experiences in Investing in the Hinterland," *Ta Kung Pao*, Nov. 24, 1994, p. 9 (Li Ka-shing speech on patterns of and opportunities for investment in China).

the end of the century.[75] Hong Kong's international bond rating has remained high (above China's) partly on the strength of foreign confidence in "the much more certain system of legality in Hong Kong."[76] On the other hand, others seemed unruffled by the prospect that China and Hong Kong would become more alike. Many Western investors have begun operating "under the assumption that they are already investing in China, not a separate entity."[77]

Taking the offensive, China and pro-China sources have argued that a cozy relationship between favored companies and government authorities is not a distinctly PRC phenomenon, but has in fact characterized Hong Kong business practices all along. When Patten accused China of using political considerations to grant franchises for new container terminals, the New China News Agency's Hong Kong branch characterized it as a "self-confession" that described "exactly what he's doing."[78] On another issue, Lu Ping said, "The British side keeps saying that they have separated economics from politics. In fact, it is precisely the British side that has mixed economics and politics."[79] Such statements imply that Hong Kong business has already survived handsomely under something like a China Model of the rule of law, and thus that, for business, the only prospective changes are redistributive – from the favorites of the territory's former political overlords to the favorites of its new rulers.

Persuading Business. The PRC and its Hong Kong allies do not, however, dismiss completely their antagonists' claims about the Hong Kong business community's views on the rule of law. China's public intransigence on liberal and democratizing reforms would seem to imply something more than an oddly unarticulated view of what (minimal) form of legality Hong Kong needs in order to prosper, and something other than a gratuitously harsh expression of indifference to what the territory's business interests consider as necessary to

---

[75] "US Businesses Confident on Hong Kong and China," Reuters, Nov. 23, 1995; Bruce Gilley, "Red Flag over Hong Kong," *FEER*, Dec. 7, 1995, p. 72. The 1996 survey showed confidence levels still on the rise, with over 90 percent of respondents declaring Hong Kong's business environment "favorable" or better. (For China the number was 95 percent.)

[76] Jonathan Sprague, "S&P Says HK Credit Safe amid Sino-UK Rows," Reuters, Feb. 13, 1995.

[77] "The Shadow over Hong Kong," *The Economist*, Apr. 3, 1993, p. 37; "Hong Kong: Business Community Maintaining Optimism," op. cit.

[78] Chris Yeung & Connie Law, "China Hits Patten for Deal with Jardines," *SCMP*, Sept. 14, 1994, p. 1.

[79] "Britain Like a Barber with only a Stove but No Water Barrel on His Shoulder Pole," *Ta Kung Pao*, Jan. 18, 1994, p. 2; see also, Gary Silverman, "Miles to Go," *FEER*, June 13, 1996, p. 69 (PC member and pro-China think-tank head Shiu Sin-por's suspicions of British handling of contracts for new railway).

its economic health. The calculus, although not openly stated, appears to have been that, once China made clear its resistance to such moves, Hong Kong's key business actors would forgo any inclination to support a strongly reformist rule of law agenda.[80]

In bringing pressure to bear on Hong Kong's business interests, China has also played effectively on their strong aversion to uncertainty. Thus, China's throwing lucrative contracts and key infrastructure projects into protracted limbo sharpened business opposition to Patten's political reforms, and its promise to delay work on a number of concrete transitional issues of interest to business gelled business acceptance of the troubling resolution to the Court of Final Appeal issue.

This business sector–wide approach has been backed by China's considerable array of carrots and sticks. Everyone in Hong Kong's business community understands that China will reward its supporters and punish its opponents. Xinhua's virulent attack on Jardine Matheson for its support of the Patten electoral reforms, coinciding with China's opposition to Jardine's participation in the new container terminal project, exemplified the "stick" approach,[81] while the awarding of sought-after government contracts – such as the concession to print SAR passports – to established friends of Beijing in the territory represented the "carrot."[82]

In a different vein, China and its allies in the territory have sometimes sought – though often ineptly – to reassure businesses that the economy-focused rule of law they require will be provided. For example, PRC sources have argued that the perceptions of a Chinese threat to scuttle transition-bridging contracts were misplaced, for "the Chinese side has always adopted a positive and responsible attitude to contracts straddling 1997" and has "no intention of intervening in any economic affairs of the SAR."[83] China's Joint Liaison Group leader Zhao Jihua expressed confidence that the 1995 Court of Final Appeal bill would avoid a "judicial vacuum" and assure Hong Kong "an independent and complete judicial system." A pro-China Legco member argued

---

[80] Lest business miss the point, pro-China Hong Kong newspaper commentaries cautioned that Patten's reforms would surely "shock" the community and "jeopardize prosperity and stability" and harm the economic interests of foreign and domestic investors – all results that would be brought about, or exacerbated, by China's taking its announced hard line on the reforms. See, for example, "Mr. Patten's Choice," *Ta Kung Pao*, Oct. 18, 1992, p. 2.

[81] Huang Chen-ya, "Jardines Salvo," op. cit., p. 11; Bruce Gilley, "Brass Tacks," op. cit., p. 14.

[82] Bruce Gilley, "Red Flag," op. cit., p. 72.

[83] "China Has Final Say on Right of Abode in HK," Xinhua, BBC Monitoring Service: Far East, Feb. 11, 1996; Liu Shih-hsin, "Lu Ping Talks with Visiting Textile Delegation," op. cit., p. 2.

that the bill should cause no alarm because the Basic Law assures that common-law practices will be fully considered when the NPC decides whether a case is within the court's jurisdiction.[84] Moreover, China's Foreign Minister argued, the provisional legislature that would be established to succeed Legco on July 1, 1997, would avoid a "legislative vacuum" and assure the social stability and "normal operation" of the SAR that business required.[85] One of China's senior Hong Kong spokesmen stressed that there was no need to fear that China would politicize the civil service, whose neutrality and competence have been so vital to Hong Kong's favorable business environment.[86]

A senior Beijing official reportedly assured Paile Cheng, chairman of the prominent British firm Inchcape Pacific, that China understood the perils of importing PRC methods to Hong Kong, noting that land values in Macau were lower than in Hong Kong because China had been "far too involved" in the Portuguese colony since the 1970s.[87] Politburo Standing Committee member Li Ruihuan made a similar point more colorfully, describing Hong Kong as an *yixing* teapot which would lose its value if it were scrubbed aggressively in an effort to clean it.[88] In addition, senior Foreign Ministry officials have frequently reassured foreign businesses that their interests will continue to be protected by Hong Kong's current laws after 1997.[89]

Another appeal to the self-interest of the Hong Kong business community has shown an appreciation for nascent democratic politics in Hong Kong. China and its allies have played on the business community's fears of what democratization might bring. Democratic Alliance for the Betterment of Hong Kong (DAB) leader Tsang Yok-sing warned of concern in the business community that under the Patten reforms, "you'll get a lot of radicals in the legislature."[90] Shiu Sin-por, head of a pro-China think tank in Hong Kong, sought to persuade business of the merits of the provisional legislature that Beijing

[84] *Wen Wei Po*, June 10, 1995, p. A2; "China Hopes Court Deal Will Boost Sino-British Ties," *AFP*, June 13, 1995; Chris Yeung, Louis Won, & Catherine Ng, "Fight Not Over," op. cit., p. 1.
[85] "Provisional Legislature Must Be Set Up as Scheduled," *Ta Kung Pao*, Oct. 8, 1996, p. A2.
[86] *Wen Wei Po*, Dec. 29, 1996, p. A3 (quoting Zhang Junsheng, Deputy Director of Xinhua's Hong Kong office); *Wen Wei Po*, June 25, 1995, p. A4 (text of Qian Qichen speech to Preliminary Working Committee).
[87] Bruce Gilley, "Red Flag," op. cit., p. 73.
[88] *Wen Wei Po*, Mar. 14, 1995, p. B5 (text of Li's remarks to Hong Kong and Macau delegates to China's principal united front organ).
[89] See, for example, *Wen Wei Po*, July 24, 1996, p. A12 (quoting Foreign Minister Qian Qichen).
[90] Louise do Rosario, "Patten's Progress," op. cit., p. 20; Louise do Rosario, "Thorn in the Side," *FEER*, Apr. 20, 1994, p. 28 (noting criticisms of Democrats for raising populist expectations of tax cuts and welfare spending).

would establish in 1997, arguing that "[b]usiness will find it a blessing to have a legislature which is supportive of the [SAR] administration" and not dominated by the Democrats.[91] PRC sources have repeatedly invoked the specter of expanded social welfare spending under a Democratic Party–dominated Legco and a like-minded governor.[92] In doing so, they have sought to draw on Hong Kong business elites' strong aversion to fiscal profligacy and government regulation as a source of opposition to liberal, rule of law–supporting reforms.

More broadly, China and its allies have sought to tap into business' fears of the politicized, disorderly society that the colonial authorities' moves to implement elements of the Augmented Hong Kong model arguably portended. They cautioned that Patten's political reforms and later legislation to relax restrictions on public political gatherings and the establishment of political organizations risked transforming Hong Kong into a "political city" plagued by worsening social unrest and declining prosperity.[93]

Beijing and its loyalists have played their own version of the "popular opinion card" as well. China helped to fund and nurture the DAB as a pro-PRC political party; it established a Hong Kong branch of the All-China Federation of Youth. Such organizations joined the long-established pro-China press and pro-China trade unions in providing a regular voice sympathetic to the PRC's position in the increasingly tumultuous politics of the territory.[94] More negatively, China derided apparent popular support for an Augmented Hong Kong Model by dismissing it as shallowly rooted and the product of a propaganda apparatus controlled by the colonial government and its sympathizers, and

---

[91] Chris Yeung & Fannie Wong, "When the Lights Go Out at Legco," *SCMP*, Oct. 15, 1994, p. 21.

[92] Jonathan Karp, "Money Talks," *FEER*, Mar. 17, 1994, p. 18 (quoting Bank of China economist); Jonathan Karp, "Man in the Middle," *FEER*, Oct. 13, 1994, p. 16 (quoting Wang Fengchao, Deputy Director of Hong Kong and Macau Affairs Office); William McGurn, "Diminishing Returns," *FEER*, June 13, 1996, p. 62 (quoting Joint Liaison Group member Chen Zuo'er); "Increasing Tax in Disguised Form, and Shifting Misfortune to the Special Administrative Region," *Wen Wei Po*, Dec. 17, 1993, p. 2.

[93] "Tung Chee-hwa Says Proposals of Legal Sub-Group Are Good," *Ta Kung Pao*, Jan. 24, 1997, p. A2 (Hong Kong government's amendment of the Public Order Ordinance and Societies Ordinance invites foreign political forces into the territory and undermines social order and stability); "Vigilance Against Instigating Political Confrontation," *Ta Kung Pao*, July 10, 1996, p. A2 (Patten's purpose is to make Hong Kong a "political city"); "Deng's Remarks Have Practical Significance," *Wen Wei Po*, Sept. 27, 1993 (Patten's political reform program has caused "turbulence" in Hong Kong and harm to the economy).

[94] Louise do Rosario, "Board Game," *FEER*, Sept. 8, 1994, p. 18; *Ta Kung Pao*, May 19, 1992 (interview with DAB leader Tseng Yu-cheng); *Wen Wei Po*, May 9, 1990 (editorial describing comments of State Council Hong Kong and Macau Affairs Office Director Ji Pengfei).

thus, implicitly, as something business interests need not take seriously.[95] Relatively poor voter turnout rates in elections held under expanded franchise have provided China and its allies ammunition for this argument.[96]

Claiming to Be Right. Finally, China and pro-China elements apparently believe that, even if China's assessments of business' preferences prove to be incorrect and efforts to effect a change in preferences fail, post-1997 events will prove doubters wrong: The territory will continue to thrive economically without a strong and expansive rule of law. The indications of this view are fragmentary yet telling. If China truly accepted that nothing less than an Augmented Hong Kong Model would sustain prosperity, it would not have expended so much effort in fashioning and trying to "sell" a more modest legal regime for the economy in the SAR. Nor would it have let slip remarks (typically from those not involved directly in the management of Hong Kong affairs) to suggest that law has made only modest contributions to Hong Kong's success. Striking examples of this phenomenon include Jiang Zemin's comment that "Hong Kong's prosperity in the past cannot be attributed . . . to an independent judiciary and a free system of the press, but mainly to the creativity of the Hong Kong people themselves," and an assertion in the territory's pro-China press that China's growing wealth and strength are the "fundamental guarantee" of Hong Kong's continued prosperity.[97]

THE SINGAPORE MODEL AND THE QUESTION OF POLITICAL CONTEXTS

In the battle over Hong Kong's business community, both sides' failure to push for a "Singapore Model" of the rule of law seems puzzling. After all, the territory's business elites have reacted negatively to developments portending either

[95] "Just Keep a Watch over Mr. Chris Patten's Performance," *Wen Wei Po*, Oct. 21, 1992, p. 2 (describing Patten's possible success in temporarily fooling people into thinking his reforms were not harmful); "Tung Chee-hwa Says Proposals of Legal Sub-Group Are Good," *Ta Kung Pao*, Jan. 24, 1997, p. A2 (arguing that Patten has duped some Hong Kongers into opposing planned post-1997 repeal of late colonial amendments that liberalize laws restricting political organizations and public speech).

[96] Louise do Rosario, "Sharp Distinction," *FEER*, Sept. 7, 1995, p. 29; Bruce Gilley, "Red Flag," op. cit., p. 72; Louise do Rosario, "Stand Up and Be Counted," op. cit., p. 16; Chen Chien-ping, "Lu Ping Stresses Basic Law Cannot Be Amended Before 1997," *Wen Wei Po*, Oct. 9, 1991.

[97] Frank Ching, "Danger Signals for Hong Kong," *FEER*, Oct. 17, 1996 (quoting Xinhua summary of Jiang interview); "Preparation Means Success; No Preparation Means Failure," *Wen Wei Po*, Dec. 12, 1993, p. 2. In the same vein, Politburo Standing Committee member Li Ruihuan argued that Hong Kong's success is attributable to the Hong Kong people themselves and not to anything they have received from the British. See *Wen Wei Po*, Mar. 14, 1995, p. B5.

the Augmented Hong Kong Model or the China Model, suggesting the appeal of a middle ground. Moreover, common sense suggests that Hong Kong business interests would prefer a robust and autonomous legal order for commerce, and something much less in the realm of politics. The formation in 1995 of a "Hong Kong–Singapore Club," linking business leaders from the two city-states,[98] and the transfer to Singapore of some firms skittish about Hong Kong's future order,[99] attest to the appeal that Lee Kuan Yew's vision of legality has for companies doing business in Hong Kong.

Further, such a model of the rule of law is likely to appeal to two key participants in the political process of shaping Hong Kong's transition: departing British authorities seeking to duck embarrassing questions about the lack of a legal and constitutional infrastructure for political liberalism and democracy in colonial Hong Kong, and arriving Chinese rulers who have been far more comfortable with laws supporting market-oriented economic reforms than with the prospect of legal reform conducive to a political marketplace. Indeed, its assumed attractiveness to China was a key reason for the Singapore Model's popularity with some of Hong Kong's business elite, one of whom echoed Zhou Nan and Lu Ping: "If we leave them [the PRC] alone politically, they will leave us alone economically."[100] Nonetheless, a Singapore Model has received strikingly little consideration in the political battle over Hong Kong's business communities.

Also puzzling is the fact that the principal participants in that struggle have ignored significant differences among Hong Kong's major business interests. Potentially salient fault lines are obvious: The political leanings of vocal business elites have run the gamut from the unabashedly liberal and democratic commitments of entrepreneur and *Next Magazine* publisher Jimmy Lai to the "pro-China" views (as the press routinely labeled them) of property developer and Preparatory Committee member David Chu. Major firms vary in their key revenue sources – from those heavily dependent on investments in China, to those relying on Hong Kong sources of income, to those merely using Hong Kong as a base for regional or global operations. Key companies are also concentrated in significantly different economic sectors, ranging from the relatively low-tech manufacturing based in Guangdong and focused on exports, to the

---

[98] Katsu Hiizumi, "Hong Kong Ponders," op. cit., p. 3.

[99] "Growing Chinese Influence Fuels Jitters on HK's Future," *Asian Political News*, July 10, 1995; Bruce Gilley, "Courting Qualms," *FEER*, Apr. 25, 1996, p. 55.

[100] Robert Tyerman, "Hong Kong Awaits the Dragon," op. cit. (quoting John Hung, director of Wheelock Group).

mobile world of international financial and investment services. Instead of targeting segments of this diverse community in search of support for their preferred model of the rule of law, the antagonists in the battle over business have chosen to treat business as a near-monolith.

Both of these puzzles – both sides' failure to push for a Singapore "compromise" Model and their failure to exploit differences among key business elites – can be explained by the broader clash between opposing visions of sovereignty and legal authority that has defined the context in which the battle over business has been fought in the quest for a prosperity-supporting rule of law regime for Hong Kong after reversion. Concerning the first puzzle, the visions framing the narrower conflict are, at best, ambivalent about the Singapore Model. Relevant to the second puzzle, the broader clash is not conducive to the politics of coalition-building and horse-trading. Especially as the endgame for the vital pre-reversion phase draws near, the political struggle concerns what is "right," "true," and acceptable as a matter of principle, not what will win over a particular constituency. Understanding the battle over business and the rule of law, therefore, requires us to pay attention to those broader perspectives.

A "Strong Sovereignty" Perspective and the Rule of Law

China has been obsessed with securing an arrangement that recognizes and assures its sovereignty – "sovereignty" in the classical sense of China's holding plenary and non-derogable governmental authority and legal jurisdiction over the territory and people of Hong Kong. At the level of international law, the Joint Declaration says as much. Stating that the PRC "has decided to resume the exercise of sovereignty over Hong Kong, effective from July 1, 1997," it implicitly reiterates China's long-standing position that the nineteenth-century treaties ceding Hong Kong Island and Kowloon and leasing the New Territories to Great Britain were "unequal," invalid treaties that did not effect any transfer of sovereignty.

This strong notion of sovereignty has driven China and its allies to reject the Augmented Hong Kong Model of the rule of law. Instead of seeing close connections, they perceive a sharp disjunction between internationally binding promises concerning "economic" and "political" aspects of Hong Kong's legal and institutional order. Indeed, China has had relatively few qualms about pledging, as in the Joint Declaration, that Hong Kong will continue to enjoy monetary and fiscal autonomy, and that its rules of private property and ownership as well as its status as a free port will be upheld. Such arrangements do not obviously threaten the core requisites of sovereignty, as China sees it, over Hong Kong.

A treaty-like promise to grant the SAR independent authority to participate in international trade regimes, enact its own economic laws, and maintain an independent judiciary to enforce them is potentially troubling. To a certain extent, however, such a risk is unavoidable if a Singapore Model, and perhaps even a China Model, of the rule of law is to be established in the interest of safe-guarding Hong Kong's prosperity. Once the PRC accepted the initial premise of an internationally open, capitalist enclave within its borders, promising the SAR some discretion in shaping its economic legal order (including interna-tional ties) was a relatively modest additional step.

Pledges to give the SAR broader authority to operate independently in for-eign affairs, or to engage in autonomous self-government (much less self-deter-mination) would be unacceptable, however. To promise autonomy with respect to such "political" matters is to risk sovereignty, in the unitary, indefeasible sense in which China understands it.[101] The Joint Declaration's promises of a "high degree of autonomy" and government by local residents, therefore, can-not be allowed to sweep so broadly.

In some respects, China's view of sovereignty in international law casts doubt on China's willingness even to provide the more modest requisites of a Singapore Model. Although acceptable in theory, a promise to maintain the legal framework that has supported international economic openness and inter-nal capitalism in Hong Kong could threaten, in practice, to undermine China's authority over the territory. To go even further by implementing an interna-tional legal undertaking in order to give Hong Kong substantial autonomous authority to pursue its own agenda in domestic economic law-making and

---

[101] Promises, at the international level, to permit continuity regarding the aspects of Hong Kong's laws and legal system that deal with political rights could have presented a milder version of the same problem for China. In practice, the Joint Declaration process did not bring the ques-tions much into focus. This was largely a result of the fortuitous combination of Hong Kong's laws, circa 1984, which fell well short of liberal democratic ideals and China's constitution, as of 1982, promising (if not delivering) a laundry list of rights conforming to those ideals. With continuity thus appearing to require relatively little, and threats of formal retrenchment likely to throw a spotlight on China's shortcomings, the Joint Declaration finessed the one obvious sticking point, stating that the International Covenant on Civil and Political Rights and the International Covenant on Economic, Social and Cultural Rights would "remain in force" in Hong Kong.

international economic relations, could pose an even more serious version of the same threat.

Moreover, Beijing's growing concern about losing central control (especially in regions near Hong Kong) makes it more likely that China will construe "sovereignty" to require the jettisoning of objectionable promises concerning post-1997 Hong Kong. Such a move would not fundamentally undermine international legality, as China defines it. On this view, it would be perfectly consistent and lawful to reject some formally proper obligations on the grounds that they undermine the core requisites of China's sovereignty while remaining fully committed to formally identical international legal undertakings that do not pose such problems. Although promises that appear to address such "political" questions as governmental autonomy or civil liberties might be particularly vulnerable, nothing turns on such labels in principle, and pledges on "economic" matters could prove vulnerable to an expansive official Chinese view of what threatens to erode sovereignty.

China's sense of sovereignty in international law accords the sovereign great discretion in exercising its plenary authority in the *domestic* arena. The validity of China's domestic laws – including those for Hong Kong – does not depend on their fit with some set of substantive principles, whether capitalist or socialist, or with any particular model of prosperity-supporting rule of law. What matters is that the laws are issued by an institution with sufficient formal powers and according to legal and constitutional procedures – which can themselves be freely changed by proper exercise of sovereign authority.[102]

Any number of "rule of law" arrangements could be adopted via the Basic Law or other legislation applicable to Hong Kong. No principle forbids – or requires – the Basic Law to delegate substantial law-making, administrative, or adjudicative authority to the SAR government or to mandate that Hong Kong's distinctive "systems" remain basically unchanged. Similarly, nothing in the Chinese perspective bars arrangements that provide for extensive continuity in, or grant considerable autonomy to govern, economic activity while declining to confer similar authority or to promise equivalent continuity in the political sphere. While China could, in theory, mandate a relatively robust version of the

---

[102] This aspect of China's perspective – although sometimes honored only in the breach – is reflected in China's having rather punctiliously established a constitutional basis for the SAR, in passing the Basic Law itself, and implementing and interpretive resolutions, in accordance with constitutional procedures, and in arguing about many proposed Hong Kong reforms in terms of their incompatibility with the text of the Basic Law.

rule of law, any such arrangement would exist only as China's prudential accommodation, accepted for its instrumental value as a route to a Hong Kong that is prosperous and stable, but also unquestionably subject to Chinese sovereignty.

This minimally proceduralist perspective supports a more substantive dimension of China's conception of domestic law, one that indicates more clearly why an Augmented Hong Kong Model of the rule of law is problematic: No allocation of authority and no substantive commitment in domestic law can have the effect of irretrievably delegating the Chinese sovereign's discretionary authority in ruling Hong Kong. Put broadly, potentially runaway promises of autonomy for the SAR, especially concerning political rights and legislative authority, must not be undertaken lightly. Put more narrowly, because one aim of proceduralist legitimacy is to assure and enhance the sovereign's capacity to make laws that reflect its preferred policies, China cannot countenance binding or irrevocable promises allowing Hong Kong to establish legislation or institutions that could undermine China's Hong Kong policies (which are potentially malleable and do not accord prosperity a lexical priority).

Thus, domestic Chinese law for Hong Kong must keep decisive authority in PRC institutions and PRC-controlled processes. Accordingly, the Basic Law and other legal provisions implementing a "high degree of autonomy" for the SAR or "basic policies regarding Hong Kong" reserve – both in the text of the Basic Law and under the Chinese constitutional theory that permits legislation of equal dignity to alter the Basic Law – to the National People's Congress, its Standing Committee, and the Central People's Government such vital functions as amending the Basic Law, guiding interpretation of its most sensitive provisions, and enacting national legislation applicable to Hong Kong. On China's view of such matters, any commitments made in domestic law – whether addressed to economic or political matters, whether promising continuity with Hong Kong's late colonial ways or pledging freedom from Beijing's interference – are, on this view, equally and legitimately vulnerable to changes wrought by later law-making. Such changes are obligatory if they prove necessary to protect China's enjoyment of sovereignty over the territory.

In sum, Beijing's conception of sovereignty and legality, together with its emphasis on preserving Hong Kong's prosperity, have generated an affinity for a rule of law for Hong Kong that keeps a safe distance from the expansive "political" promises of autonomy, liberalism, and democracy demanded by the Augmented Hong Kong Model, and that remains very wary of the Singapore Model's potential for, in practice and "unintentionally," eroding sovereignty.

Jacques deLisle and Kevin P. Lane

A "Liberal Order" Perspective and the Rule of Law

From the perspective broadly shared by Great Britain, the Hong Kong government, and Hong Kong's liberals and "pro-democracy" politicians, the picture looks profoundly different. At the level of international law, the obligatory force of promises affecting Hong Kong's future legal order depends principally on formal concerns, particularly that the parties to the Joint Declaration held the necessary authority and followed appropriate procedures for concluding an agreement addressing such matters. Nothing is inherently suspicious about an international agreement between Great Britain and China that provides the requisites of a particular rule of law model for the Hong Kong SAR. As long as the two parties could come to an agreement and embody it in proper legal instruments, they were free to adopt the China, Singapore, or Augmented Hong Kong Models (or any other arrangement).

Once the Joint Declaration enshrined specific undertakings – such as a high degree of governmental and economic autonomy, continuity in Hong Kong's economic and legal systems, a list of specific civil rights, and elections for key SAR posts – in a treaty-like document, such flexibility vanished. Put simply, a valid contract between sovereigns must be fully performed. Under this classically liberal and contractarian perspective, all significant provisions serve as equally good barometers of a partner's worthiness and reliability. At the outset of the bilateral discussions on Hong Kong's future, British Prime Minister Margaret Thatcher articulated the basic point underlying this position. Insisting that accepting the validity of the nineteenth-century treaties ceding parts of Hong Kong was a necessary starting point for negotiating a treaty effecting the return of those lands, she warned that a nation that failed to honor one treaty could not be counted upon to abide by others.

On this view, each instance of China's failing to abide by – or seeking to reinterpret fundamentally – a promise made in the Joint Declaration looms as a harbinger of its likely disregard for the full range of China's international undertakings concerning the territory. The PRC's apparent reneging on a pledge to provide governmental autonomy or political democracy meant more than undermining an Augmented Hong Kong Model of the rule of law; it meant casting doubt as well on China's narrowly economic guarantees, without which less expansive models of the rule of law could not flourish.

The domestic-law face of this conception of sovereignty is also profoundly at odds with the conception advanced by Beijing and its allies. To varying degrees and at various times, liberal and pro-democracy elements in Hong Kong, the territory's governor, and officials in London have come to see the provisions for the SAR's internal legal and institutional order that China has promised to accept, and additional arrangements that China has been determined to reject, as part of an inseverable package of principles that a sovereign is duty-bound to protect. Although there has been no consensus about exactly what the package entails, there has emerged a pervasive sense that it provides something more (especially in the way of civil and political liberties) than a Singapore Model, and perhaps the full requisites of the Augmented Hong Kong Model.

On this view, the Basic Law, as well as domestic Hong Kong law before and after June 30, 1997, is to be judged by its conformity to standards of what just and good laws must be. Great Britain's professed "moral obligation and duty to the people of Hong Kong" means a commitment to work with like-minded citizens of Hong Kong to ensure that economic liberties, liberal political values, and sound mechanisms of democratic accountability are embodied in the post-1997 legal and institutional order. These goals could be achieved through such means as the enactment and implementation of a Bill of Rights, the once-hoped-for establishment of a Court of Final Appeal before 1997, and the election of a semi-democratic Legco that could "ride the through train" to become the SAR's first legislature. To the extent that the Basic Law was – or was interpreted by China to be – at odds with this project, it was illegitimate.

Maintaining the "continuity" of Hong Kong's prior achievement of a rule of law approximating these exacting standards (and the level of prosperity it reliably supported) would require more than standing still. It would take substantive change to expand Hong Kong's autonomy in the political realm in order to replace the vicarious democratic accountability that Parliament had provided, and to establish clear checks on governmental abuse that had been absent from the letter of colonial legislation. As proponents of strong versions of this view have put it, where the British parliament previously has provided the democratic basis for Hong Kong's rule of law, an indigenous democratic legislature is the necessary replacement. Others, including Patten, have been more capacious, arguing that no institutional and legal order that fails to provide mechanisms for reflecting the will and values of the people of Hong Kong can suffice.

In sum, the perspective on sovereignty and legality voiced by China's antagonists and negotiating partners implies a commitment to a robust notion of the rule of law for Hong Kong, requiring more than a Singapore Model (even assuming the Singapore Model would be adequate to preserve prosperity). At the level of domestic law, the conception of sovereign obligation demands nothing less than the Augmented Hong Kong Model's central elements. At the level of international law, the Joint Declaration now obliges China to provide much of what that model requires, by virtue of provisions that are at least compatible with the laws and institutions that a good and just sovereign is obliged to provide.

Potential Agreement and the Perils of Misperception

As the moment of Hong Kong's reversion approaches, the political process that has been shaping the prospects for the rule of law in Hong Kong will continue; it will continue to swirl around the territory's principal business communities. Whether it will yield a rule of law regime that is acceptable to relevant political actors and to business interests remains uncertain.

A solution potentially acceptable to all is conceivable. Adherents to the two different visions of sovereignty might find common ground in a regime that provides something more than the China Model, something less than the Augmented Hong Kong Model, and something other than the Singapore Model. Some such middle ground appears to accord with the positions of many of the most important (if not the most audible) participants in the political debate and among the business audience: the colonial authorities who have hailed quite modest accords on the Court of Final Appeal, and offered minor moves toward democratization;[103] members of Parliament and the Foreign Office in London and occasionally the Prime Minister, who have at times distanced themselves from Patten's reforms;[104] Chinese officials who have promised something more formidable than a China Model of legality; the DAB and other pro-China elements in Hong Kong who have sought to persuade their mainland backers of the wisdom or necessity of supporting some modicum of democratic reform and political liberties;[105] the many pieces of the fragmented business commu-

---

[103] Kevin Hamlin, "Law: Agreeing with Whatever Peking Wants," *The Independent*, Dec. 20, 1991 (quoting Hong Kong Attorney General Jeremy Mathews's defense of the Sino-British deal on a Court of Final Appeal limiting the number of foreign judges to one).

[104] Bruce Gilley, "Back on Track," *FEER*, Oct. 19, 1995, p. 16.

[105] See, e.g., Teresa Poole, "Pro-China Alliance," op. cit., p. 11 (quoting DAB's Tsang Yok-sing; Louise do Rosario, "Winners and Losers," *FEER*, Sept. 28, 1995, p. 17 (noting the DAB position in 1995 elections favoring an elective rather than appointive provisional legislature); Tai Ming Cheung, "Common Front," *FEER*, Dec. 17, 1992; Bruce Gilley, "Red Flag," op. cit., p. 22 (DAB's opposition to China's plan to gut the Bill of Rights).

nity, and the politicians who represent them, none of whom had shown much love for the potentially destabilizing project of pursuing a "pure" Augmented Hong Kong or China Model of the rule of law; and perhaps even some of the pro-democracy activists in Hong Kong who once sought to craft a compromise version of the Patten reforms that Beijing would accept.[106]

Moreover, apparent rejections of the middle ground – notably by Hong Kong's most visible pro-democracy politicians and by Chinese central government officials – may prove disingenuous or irrelevant. In Hong Kong's colonial end game, proponents of extreme solutions to the rule of law problem probably have demanded more than they thought necessary, as part of a strategy of bargaining with their antagonists in the political struggle or in an attempt to persuade business interests to take sides in that struggle. Some Hong Kong liberals may reconcile themselves to the notion that Hong Kong – or at least Hong Kong's prosperity – can survive a relatively modest rule of law regime. And the most intransigent voices from the PRC may prove to be willing to exercise Chinese sovereignty in a more law-governed way than they have indicated.

Nonetheless, a more pessimistic scenario remains possible, even likely. Any broadly acceptable "rule of law" solution will necessarily be the product not of consensus but of overlap among the visions of sovereignty animating the principal political participants and the interests and preferences shaping the reactions of key businesses. Where such fundamental differences in perspective lie just beneath the surface, the potential for mutual misunderstanding, imputations of bad faith, and perceptions of provocation is high. Any deal is vulnerable to unravelling. In addition, the "extremist" posturing and atmosphere of crisis may lead to a failure to perceive opportunities for agreement – whether between political antagonists who have embraced opposing visions of sovereignty, or between members of a political camp and substantial segments of a non-unitary business community.

The potential for such an accord may be illusory, however. Claims from the colonial authorities that they are leaving behind the necessary conditions for survival of a strong and prosperity-supporting rule of law may be nothing more than Great Britain's attempts to save face where it knows it has failed. Many business interests may have been overstating their satisfaction with a weak form of the rule of law, in an effort to curry favor with China. And the less-than-unified voice from China may have promised more than it intends, or will be

---

[106] Tai Ming Cheung, "Silent Night," op. cit., pp. 8–9 (describing proposals from the Hong Kong Democratic Foundation and the Association for Democracy and People's Livelihood).

able, to deliver in a volatile era of systemic transformation and leadership transition on the mainland.

Whether it will prove possible in practice to cook the rice without cooking the goose depends on the still-unanswerable questions of which side of this "balance sheet" will predominate, and whether proponents of an Augmented Hong Kong Model are right to insist that something more than China seems willing to tolerate is necessary to maintain Hong Kong's prosperity.

3

Hong Kong Faces 1997

Legal and Constitutional Issues

JAMES V. FEINERMAN

INTRODUCTION

The British dependent territory of Hong Kong will become a Special Administrative Region (SAR) of the People's Republic of China (PRC) on July 1, 1997. This transfer of sovereignty, ordained by both historical forces and a more recent international agreement between the United Kingdom and the PRC, will be an epochal event in international legal history. Never before, even during the spate of decolonization during the late 1950s and early 1960s, has a new entity been created with such attention to its legal underpinnings. Beginning with the international agreement determining the basic features of the PRC's resumption of sovereignty, to a "mini-constitution" created to govern Hong Kong, to supplemental undertakings providing substantial details of such bodies as the new Court of Final Appeal – legal arrangements have been critical to every stage of determining Hong Kong's new status as an SAR of the PRC. Intended to guarantee the promised "high degree of autonomy" for Hong Kong after 1997 and to maintain Hong Kong's current polity, economy, society, and culture for at least fifty years after the PRC takeover, these legal instruments will likely be tested repeatedly in the months and years immediately following July 1, 1997.

Since the crackdown by the Chinese government in 1989, imposed after months of demonstrations in and around Tiananmen Square, the international community – as well as many residents of Hong Kong themselves – have become increasingly concerned. They perceive that the Chinese government is not receptive to Hong Kong's desire to establish a modicum of political democracy before the government of the PRC assumes sovereignty over the territory in 1997. Hong Kong's future was problematic even before the 1989 crackdown on demonstrators in and around Tiananmen Square and the sympathetic reaction of many Hong Kong residents to the student protesters and the goals of pro-democracy forces in the PRC. Fundamental differences between the people of Hong Kong and the PRC in their understanding of the 1984 Sino-British treaty and subsequent legal enactment reflected divergent experiences of both political rule and economic life. Some of the PRC's officials dealing with the Hong Kong issue proved poorly skilled in handling a democratic, and boisterous, international and local press based in Hong Kong. Harsh rhetoric from Beijing addressed to those in Hong Kong who publicly voiced their support for dissident elements inside the mainland boded ill for the enjoyment of promised civil liberties after 1997.

Notwithstanding these concerns, the return of Hong Kong to Chinese sovereignty is inevitable; most residents of Hong Kong are resigned to it, and many have been working for some time to accommodate themselves to the coming new order. Depending upon individual interests and experiences, many Hong Kong residents have decided to rely upon the assurances of the body of law now in existence to preserve their civil and political rights as well as their economic system and the prosperity they have enjoyed for several decades. This chapter examines the record to determine whether optimism, concern, or some admixture is justified by not only the content of the legislation but also the spirit in which it was enacted and promises to be implemented.

More immediately threatening was the protracted series of negotiations leading to the adoption of a "mini-constitution" for post-1997 Hong Kong. Three successive drafts were circulated, and public comment was invited. Strong public reaction to the undemocratic nature of the government proposed for Hong Kong after 1997 led to strident statements from both PRC and Hong Kong representatives. Officials from China threatened to impose a framework on Hong Kong unilaterally if its representatives persisted in their "intransigence."

One further worry has been the prospect that the United Nations International Covenant on Civil and Political Rights, currently in force in Hong Kong as a result of British colonial rule, will no longer apply after the Chinese takeover, since China is not a signatory. Although British attention to human rights in Hong Kong has been rather limited, the removal of this basic underpinning for civil liberties is troubling. Expectations for adherence to international human rights standards and the conventions enunciating them are minimal.

Hong Kong Faces 1997

On July 1, 1997, when the United Kingdom relinquishes sovereignty over Hong Kong to the PRC, it will do so according to an agreement between those two nations reached in 1984.[1] As an international agreement between the two nations which have the most direct control over Hong Kong's fate, this document is the starting point for any analysis of Hong Kong's post-1997 legal system. Yet, the Joint Declaration itself merely anticipated the construction of a new framework to implement the broadly worded, precatory document that established the process for the transfer of sovereignty.

This agreement was predicated upon an earlier legal document, the then-recently enacted 1982 Constitution of the People's Republic of China,[2] which first authorized the creation of SARs. Article 31 of the 1982 Constitution, very simply, provides as follows: "The state may establish special administrative regions when necessary. The systems to be instituted in special administrative regions shall be prescribed by law enacted by the National People's Congress in the light of specific conditions."[3]

As a result of this provision, new to the 1982 Constitution and lacking any analogue in the PRC's three previous constitutions, it became possible for the PRC government to negotiate an agreement with the United Kingdom to provide SAR status for Hong Kong following its reversion to PRC rule. On the other hand, the novelty of this provision and the fact that no other SAR was then in existence immediately raised concerns as to the nature and extent of the autonomy to be provided to SARs when one was established pursuant to the new constitutional provision. After all, the PRC contained a number of autonomous regions – equivalent in size and population in some cases to provinces – which enjoyed precious little autonomy. Many of them were in border regions, populated largely by non-Han ethnic groups and thus suspect to the dominant PRC ethnic majority; as a result, they in fact often possessed even

---

[1] Joint Declaration of the Government of the United Kingdom of Great Britain and Northern Ireland and the Government of the People's Republic of China on the Question of Hong Kong, Dec. 19, 1984, Gr. Brit. Treaty Series No. 20, reprinted in Vol. 23, *International Legal Materials*, p. 1366 (1984) [hereafter, "Joint Declaration"].

[2] *Zhonghua Renmin Gongheguo Xianfa* [Constitution of the People's Republic of China], promulgated for implementation by the Proclamation of the National People's Congress on Dec. 4, 1982, translated in *The Laws of the People's Republic of China, 1979–1982*, pp. 1–32 (Beijing: Foreign Languages Press, 1987).

[3] Ibid., p. 11.

less autonomy and were even more tightly controlled than ordinary provinces and other political subdivisions which were not denominated as "autonomous."

On April 4, 1990, the Chinese National People's Congress in Beijing passed a Basic Law for the Hong Kong SAR, which will come into effect in 1997; the president of the PRC subsequently promulgated this law.[4] Among other provisions, this Basic Law contains guarantees of individual rights, leaving to future determination the precise means for enforcement of these rights. Article 2 of the Basic Law restates the promise of the Joint Declaration that the Hong Kong SAR will enjoy "a high degree of autonomy," along with executive, legislative, and independent judicial power – including the power of final adjudication, as provided in the Basic Law. In form and substance, the Basic Law is intended to implement the terms of the Joint Declaration, providing greater detail for the basic policies enunciated in that document. In effect, it is a "mini-constitution" pursuant to the authorization contained in Article 31 of the PRC's 1982 Constitution for the new Hong Kong SAR.

Like most constitutions around the world, the Basic Law contains a long list of rights (Chapter III, "Fundamental Rights and Duties of the Residents"), covering everything from equality before the law, freedom of speech and religion, and freedom to travel, to rights to social welfare, and to choice of occupation. Most important, Article 39 of the Basic Law states that the provisions of the International Covenant on Civil and Political Rights, the International Covenant on Economic, Social and Cultural Rights, and international labor conventions which already apply to Hong Kong as a British dependent territory as a result of the United Kingdom's accession to these agreements "shall remain in force and shall be implemented through the laws of the Hong Kong Special Administrative Region." This provision is of particular importance, since the PRC is neither currently nor likely soon to become a party to these central international human rights treaties; thus, Hong Kong residents once reintegrated into the PRC after July 1, 1997, will enjoy considerably greater protection of their rights than do other PRC citizens.

Current Rights in Hong Kong

Despite its status as one of the United Kingdom's last remaining colonies (or "Dependent Territories," in quaint British usage), Hong Kong has come to

---

4 *Zhonghua Renmin Gongheguo Xianggang Tebie Xingzhengqu Jiben Fa* [The Basic Law of the Hong Kong Special Administrative Region of the People's Republic of China], with an English translation (Hong Kong: One Country, Two Systems Press, 1992) [hereafter, "Basic Law"].

enjoy considerable economic prosperity and rather extensive civil and political liberties during the past two decades. At present, the formal instruments of government are controlled by the British-appointed Governor; the nominal legislature, Hong Kong's Legislative Council, has hardly been a democratic body, at least until the past few years. Until the beginning of this decade, its fifty-six members were either personally selected by the Governor (twenty non-official members) or elected by professional bodies and district boards (twenty-six non-official members). An additional ten official members are public servants, who serve by virtue of their official positions. Yet, despite the previously undemocratic nature of their selection, in recent years the membership of the Legislative Council has come to include (by appointment and election) a reasonably large group of younger, outspoken members who have voiced the concerns of the Hong Kong citizenry. Moreover, the obvious concern of the Hong Kong government for the well-being of its people – manifest in its commitment to public housing projects, mass transit, and other infrastructural improvements, and to public health and social welfare – has convinced the populace of the benign intentions of their unelected overseers.

As a British colonial dependency, Hong Kong enjoys many of the protections of the unwritten English constitution and common law as well as the rule of law tradition. These have, to a great extent, been transplanted to Hong Kong and have taken root. The Hong Kong judiciary, particularly at its higher levels, is scrupulously honest and independent of (and resistant to) any executive or legislative interference with its adjudication. Significant indigenization of the judiciary and the legal profession has occurred over the past twenty years; local Chinese professionals are well trained and already largely in control of these institutions. Under British rule, final appeals from the Hong Kong Court of Appeal have been taken to the Privy Council in London; to prepare for Hong Kong's return to Chinese sovereignty in 1997, a new Court of Final Appeal in Hong Kong has been proposed and established, although it will not come into practical existence until July 1, 1997. The Chinese government has, among other guarantees, promised that Hong Kong can retain this legal system for at least fifty years after China recovers sovereignty over Hong Kong.

Some Issues Arising from Hong Kong's Return to Chinese Sovereignty

As already noted, the United Kingdom and the PRC concluded a Joint Declaration with three annexes in 1984 under which Britain has agreed to restore Hong

Kong to China on July 1, 1997. Hong Kong will then become, pursuant to Article 31 of the Chinese Constitution, an SAR of China and, in the words of the Joint Declaration, "will enjoy a high degree of autonomy, except in foreign and defense affairs, which are the responsibility of the Central People's Government." Since the ratification of the Joint Declaration in 1985, the National People's Congress of China, through an appointed Basic Law Drafting Committee (BLDC), undertook the writing of a Basic Law – in effect, a constitution for post-1997 Hong Kong – which is (among other things) to ensure Hong Kong's autonomy: "[T]he socialist system and socialist policies shall not be practiced in Hong Kong, and . . . Hong Kong's previous capitalist system and lifestyle shall remain unchanged for 50 years."

In connection with the transfer of sovereignty, the British government in Hong Kong has attempted to establish a toehold for representative government in Hong Kong before 1997 by aiming for the direct election of at least ten members to the Legislative Council by 1991, with further increases possible before 1997. Members of the Legislative Council have proposed that at least 50 percent of the seats there should be directly elected by 1997, with a mechanism put in place to provide for 100 percent direct election by 2003. Governor Chris Patten proposed speeding up this timetable to provide more representative rule by 1995, leading to a tumultuous election in which the biggest winner was the Democratic Party, founded by Martin Lee, Q.C., and other anti-Beijing activists who became more vocal after the 1989 crackdown on the mainland. China threatened to "react" to any precipitous rush toward participatory democracy in Hong Kong before 1997 as a hostile act. In crude, almost scatological, language that echoed the denunciatory harangues of the worst days of the Cultural Revolution, Patten, the British, and any Hong Kong Chinese who sided with them were vilified repeatedly and at great length. Following the success of Lee's party and a disastrous defeat for pro-Beijing forces in Hong Kong during the 1995 election, the PRC indicated through its official spokesmen that the newly elected legislators, who were elected to four-year terms intended to span the 1997 transition, would see their terms end on June 30, 1997.[5]

Moreover, in response to the outpouring of popular support in Hong Kong for the mainland pro-democracy demonstrators in 1989 and thereafter, thinly veiled threats against Hong Kong individuals and groups have issued from both the Chinese government and its representatives in Hong Kong. China has stated that it will not allow Hong Kong to become a "base for subversion" against

---

[5] "China and Hong Kong Victors Square Off After the Election," *New York Times*, Sept. 19, 1995.

the PRC, although it has never made clear what activities it would deem subversive. Three successive drafts of the Basic Law were publicized, with little attempt to answer substantive criticisms of earlier drafts by responsible Hong Kong parties (and Hong Kong members of the BLDC). Two members of the BLDC who were also then members of the Legislative Council, teachers' union leader Szeto Wah and lawyer Martin Lee, were expelled from the BLDC and accused of "counter-revolutionary activities" for their involvement in protests against the 1989 Beijing massacre. A Bill of Rights for Hong Kong, which was supposed to be published in January 1990 by the Hong Kong government, was delayed because of mainland pressure. When it was eventually adopted in June 1991, the Chinese authorities announced that it would not bind them after 1997 and that they felt free to reject any or all of it after the resumption of Chinese sovereignty, raising numerous concerns about the continuity of Hong Kong's pre-1997 legal system and whether it would indeed remain in force under PRC administration.

PRC Attempts to Intervene in Hong Kong Governance

Almost immediately after the establishment of the PRC on the mainland in 1949, the Chinese government began a program of infiltration and sought to wield influence over the affairs of the British colony which remained in Hong Kong. Once it became clear that the British were not leaving Hong Kong, China reached a modus vivendi with the British colonial government which permitted China, isolated from much of the world after the Korean War, to use Hong Kong as a kind of entrepot for contact with the non-socialist world. Much of China's foreign exchange was earned through Chinese-controlled enterprises based in Hong Kong and from direct sales to Hong Kong of basic commodities. Surplus population and individual malcontents were allowed to flee across China's border with Hong Kong; almost 2 million refugees entered Hong Kong from 1949 until the late 1960s. Whatever hopes China might have had that such an influx would destabilize Hong Kong and encourage the British to leave were dashed by Hong Kong's resilience; resources were mobilized to house and maintain at a subsistence level the colony's swelling population.

At the end of the 1960s, China's "Great Proletarian Cultural Revolution" washed over into Hong Kong briefly, as political radicals sought to achieve – in line with then-current political thinking on the mainland – the immediate revolutionary transformation of Hong Kong and the expulsion of the colonial power. Militant trade unionists and other pro-mainland activists tried their best to turn the populace against the British, but to no avail. After a brief period of disorder, the government firmly reestablished its control. Successive temporary waves of immigrants from the mainland recurred, but they were easily absorbed by Hong Kong's growing economy.

By the early 1980s, attention began to focus on the 1997 deadline for return of the leased New Territories (which account for over 90 percent of Hong Kong's total land area) to China under the terms of an 1898 treaty. China made it clear that it would not countenance any continuation of British control and that it intended to resume sovereignty. As a practical matter, the rest of Hong Kong would have to revert along with the New Territories. Initial resistance to China's stance, contemplated by Mrs. Thatcher (flush from her victory in the Falklands), was later prudently abandoned in the face of Chinese resolve. A handful of senior Chinese officials in Hong Kong were promised full British passports and residency in Great Britain, but only a small number availed themselves of the offer. On the other hand, the basic human rights of the rest of Hong Kong's people have been left to the determination of the Chinese leaders who ordered the Beijing massacre. From an international human rights perspective, this is clearly unacceptable; however, the international community, which can scarcely bestir itself to worry about Bosnia and Somalia in the throes of all-out war, has proved unable to focus upon a possible crisis in Hong Kong still (possibly) years ahead.

CAUSES FOR CONCERN OVER HONG KONG'S POST-1997 LEGAL ORDER

In the Joint Declaration, the governments of China and the United Kingdom agreed that (1) "[T]he legislature of the Hong Kong Special Administrative Region shall be constituted by elections,"[6] and (2) "[T]he power of final judgment of the Hong Kong Special Administrative Region shall be vested in the court of final appeal in the Hong Kong Special Administrative Region, which may as required invite judges from other common law jurisdictions to sit on the court of final appeal."[7]

Once the National People's Congress passed the Basic Law on April 4, 1990, the PRC provided a legal framework for the Hong Kong SAR, to take effect on July 1, 1997. In this respect, Articles 66–79 and Annex II of the Basic Law describe the future legislative framework, and Articles 80–96 outline the

6 Joint Declaration, Annex I, Section I, op. cit.
7 Joint Declaration, Annex I, Section III, op. cit.

judicial framework.[8] Given this legal background, it is necessary to consider the subsequent developments in both areas, for there have been continuing legal disputes over the proper establishment of the legislative and judicial branches to govern the Hong Kong SAR. Although the establishment of both the Court of Final Appeal and the Provisional Legislative Council has generated considerable controversy, of the two, the Provisional Legislative Council remains more problematic, since both sides still disagree forcefully about the issue. The disputes surrounding the Court of Final Appeal have been resolved by both sides – to the dismay of many residents of Hong Kong. Although these two critical components of the future Hong Kong SAR government are by no means the only controversial aspects of the Hong Kong transition, limitations of time and space require a focus on these two institutions and their development as emblematic, and possibly predictive, of the future.

The Court of Final Appeal

Unlike the pending controversy over the Provisional Legislative Council, the issue of the Court of Final Appeal (CFA) has been resolved with legislation. A decade after the signing of the Joint Declaration, the agreement between China and the United Kingdom to establish the CFA was finalized on June 9, 1995.[9] Pursuant to the Joint Declaration, both sides agreed that Hong Kong's judicial system would remain intact, except for necessary changes to include the CFA. The court system of the Hong Kong SAR would continue its common-law tradition and "exercise judicial power independently and free from any interference";[10] moreover, the "power of final judgment" would be vested in Hong Kong. Until the establishment of the CFA, however, the power of final judgment remains with the Judicial Committee of the Privy Council, located in Great Britain.[11]

Signed in 1995 by the Senior Representatives of the Sino-British Joint Liaison Group (JLG),[12] the CFA Ordinance culminated years of negotiations and the settling of disagreements between the two sides. Of course, not everyone was happy with the Sino-British agreement; many pro-democracy supporters

---

[8] Basic Law, op. cit.

[9] The Hong Kong Court of Final Appeal Ordinance, vol. 35, *International Legal Materials*, p. 207 (1996) [hereafter, "CFA Ordinance"].

[10] Joint Declaration, op. cit.

[11] David Schlesinger, "Hong Kong Governor Defends Court Deal with China," Reuters News Service–Far East, June 9, 1995 (available in LEXIS-NEXIS Service database).

[12] As authorized in the Joint Declaration, Annex II.

of Hong Kong voiced their dissatisfaction with what they saw as too many British concessions. In this respect, "almost all of the 18 directly elected Legco members voted against the CFA bill,"[13] which nevertheless received endorsement by the sixty-member Legislative Council (by a margin of about two to one). Martin Lee, leader of the Democratic Party, described the agreement as a "sell-out of the rule of law"[14] that would create a "useless" court. He and his supporters opposed the agreement based on three primary objections:

1. The CFA comes into force on July 1, 1997, rather than earlier.
2. The CFA is limited to having only one overseas judge.
3. Undefined "acts of state" are removed from the jurisdiction of the CFA.[15]

While the first issue may appear to be less substantive, the second and third issues raise fears among opponents as to the true nature of judicial independence in the future Hong Kong SAR court system.[16]

Issue 1: Early Establishment of the CFA. The CFA Ordinance represented a series of compromises by Chinese and British negotiators over issues that had been debated ever since the adoption of the Joint Declaration. In February of 1988, the British proposed establishing the CFA before the July 1, 1997, turnover of Hong Kong.[17] The purpose of such early establishment would be to "gain experience and win public confidence."[18] In response, consultation between the Chinese and British led to an accord in 1991, which included the agreement to establish the CFA before 1997. However, the Legislative Council rejected that 1991 agreement, which also outlined the composition of the CFA.[19] Whether the unfortunate delay

---

[13] Robin Fitzsimons, "Is Hong Kong Facing a Legal Sell-out?" *The Times*, Aug. 1, 1995.

[14] Sally Blythe, "Appeasement Carries the Day," *Eastern Express*, June 10–11, 1995, p. 2.

[15] Diane Stormont, "HK Legislators Pass Final Appeal Court Bill," Reuters Financial Service, July 26, 1995.

[16] See the Introductory Note by Frankie Fook-Lun Leung to the Hong Kong Court of Final Appeal Ordinance, 1996, vol. 35, *International Legal Materials*, p. 207.

[17] Zhao Jihua speech on signing the Court of Final Appeal agreement, *Wen Wei Po*, June 10, 1995, p. A2 (translated in LEXIS-NEXIS Service database).

[18] "China's Day in Court," *The Times*, June 10, 1995.

[19] "Case of Court of Final Appeals Is a Bad Precedent," *Ta Kung Pao*, Mar. 7, 1993, p. 2 (translated in LEXIS-NEXIS Service database). The editorial criticizes the UK for backing away from the 1991 diplomatic agreement with China based on the Hong Kong legislature's disapproval. It argues that the United Kingdom wrongfully fabricated a "three-legged stool" structure, by attempting "to upgrade the Legco" (Legislative Council) and involve it in the affairs of the Chinese and British governments.

in establishment of the CFA (until July 1, 1997) was avoidable and who caused the delay are essentially moot issues at this time. As Governor Patten stated, "[W]e would have very much liked to have set up the court not just now but two or three years ago . . . the choice that we had was whether to go ahead with an agreement with the Chinese that would stick or whether to do nothing at all, or chance setting up a court which would be dismantled by the Chinese."[20] Nevertheless, the delay remains a sticking point for the ordinance's opponents. For good reasons or bad, it is clear that the CFA will not come into effect before the 1997 transfer, as originally planned. As a result, there will be no opportunity to establish a track record under British administration before the CFA comes under Chinese sovereignty. More important to many observers than the implementation date, however, are the second and third issues of contention: the Court makeup and the vague phrase "acts of state."

Issue 2: Court Composition and Foreign Judges. The 1991 accord specified that the number of foreign judges permitted to sit on the CFA would be limited to one, and that although the Court could invite foreign judges, it was not required to do so. Such an agreement undermined the judicial independence of a multinational Court of Appeal which Martin Lee envisioned in 1983. To the dismay of the Hong Kong opponents, four more years of negotiations leading to the eventual CFA Ordinance did not change these contested provisions; the CFA remains limited to only one foreign judge out of the five, and the CFA Ordinance merely states that the

---

[20] David Schlesinger, "Hong Kong Governor Defends Court Deal with China," op. cit. See also Robin Fitzsimons, "Hong Kong Facing a Legal Sell-Out?" op. cit.,who adds, "But China itself caused delay by spending most of 1994 refusing to consider the Bill." Similarly, Ambassador Zhao remarked:

As to the timing of the establishment of the court, one has to take into consideration that it is no longer feasible to establish the court at an early date, say in 1992 or 1993, as was envisaged in 1991. Even if it were established in great haste now, it would not have been possible to try a few cases first in order to accumulate experience for the future Court of Final Appeal as had been intended. What is more important is that both sides must now face the reality that the Preparatory Committee of the Hong Kong Special Administrative Region and the team designate of the Hong Kong Special Administrative Region will be elected in 1996. Since the team designate will already have been in place some time before the establishment of the Special Administrative Region on 1st July 1996, it is only natural that it should be given the task of making preparations for the establishment of the Court of Final Appeal. (Zhao Jihua, speech on signing the Court of Final Appeal agreement, *Wen Wei Po* [translated] June 10, 1995, p. A2.)

CFA "may as required invite judges from other common law jurisdictions." The new judges will be chosen by a commission, whose members will include the nominees of the 1997 Chief Executive elect. Ironically, by rejecting the 1991 agreement and hoping to ensure judicial independence from China, the opponents (including the Legco, Bar Association, and Law Society) felt the "key was the inclusion of foreign judges on the CFA" – not one foreign judge, but more, including the possibility of a foreign majority. The CFA Ordinance enacted in 1995, maintaining the same restriction on foreign judges as the ill-fated 1991 agreement, actually received support from earlier opponents. As legislator Jimmy McGregor stated, "I don't see one possibility of China changing its view, or of Britain being able to change its view. . . . There is no option. Either we have the court under the four-one formula or we don't have a court at all." Moreover, pro-China residents of Hong Kong did not view the foreign judges as necessarily linked to the Court's independence. Rather, they felt the "main reason for their inclusion was to augment Hong Kong's small pool of judges with outside expertise." Outside of Hong Kong, British Professor Sir William Wade has stated that the four to one ratio is not "a cause for practical concern." [21]

Whether or not the limitation on foreign judges actually affects the judicial independence of the CFA remains to be seen. Yet, coupled with the composition factor[22] is the interdependence of the independent judicial branch with the executive and legislative branches. Given China's position on disbanding the current Legislative Council as of July 1, 1997, the confirmation of the CFA judges becomes an important issue to consider, as this process poses a further threat to the CFA's independence. Given the controversy and discussion over the appointed provisional legislature and, more generally, the Hong Kong SAR's future "elected" legislature, the allocation of political power among these competing branches will likely involve a contest of wills.

Issue 3: Acts of State. Perhaps the most troublesome issue in the discussion of the CFA is the true power and jurisdiction of the independent judicial branch of the Hong Kong SAR. Indeed, the language of the Joint Declaration and Basic Law seems to ensure an independent judiciary, but given the language of the PRC Constitution and the CFA Ordinance, the

---

[21] Jonathan Sprague, "Hong Kong Wonders When It Will Have Top Court," Reuters North American Wire, Jan. 15, 1995.

[22] See Articles 88–90 of the Basic Law for the selection guidelines.

Court's mandate becomes less clear. Section 4(2) of the CFA Ordinance specifically states, "The Court shall have *no jurisdiction over acts of state such as defense and foreign affairs* [emphasis added]."[23] The inclusion of the ambiguous words "such as," has left the Court vulnerable to China's definition of "acts of state." While the standards of international or English common law seem to define "acts of state" in a narrow fashion, it is possible that China, after 1997, might reinterpret that meaning.

The former British Ambassador to China, Sir Percy Cradock, has called the provision "dangerously broad," while International Commission of Jurists Justice Michael Kirby (also President of the New South Wales Court of Appeal) stated, "any reference to an Act of State exemption in a society such as the People's Republic of China is fraught with danger."[24] In her testimony to Congress, Dinah Pokempner of Human Rights Watch stated:

Nor will the Court of Final Appeal be able to establish its authority through precedent before the switch to Chinese rule. The Court of Final Appeal's jurisdiction is in the hands of the Chief Executive, who may issue certificates stating an issue involves an "act of state" and is therefore unreviewable. Should the Hong Kong courts challenge this judgment, their decision may be reviewed ultimately by the Standing Committee of the National People's Congress in Beijing under its power to interpret Hong Kong's Basic Law. Thus the finality of judgments from the Court of Final Appeal is also uncertain. It is unlikely that China will adopt the narrow and constrained view of the common law doctrine of "acts of state." Issues ranging from commercial disputes with state-owned enterprises to habeas corpus actions could be interpreted in light of national security concerns to involve "acts of state."[25]

[23] The CFA Ordinance, 1996, vol. 35, *International Legal Materials*, p. 207. Article 19 of the Basic Law also describes the Hong Kong court system's jurisdiction – denying jurisdiction in "acts of state such as defense or foreign affairs."

[24] See "China's Day in Court," op. cit., where the author states, "International common law limits these acts (of state) to such clear exercises of the sovereign prerogative such as treaties, acts of war or blockade but China spreads the net far wider." See also Robin Fitzsimons, "Is Hong Kong Facing a Legal Sell-out?" op. cit.

[25] Prepared Testimony of Dinah Pokempner before the House Committee on International Relations, Subcommittee on Asia and the Pacific, July 27, 1995, provided by Federal News Service, July 27, 1995 (available in LEXIS-NEXIS Service database). The declaration obliges future Hong Kong courts to follow English common-law precedent.

James V. Feinerman

While opponents of this ordinance provision make a valid point concerning the vague terminology, others have dismissed such worries. Paraphrasing Sir William Wade's analysis of this issue, Robin Fitzsimons noted, "Fears regarding Acts of State exemptions are unfounded." Moreover, Sir William states, "The law of Acts of State is a well-known branch of English law in which it is quite clear that what is or is not an Act of State is decided by the court. That law is intended to continue (in Hong Kong). So there is no possibility of the Chinese being able to say that whatever they like to call an Act of State is an Act of State and so withdraw it from the jurisdiction of the CFA."[26] Whether or not one believes that such clear assertions of legal principle will hold sway after 1997 is another matter. However, the British maintain that there are some limits to China's power:

> China has agreed that an "act of state" will not include decisions on the constitutionality of laws, where the court will have jurisdiction. China has also dropped its demands for a "post-verdict remedial mechanism" giving the Chief Executive power to overturn court decisions.[27]

Nevertheless, what China views as an "act of state" remains a grave concern for the people of Hong Kong. Despite the language of the Joint Declaration, Basic Law, and CFA Ordinance preserving the independent "common law" legal system in the Hong Kong SAR, what happens after 1997 is largely speculative. As Hong Kong lawyer and sometime professor Frankie Leung has pointed out, acts of state include "purely political" acts in the Chinese view, while Martin Lee has called it "common law with Chinese characteristics . . . subject to political whim." In addition, pro-China legislator Tam Yiu Chung specifically told members of the Legislative Council that the PRC's National People's Congress would decide what common law falls within CFA jurisdiction. Statements such as these make the future of an independent judiciary branch in Hong Kong unclear.[28]

---

[26] Robin Fitzsimons, "Is Hong Kong Facing a Legal Sell-out?" op. cit.

[27] "China's Day in Court," op. cit. The issue of constitutionality remains unresolved, given the language conflict within the Basic Law. Although Article 82 vests the CFA with the power of final adjudication, Article 158 of the same Basic Law states that the "power of interpretation of this Law shall be vested in the Standing Committee of the National People's Congress." Clearly, such conflicting language presents troubling questions. The "post-verdict remedial mechanism" appears to be the one concession that China made in this agreement.

[28] "China's Day in Court," op. cit. See also Robin Fitzsimons, "Is Hong Kong Facing a Legal Sell-out?" op. cit.

Hong Kong Faces 1997

The Provisional Legislative Council

The establishment of a provisional legislature is a result of an ongoing dispute between the British and Chinese over the proper interpretation of the Joint Declaration, Basic Law, and other agreements. Both sides are firm in their respective stances – arguing that the other side has violated international agreements and promises. To analyze the status of the provisional legislature properly, it is necessary to see it in the context of Sino-British relations and negotiations over the past twelve years – starting with the Joint Declaration.

The 1984 Joint Declaration left many points to be resolved between the two sides – including the actual political system. Indeed, it specifically states that the Hong Kong SAR legislature "shall be constituted by elections."[29] What the British government (and Hong Kong residents) considered "elections" likely differed from the Chinese interpretation.[30] Nevertheless, given the contrasting views, the Joint Declaration also spelled out an agreement that both sides would work together to resolve their differences, particularly in the second half of the transition period. The purpose was to ensure a smooth transition – laying the groundwork for a "through train."[31] As a result, negotiations between the two sides were carried out throughout this period to resolve the electoral arrangements.[32] Nonetheless, as stipulated in the Joint Declaration, the administration of Hong Kong up until the transfer of power remained solely in the hands of the British. Thus, neither the PRC government nor the Joint Liaison Group had any official power in administering Hong Kong's political affairs. While the Joint Declaration points out that both governments would cooperate and work to ensure a smooth transition (i.e., through the Joint Liaison Group or other government consultation), the British would clearly retain sovereignty over Hong Kong until 1997.

[29] Joint Declaration, Annex I, Section 1.

[30] See Mary Kwang, "An Uneasy Settlement," *The Strait Times* (Singapore), Sunday Review, Dec. 18, 1994, p. 20.

[31] Joint Declaration, Annex II, outlining the goals and functions of the Sino-British Joint Liaison Group. In particular, it states in Section 5 that: "The two Governments have agreed that in the second half of the period between the establishment of the Joint Liaison Group and 1 July 1997 there will be need for closer cooperation, which will therefore be intensified during that period."

[32] The term "through train" essentially meant that the pre-transfer Legislative Council could continue in place through the transfer of sovereignty. Its origin is less clear, although it is likely borrowed from the Hong Kong–Guangzhou non-stop railway connection that crosses the international border. The "smooth transition" seems implicit in the Joint Declaration, and became more explicit later, in the 1990 negotiations.

Vested with this administrative power, the British maintained consultations with the Chinese throughout the ensuing decade. In January of 1986, Britain suggested "convergence between pre- and post-handover systems." Moreover, in February of 1988, the British postponed direct elections in Hong Kong until 1991. However, the next few years played havoc with Sino-British relations and, in particular, with planning for the new Hong Kong legislature.

The Joint Declaration (Annex I) stipulated that the Basic Law would serve as the "mini-constitution" of the Hong Kong SAR. Included in the Basic Law were provisions governing the election process of the Hong Kong SAR legislature (Chapter IV, Section 3, Articles 66–79, and Annex II). While observing the language of the Joint Declaration ("The Legislative Council of the Hong Kong SAR shall be constituted by elections"), Article 68 further states that "the ultimate aim is *the election of all the members of the Legislative Council by universal suffrage* [emphasis added]." Thus, under the Basic Law, there is no guarantee, but only an "ultimate aim" of direct democracy. In addition, under this "gradual and orderly approach" to elections for the Legislative Council, the First Legislative Council would not necessarily be selected through election, but rather "in accordance with the "Decision of the National People's Congress on the Methods for the Formation of the First Government and the First Legislative Council of the Hong Kong Special Administrative Region." Moreover, for the second and third terms, Annex II of the Basic Law provided that only up to half of the sixty-member Legislative Council would be directly elected. Prior to the Basic Law's passage in 1990, the tragic events of the spring of 1989 occurred in Beijing, shocking the residents of Hong Kong, who rallied in support of the Chinese demonstrators. To boost the people's confidence and safeguard the territory's interest, the British took steps to increase democratization in Hong Kong. As a result, the 1991 elections for the Legislative Council were to include twenty directly elected seats, and the 1995 elections would include thirty directly elected members.[33]

China, fearing the ramifications of a large, directly elected body of anti-Beijing liberals, preferred a slower pace of democratization.[34] Therefore, in its secret negotiations with the British in February of 1990, the Chinese agreed to allow eighteen (not twenty) directly elected members of the 1991 Legislative

[33] Mary Kwang, "An Uneasy Settlement," op. cit.
[34] To address the issue of anti-Beijing, pro-Tiananmen-democracy supporters in Hong Kong, the mainland Chinese NPC added an anti-subversion clause to the Basic Law in January of 1990.

Council and twenty (not thirty) members in the 1995 elections. In addition, they agreed to the "through train" policy, whereby those members directly elected in 1995 could remain members through the transfer of sovereignty and up until 1999.[35]

After this secret agreement was completed, the British appointment of Christopher Patten as Governor of Hong Kong changed the Sino-British relationship significantly. While the Tiananmen tragedy complicated the delicate relations between the two sides, the reform measures of Governor Patten resulted in an overall breakdown in Sino-British negotiations, and a bleak future for the Legislative Council. Governor Patten's constitutional reform package included the revamping of the district board elections, municipal council, and Legislative Council. More important, the electoral reforms were "duly adopted through the law-making process in Hong Kong."[36] Given British sovereignty, the actions in Hong Kong were legitimate under law. Nevertheless, China opposed all the reforms carried out; the response was harsh.

As Lu Ping stated in January of 1993, "[T]he Chinese side will not accept any proposals that are patched together on the basis of the Patten package. All such proposals are not proposals for convergence and will not be allowed to take the through train to beyond 1997."[37] From April to November of 1993, the two sides held fruitless rounds of negotiations over the 1994/1995 elections proposals.[38] Without a deal, the "through train" arrangements ended, as the

[35] Mary Kwang, "An Uneasy Settlement," op. cit. (available in LEXIS-NEXIS Service database). See the Basic Law, Annex III, outlining the selection process of the First Legislative Council, and allowing for the "through train" of pre-handover members, provided that those members meet certain requirements and are confirmed by the Preparatory Committee. See also "Throwing in the Towel Before Entering the Ring," *South China Morning Post*, Mar. 6, 1990. One month after the Sino-British agreement, it stated: "If things continue in the same vein in the next five years, it is hard to see how Beijing is going to accept the 1995 Legislative Council. This means either of two things: China is going to do her best to shape Legco in the next five years to something more to her liking; or China will find some way to modify the agreed through-train principle."

[36] Tsang Yok-sing, "Clearing up Some Political Questions," *South China Morning Post*, Sept. 12, 1995, p. 18.

[37] "Excerpts of Interview with Lu Ping by Hong Kong Television Broadcasts Limited on January 2, 1993," reprinted and translated in "China 'will be forced to take measures' to 'gain mastery,'" *Wen Wei Po* (in Chinese), Jan. 4, 1993, p. 11 (available in LEXIS-NEXIS Service database).

[38] See full text of "Facts about a Few Important Aspects of Sino-British Talks on 1994/95 Electoral Arrangements in Hong Kong," made public by Chinese Foreign Ministry, Feb. 28, 1994, reprinted by New China News Agency domestic service (Xinhua) (in Chinese), Mar. 1, 1994, translated in *BBC Summary of World Broadcasts*, Mar. 2, 1994.

Eighth National People's Congress voted to terminate all British Hong Kong legislative bodies on June 30, 1997.[39]

As a result of this decision and the breakdown of discussions between the two sides, the likely outcome of the issue was determined. There was little to zero likelihood that the democratically elected members of the 1995 Legislative Council would continue to serve after the transfer of sovereignty. It is within this setting that the controversial matter of the provisional legislature arises.

The Birth of the Provisional Legislature. Although the parties to the Joint Declaration ostensibly agreed to work together to ensure a "smooth transition," the breakdown in negotiations and end of the "through train" have made this transition less "smooth," to say the least. As early as January of 1993, prior to the failed negotiations and termination of the "through train" agreement (the Eighth NPC adopted its vote to terminate the British bodies on August 31, 1994), Director Lu Ping discussed the idea of a provisional legislature:

> It is stipulated in the NPC decision that the committee will be established in 1996 so we will strictly follow the decision. In addition, *some Hong Kong friends have proposed establishing an organization* [provisional legislature] to ensure a smooth transition. It is unlikely that this organization will become a second organ of power in Hong Kong before 1997. . . . As to the exact date of its establishment, we are still soliciting opinions from the Hong Kong people. . . . Because the Hong Kong government will be responsible for administration before 1997 as is stated in the Sino-British Joint Declaration, this organization will not interfere in any routine administrative affairs. [emphasis added][40]

Indeed, after the eventual breakdown, China took steps to establish the provisional legislature. First, China appointed "advisors to form the Preliminary Working Committee (PWC) to lay the groundwork for the SAR government."[41] The PWC took charge of the proposal to create a provisional or "caretaker leg-

---

[39] Duanmu Laidi, "Ensure Hong Kong's Smooth Transfer of Government and Its Smooth Transition – Commenting on the Preparatory Committee's Decision to Establish a Provisional Legislative Council," Xinhua News Agency domestic service (in Chinese), Mar. 25, 1993, translated in *BBC Summary of World Broadcasts*, Apr. 1, 1996.

[40] "Excerpts of interview with Lu Ping," op. cit. The fact that this statement was made so early – prior to the failure of the negotiations – is interesting. It is still unclear whether it raises questions about the sincerity of the PRC concerning a real "through train," or was made contingent on a failure in negotiations.

[41] Mary Kwang, "An Uneasy Settlement," op. cit.

88

islature . . . to fill the legislative vacuum resulting from the disbanding of the council to be elected next (1995) September."[42]

On March 25, 1996, the second plenary session of the Hong Kong SAR Preparatory Committee "adopted a decision to establish a provisional legislative council,"[43] including detailed suggestions on its "formation, election, qualification of members, working time and other tasks of the council."[44] The adoption of such a provisional legislature raised two questionable issues, despite its stated intent of aiding the "smooth transition."

First, the appointed body would supplant the First Hong Kong SAR Legislative Council, which is specifically provided for in the Basic Law. While it is uncertain how long the provisional legislature will remain in place, one member of the Chinese PWC stated that "the provisional legislature will have *full powers to make laws for an expected term of nine to twelve months* [emphasis added]."[45] Second, "Beijing has said the provisional legislature could be up and running early in 1997, months before China actually resumes sovereignty over the colony on July 1, 1997."[46] In fact, the Chinese submitted a request to the Hong Kong government to "provide a venue and other assistance to the provisional legislature" which was routinely denied.[47]

Although the British and Hong Kong governments refused to assist the Chinese, it became clear in only a few months that the establishment of the provisional legislature would become a reality. In early November 1996, the Preparatory Committee picked "340 electors out of 409 Hong Kong candidates . . . short-listed from more than 5,000 nominees" to the Selection Committee.[48] The other 60 members of the Selection Committee "will be chosen by Beijing from mainland deputies to China's National People's Congress and the Chinese People's Political Consultative Conference." This Selection Committee will choose both Hong Kong's first chief executive and the members of the

[42] Linda Choy & So Lai-Fun, "Vice Premier Backs Caretaker Legislature," *South China Morning Post*, Dec. 9, 1994, p. 1.

[43] Danmu Laidi, "Ensure Hong Kong's Smooth Transfer of Government," op. cit.

[44] Ibid.

[45] Simon Holberton & Peter Montagnon, "1,000 Days of Uncertainty: It Is China That Will Call the Shots on the Handover of Hong Kong," *Financial Times*, Dec. 3, 1994, p. 6.

[46] Mary Binks, "HK Advisor to China Blasts Beijing over Legislature," Reuters North American Wire, Apr. 11, 1996.

[47] "Hong Kong Government to Ask Chinese Side to Discuss Cooperation List Next Week, Has Reservations about Some Demands," *Sing Tao Jih Pao* (in Chinese), Apr. 19, 1996 (available in LEXIS-NEXIS Service database).

[48] "Preparatory Committee on H.K. to Select Electors," *Asian Political News*, Nov. 4, 1996 (available in LEXIS-NEXIS Service database).

new provisional legislature. While this committee includes many of Hong Kong's wealthy businesspeople, noticeably excluded are members of Hong Kong's largest political party – the Democratic Party.[49] The candidates registered between November 18 and December 9, requiring the endorsement of at least 10 members of the Selection Committee.[50] As a result of this process, Hong Kong's first new Chief Executive under the Joint Declaration and Basic Law was announced December 11, 1996: pro-China shipping magnate C. H. Tung.[51] He far outpolled rivals Yang Ti Liang, retired chief justice, and businessman Peter Woo.

Despite these developments, there remains much controversy over the appropriateness of the provisional legislature, which is now inevitable. The Chinese maintain it is the best option to ensure a smooth transition, while the British continue to question its legality. Perhaps more important, the residents of Hong Kong are divided on the issue: The Democratic liberals firmly oppose it, but others – realizing its inevitability – are at least accepting, if not embracing, it.

Analysis of PRC and UK Positions on the Provisional Legislative Council. Both sides have expressed concerns primarily over the legality and timing of the establishment of the new Provisional Legislative Council. As to its legality, the Chinese have continuously maintained the position that Britain's unlawful actions caused them to create the provisional legislature. In particular, they place the blame on Governor Patten's unilateral electoral reforms, which ultimately ruined any possibility of the "through train" arrangements with the 1995 Legislative Council elections. Because those reforms did not conform to the language of the Basic Law – outlining the electoral process for the Legislative Council – the Chinese felt that they violated the spirit of the Joint Declaration requiring both sides to work to a "smooth transition."

Indeed, without the "through train," the Chinese have stated, the provisional legislature is necessary to fill a "legal vacuum" and allow Hong Kong to operate smoothly immediately after the handover of sovereignty. They have admit-

[49] "Top Hong Kong Party Turns Its Back on Post-handover Legislature," Agence France Presse, Apr. 23, 1996 (available in LEXIS-NEXIS Service database).

[50] "China to Start Selection Process for Provisional Legislature," Agence France Presse, Nov. 4, 1996 (available in LEXIS-NEXIS Service database).

[51] Keith Richburg, "Pro-China Tycoon Chosen for Top Hong Kong Post," *Washington Post*, Dec. 12, 1996, p. A33.

ted its imperfections but reiterated their belief that this is the best option available.[52] Moreover, and potentially a sign of things to come, the Chinese have even threatened the Hong Kong people over this issue. According to Foreign Minister Shen Guofang, "Senior officials who want to have responsibility after 1997 must endorse the provisional legislative council and cooperate with it."[53]

It is interesting to consider the justifications presented in the Xinhua article:

> [A]ccording to the stipulations of the Basic Law, a Basic Law committee should be set up at the time the Basic Law comes into effect with its Hong Kong members nominated by the SAR chief executive, the Legislative Council president and the Court of Final Appeal judges. Without any legislative body, the election of Hong Kong members of the Basic Law Committee would be problematic, as would the appointment of the Court of Final Appeal and High Court chief judges, the examination and approval of financial budgets and the approval of taxation and public spending, all of which require legislative action.
>
> Moreover, some laws are indispensable after 1 July 1997. . . . They all require the involvement of a legislative body. Moreover, even after the NPC Standing Committee declared Hong Kong laws invalid in contravention of the Basic Law, there are existing Hong Kong laws that still require legislative involvement. Establishing the provisional legislative council is the most suitable way to signal the Chinese government's resumption of sovereignty over Hong Kong. . . .[54]

In essence, the appointed provisional legislature, even if in existence for only a short time, will be allowed to affect the future of the Hong Kong SAR greatly, given its inordinate law-making power. Lu Ping admitted that between the handover and election of the first legislature, "the provisional legislature had many issues to deal with, including nationality laws, right of abode and the

---

[52] See "When the Lights Go out at Legco," *South China Morning Post*, Oct. 15, 1994, p. 21, where the article lists the other three options as "giving the legislative powers to the Chief Executive, the Preparatory Committee or the National People's Congress." It is interesting to note that while the Chinese fault the British for not observing the Basic Law in its electoral reforms, the Chinese seem to ignore the provisions outlining the First Legislative Council of the Hong Kong SAR, by establishing a provisional legislature.

[53] "China Defends Its Position on Hong Kong," Agence France Presse, Apr. 2, 1996 (available in LEXIS-NEXIS Service database).

[54] Duanmu Laidi, "Ensure Hong Kong's Smooth Transfer of Government," op. cit.

appointments of Court of Final Appeal judges."[55] Such involvement by the Provisional Legislative Council is clearly a major issue which will affect the rule of law and judicial interpretation of Hong Kong SAR laws.

As for the timing question, in response to the concerns of the opponents regarding the early implementation of the Provisional Legislative Council, the Chinese have promised that it would not rival the currently sitting and elected Legislative Council.[56] However, whether these promises mean anything is another matter. For practical purposes, an appointed provisional legislature with guaranteed power starting on July 1, 1997, causes the existing legislature to become a lame-duck body. In fact, one prominent PRC supporter, Sir See-yeung Chung, contradicted the official Chinese position – predicting that a provisional legislature "would be established in early 1997 to shape policy, draft bills and prepare budgets – not just observe the outgoing British-backed bureaucrats," suggesting creation of an establishment to rival the official Legislative Council.[57] Qualifying that statement somewhat, Qian Qichen has written:

> Although the provisional legislature will be set up before 1st July 1996, the laws it approves will not come into force until 1st July 1997. Therefore, there is no question of two legislative organs existing simultaneously in Hong Kong.[58]

The British position with respect to legality is perhaps equally entrenched. The British government has remained firm in its position that the Provisional Legislative Council is inconsistent with the Joint Declaration, which calls for an elected legislature in the Hong Kong SAR. However, British opposition to the legality of the provisional legislature is based less on its actual existence than on its timing. In theory, the establishment of the Provisional Legislative Council after July 1, 1997, would no longer be an issue for the British, since at that point, China will retain complete sovereignty over the Hong Kong SAR. Of course, the British have pointed out the lack of any provisions for such an

---

[55] Angela Li, "Lu Ping's Legco Pledge," *South China Morning Post*, Oct. 15, 1996 (available in LEXIS-NEXIS Service database).

[56] Ibid.

[57] "HK Criticizes Plan for Shadow Government," U.P.I. International, Nov. 22, 1995 (available in LEXIS-NEXIS Service database).

[58] Excerpted from "Provisional Legislature Must Operate Before 1997" (editorial), *Wen Wei Po* (in Chinese), Aug. 31, 1996, p. A2 (available in LEXIS-NEXIS Service database).

appointed body in the Basic Law, thereby questioning its constitutionality.[59] However, Britain's main contention is that an early creation of this appointed body infringes upon British sovereignty over Hong Kong.

Governor Patten has repeatedly stated his opposition to an early creation of the Provisional Legislative Council: "[W]e certainly won't be prepared to consider anything designed to divide the loyalties of civil servants or anything that could result in confusion or which would result in eroding the effectiveness of the government as a whole."[60] Despite the PRC's defense, the British have made clear that such an appointed body threatens the legitimacy of the Hong Kong Legislative Council, and therefore violates British sovereignty.

Hong Kong's Conflicting Positions. Perhaps more important than the lack of agreement between the British and the Chinese are the conflicting positions held by the people of Hong Kong. Given the inevitability of the Provisional Legislative Council, some residents have taken a pragmatic approach – accepting their fate, and hoping to make the best of it.[61] Others, led by the popular Democratic Party, have steadfastly remained opposed to the appointed body. Many people, including various nominees for the position of Chief Executive, have echoed the Chinese position that the Provisional Legislative Council is a "matter of necessity" to ensure the smooth transition, given the lack of a "through train" arrangement.[62] Because guidelines for the First Legislative Council of the Hong Kong SAR, according to the Basic Law, have not been finalized, some institution must be in place at the time of handover. However, while these supporters

---

[59] See the Basic Law, Annex II, on the selection of the First Legislative Council by the "Decision of the National People's Congress on the Method for the Formation of the First Government and the First Legislative Council of the Hong Kong Special Administrative Region." There is no mention of any establishment of an appointed Provisional Legislative Council to govern Hong Kong during the transition.

[60] "HK Criticizes Plan for Shadow Government," U.P.I., op. cit. See "China Defends Its Position on Hong Kong," Agence France Presse, op. cit., where Shen Guofang made the extraordinary threat that civil servants who opposed the provisional legislature would be fired.

[61] See Tsang Yok-sing, "Realism Needed over SAR Deadlock," *South China Morning Post*, Apr. 23, 1996, p. 16. Tsang argues for a pragmatic approach, stating that "[I]t makes more sense to ensure the provisional legislature will only do the right thing, than it does to discredit it before its formation. For it will be formed anyway, and it will make laws which everyone must obey."

[62] Tsang Yok-sing, "Clearing up Some Political Questions," *South China Morning Post*, Sept. 12, 1995, p. 18.

see the need for the appointed body, many oppose its creation prior to the July 1, 1997, transfer.[63]

Led by Martin Lee and the popular Democratic Party, others in Hong Kong worry greatly about the existence of the provisional legislature. Indeed, they fear that the body, as an appointed group, will represent the interests of China over the interests of Hong Kong. It is important to note that no members of the Democratic Party will be a part of the Selection Committee or the provisional legislature itself. As do the British, these opponents oppose the PRC's imposition of a provisional legislature on two fronts: general legality and early timing.

Hong Kong opponents view the body as a threat to Hong Kong's precious rule of law. The Democratic Party has refused to participate in the body, calling it illegal and promising instead to wait until election of the First Legislative Council as prescribed in the Basic Law.[64] As Anna Wu stated, "It's an extremely dangerous thing to have because they [Beijing] can clean, with one sweep, any laws they don't like."[65] Fears about the body include its ability to appoint judges to the Court of Final Appeal, "watering down the Bill of Rights, and defining new laws on sedition, treason, and the theft of state secrets."[66]

As Martin Lee has queried, "How can two governments function at the same time?"[67] Indeed, while in theory the Provisional Legislative Council may not actually be a rival to the Hong Kong Legislative Council in future elections in the SAR, in practice, it becomes one. "Suppose Legco [the existing Legislative Council] approves something and the provisional group rejects it. Then does the money get spent?"[68] Moreover, Dorothy Liu, a Hong Kong delegate to the National People's Congress, points out that "Setting up a provisional legislature before 1997 was never ratified by the NPC and cannot be done without the most blatant disregard for legal theory and reason. . . . it contravenes the Sino-British Joint Declaration, an international treaty which stipulates Britain is in charge of Hong Kong until midnight on June 30, 1997."[69]

---

63 Ibid. "The provisional legislature will not be involved in legislation before the SAR comes into being."

64 "Top Hong Kong Party Turns Its Back," Agence France Presse, op. cit. See Tsang Yok-sing, "Realism Needed over SAR Deadlock," op. cit., pointing out that a "worse fear is that the interim body will make electoral laws which deprive them (the Democratic Party) of a fair chance in future elections in the SAR.

65 Simon Holberton & Peter Montagnon, "1,000 Days of Uncertainty," op. cit.

66 Mary Binks, "HK Advisor to China Blasts Beijing," Reuters, op. cit.

67 "HK Criticizes Plan for Shadow Government," U.P.I., op. cit.

68 Ibid.

69 Mary Binks, "HK Advisor to China Blasts Beijing," Reuters, op. cit.

Lu Ping posed the purportedly rhetorical question, "[I]f there was no provisional legislature, how would Hong Kong operate?"[70] Given its inevitability, that question has become moot. Nevertheless, one might respond with the answer that rather than the provisional legislature, the first legislature of the Hong Kong SAR, as outlined in the Basic Law, would operate in Hong Kong on both sides of July 1, 1997. Of course, without the "through train" arrangement, the answer is not so simple. When and how the first legislature is created by the National People's Congress remains to be seen, but until then, it is clear that the Provisional Legislative Council will be actively involved in the transfer of sovereignty and immediate-future rule of law in Hong Kong.

CONCLUSION

Through its dynamic populace, vibrant economy, and commitment to the rule of law, Hong Kong has created a unique polity in the East Asian region for 6 million people which has provided inspiration for development in the Chinese hinterland adjacent to it and even farther afield. This will all be at risk after 1997 if Beijing fails to keep its word as documented in the legal enactment discussed above. While controversy over the Provisional Legislative Council and CFA has eroded some people's confidence in Hong Kong's future, others (including many Hong Kong residents) argue that once the British leave and issues of Hong Kong's governance no longer automatically assume an antithetical cast tinged with concern over Chinese sovereignty, Hong Kong's people and the PRC leadership will be easily able to reach an accommodation which will assuage PRC fears and ensure Hong Kong's continued prosperity and relative freedom. Moreover, China's continuing emergence on the world stage as a global power increasingly calls attention to its international legal behavior and reputation for observing international legal undertakings. Given the importance of the agreements to Hong Kong's future, on their own merits and with respect to PRC hopes for eventual reunification of the mainland and Taiwan, many countervailing forces may militate toward strict observance of those agreements in 1997 and beyond.

[70] Ibid.

4

The Economic and Political
Integration of Hong Kong

Implications for Government–Business Relations

YASHENG HUANG[1]

ECONOMIC INTEGRATION

IN examining the economic integration between China and Hong Kong, one needs to distinguish between two types of integration. One type involves the increasing integration of the Hong Kong economy with the Chinese economy. This integration can be trade-related – Hong Kong exports to, or imports from, China – or it can be investment-related – Hong Kong firms move their manufacturing sites to China. The other type involves control by mainland Chinese firms over assets located in Hong Kong. Although these two types of economic integration are often lumped together, they in fact have different implications for government–business relations in Hong Kong.

Trade and investment integration with China is nothing new; Hong Kong has served as a trade entrepot between China and the rest of the world since the founding of the People's Republic of China (PRC) in 1949. Investment integration came much later, beginning in the late 1970s in reaction to China's open-door policies. It is important to point out here that trade and investment ties of this kind alone have not changed in any meaningful way the manner in which Hong Kong's economy is governed. Hong Kong has remained a laissez-faire economy regardless of the fact that an increasing proportion of its trade is with one of the most illiberal economies in the world.

[1] Yasheng Huang is the author of *Inflation and Investment Controls in China: Political Economy of Central and Local Relations in China in the Reform Era* (New York: Cambridge University Press, 1996), and *Management of Foreign Direct Investment in Asian Perspectives* (Singapore: Institute of Southeast Asian Studies, 1997). The author wishes to thank Kenneth Lieberthal for his very helpful comments. Any errors are solely those of the author.

Economic and Political Integration of Hong Kong

Chinese acquisitions of Hong Kong assets are of a different order altogether: They are of far more recent vintage, closely connected with the imminent transition of sovereignty from the British to the Chinese. Chinese firms are state-owned and accustomed to operating in an environment of extremely close government–business relations. Although their increasing role in Hong Kong does not imply changes in the laissez-faire nature of Hong Kong's economy, it does imply changes in government–business relations in Hong Kong after 1997, especially given that the government of the Hong Kong Special Administrative Region (SAR) is not politically or philosophically committed to laissez-faire.

Hong Kong's Presence in China

When the British acquired Hong Kong in the nineteenth century, Hong Kong served then, as it does now, as an entrepot for trade between China and the West. In the late 1890s, more than 50 percent of China's imports and 37 percent of its exports moved through Hong Kong.[2] These figures are not significantly different from the more recent numbers. For example, in 1987, 33 percent of China's trade passed through Hong Kong.[3]

The communist revolution in China disrupted the traditional trading relationship between Hong Kong merchants and their Chinese partners. However, as the situation stabilized in China, Hong Kong began to reestablish some of its trading ties and assumed its traditional entrepot role. The more serious blow came with the Korean War, when the United States imposed a total embargo on China. This had a devastating impact on Hong Kong's economy.

For much of the 1960s and 1970s, Hong Kong served mainly as a trade conduit for China; the process of integration quickened vastly when China opened its borders for foreign direct investments. Moving manufacturing sites to China became part of the response by the Hong Kong business community to adverse economic shocks, such as rising wage costs in Hong Kong and protectionism for developed economies. In the process of investment integration, unlike trade integration, the Hong Kong business community also brought both soft- and hardware technology and management expertise to the Chinese operations. By the early 1990s, four-fifths of Hong Kong manufacturing firms had relocated to

---

[2] John P. Burns, "Hong Kong: Diminishing Laissez-faire," in Steven M. Goldstein (ed.), *Mini Dragons: Fragile Economic Miracles in the Pacific* (Boulder, CO: Westview, 1991), pp. 104–43.

[3] *Far Eastern Economic Review Asia 1987 Yearbook* (Hong Kong: Review Publishing Company Ltd., 1988), p. 120.

China. Hong Kong is, by far, the largest source of foreign capital to China. In 1995, Hong Kong firms invested US$20.2 billion in China, accounting for some 53 percent of China's total capital inflow in that year.[4] Hong Kong's investments in China are diversified, found not only in manufacturing but also in property, infrastructure, and technology. Significantly, while in the 1980s Hong Kong investing firms tended to be small, labor-intensive operations, beginning in the early 1990s Hong Kong's publicly listed firms have also invested heavily in China. Thus the investment scale per project has also increased.

Investment of this kind has reoriented Hong Kong–China trade patterns: Most trade activities are directly related to subcontracting undertaken by the Hong Kong firms in China. In 1993, 74 percent of Hong Kong's domestic exports to China were related to outward processing; of the imports from China, the figure was also 74 percent.[5] In effect, Hong Kong operates as a trading corporation that contracts out production units in China – through provisions of production designs and materials – and purchases and distributes the finished goods worldwide. One may argue that investment integration between China and Hong Kong conforms with the laissez-faire nature of the Hong Kong economy: Hong Kong essentially has accessed the vast pool of cheap Chinese labor, which has obviated the need for the Hong Kong government to play a strong role in steering industrial responses among the private firms.

China's Presence in Hong Kong

Before the economic reforms, Chinese economic functionaries in Hong Kong kept a very low profile. The Chinese firms in Hong Kong had well-defined and non-overlapping scopes of business. The Bank of China, China Resources (Holdings) Co., Ltd, China Merchants International, and China Travel Services (HK), Ltd., were the only PRC firms in Hong Kong engaged in foreign-

---

[4] The actual amount of the investments from Hong Kong is probably less than US$20.2 billion. The Hong Kong figure incorporates two sources of non–Hong Kong capital inflows. One is the investments from the foreign firms with subsidiaries in Hong Kong; the other refers to investments which actually originate in China and are then reinvested back into China. I have estimated this source of capital to account for around 30 percent of the Hong Kong investment. See Huang Yasheng, *Management of Foreign Direct Investment in Asian Perspectives*, op. cit., and State Statistical Bureau, *Zhongguo Tongji Nianjian 1996 [China Statistical Yearbook 1996]*, (Beijing: Zhongguo Tongji Chubanshe, 1996), p. 598.

[5] K. C. Fung, "Trade and Investment Relations among Hong Kong, China and Taiwan," unpublished manuscript (University of California–Santa Cruz).

exchange transactions, fossil oils and foodstuffs trade, shipping, and tourism, respectively. They operated as the business arms of the Chinese central government, seldom out of their established spheres of business.

During the reform era, the Chinese economic presence grew rapidly. According to the Hong Kong Monetary Authority, the banking group of China owned US$89.7 billion in assets as of the end of 1993. In addition, there have been new PRC players in Hong Kong that have broken the monopoly positions previously held by the four traditional Chinese firms in Hong Kong. Some of these firms are motivated to establish trade and investment links with their operations in China; others, which are growing in importance, are motivated to tap into Hong Kong's deep capital market to raise funds for their projects in China. It is likely that these PRC firms will exert a powerful influence on the Hong Kong economy as well as on its economic institutions once Hong Kong reverts to Chinese control.

China today is, in fact, Hong Kong's largest foreign investor. The number of Chinese firms investing in Hong Kong rose from 400 in 1991 to 2,000 in 1994. According to one estimate, in the early 1990s, Chinese investment in Hong Kong amounted to about US$20 billion.[6] Increasing Chinese investment in Hong Kong and increasing "China play" on the Hong Kong Stock Exchange have contributed to the rapid rise of the Hang Seng index in the past decade, hence to the economic prosperity of Hong Kong. In 1993, 39 companies listed on the Hong Kong Stock Exchange were controlled by firms from China; their total market capitalization value amounted to $US15.8 billion, accounting for 6 percent of the total capital marketization value of the Hong Kong Stock Exchange. One common investment strategy of Chinese firms is to acquire poorly performing firms at an attractive price and to establish a controlling share. Typically, the shares of these firms have not been actively traded prior to their acquisition. In 1992–1993, 19 such "shells" were purchased by PRC concerns. Using this strategy, the Chinese firms raised US$1.84 billion from the Hong Kong Stock Exchange.[7]

GOVERNMENT–BUSINESS RELATIONS IN HONG KONG

Growing integration with the Chinese economy, the rising Chinese economic presence in Hong Kong, and Chinese sovereignty over Hong Kong will deter-

---

[6] Chan Hing Lin, "Chinese Investment in Hong Kong," *Asian Survey*, no. 39, October 1995, pp. 941–54.

[7] Chan Hing Lin, "Chinese Investment in Hong Kong," op. cit., p. 945.

mine the shape of future government–business relations in Hong Kong. This section discusses the laissez-faire character of Hong Kong's economic institutions.

Hong Kong's Laissez-Faire Economy

Several indicators show that Hong Kong's economic institutions have been the most laissez-faire in the world. First, Hong Kong does not have a central bank; two private banks – the Hong Kong Bank and the Standard Chartered Bank – and the Hong Kong Branch of the Bank of China issue the currency on behalf of the government. Although the Hong Kong Monetary Authority has exercised some of the functions of a central bank since its creation in 1993, it does not have the autonomy to set monetary policies. The government has not set fiscal targets for its budget; it has a flat tax rate of 15 percent. Government consumption is below 10 percent of the gross domestic product (GDP).[8] Second, Hong Kong is a free trade port. In an aberration from patterns commonly observed elsewhere in East Asia and China, the government does not have a "developmental policy" that encourages either import substitution or export promotion.[9] Third, unlike other East Asian economies, which either restrict foreign firms (South Korea and China) or encourage them at the expense of domestic firms (Singapore), the Hong Kong government, as a matter of principle, does not discriminate between its own and foreign firms – indeed, it does not actively collect statistics on the nationalities of firms operating in Hong Kong.

The main exception to Hong Kong's laissez-faire economy is government control and ownership of land. Although Hong Kong's colonial government historically has performed basic and minimal functions, these activities cost money. To raise revenue, the colonial government became involved in land management. Today, the government owns all the land and sells it on leasehold to raise revenue. In addition, the government controls rents in a portion of the private housing market and provides public housing to roughly half the population. Government ownership and sale of land is one reason tax revenue as a proportion of gross national product (GNP) is so low as compared with other

---

[8] See *World Bank Tables 1995* (Washington, D.C.: International Bank for Reconstruction and Development), p. 333.

[9] For an in-depth analysis of the developmental state in East Asia, see Robert Wade, *Governing the Market: Economic Theory and the Role of Government in East Asian Industrialization* (Princeton: Princeton University Press, 1990).

East Asian economies.[10] Some scholars argue that the colonial government might have used control over land release to affect industrial development and control over immigration from China to influence wage costs in the colony. Even if this is true, there is no question that these do not constitute specific industrial policies, and land and immigration policies do not favor some businesses over others.

The state's minimal functions have several origins. One is simply historical. When Hong Kong was ceded to the British in the nineteenth century, it served as a base for entrepot trade. At that time, the British did not consider Hong Kong to be of overwhelming strategic value. For that reason, the British kept its colonial administration to a minimum. In addition, when the British landed on Hong Kong, the city consisted of approximately twenty villages and some scattered fishermen. The British established administrative control easily because there were no entrenched local interests.

From an economic point of view, the small size of Hong Kong would render state control of economic activities both ineffective and irrational. Hong Kong does not have its own central bank because it does not need one. Hong Kong dollars are pegged to U.S. dollars and, in effect, Hong Kong's monetary policy is made in Washington, D.C., by the Federal Reserve.[11] Because of Hong Kong's status as a free port city, excessive taxation would also drive businesses to more competitive sites elsewhere in Asia.

However, these economic factors do not automatically prevent the establishment of an activist government in economic management. Singapore, a city of similar-sized economy, has an extremely interventionist government in economic, social, and political management. The fundamental reason for the laissez-faire nature of the Hong Kong economy is philosophical and temperamental, which is why laissez-faire under Chinese rule could be quite fragile. Generations of British finance secretaries in Hong Kong have believed that the government ought to have minimalist functions in the economy. Indeed, until the 1960s, the government even refused to collect statistics on GNP lest such collection be viewed as interventionist. In addition, laissez-faire was very much in keeping with the British tradition of maintaining small colonial administrations.[12]

10 See Wade, op. cit., p. 332.
11 Before 1972, the Hong Kong dollar was pegged to sterling.
12 For a fuller discussion, see Stephan Haggard, *Pathways from the Periphery* (Ithaca: Cornell University Press, 1990).

Yasheng Huang

Laissez-Faire Economy Under Adversity

A remarkable feature of the Hong Kong economy is that, until now at least, government–business relations have retained their arm's-length character despite the fact that economic adversity has led other countries to resort to government intervention in a variety of ways. The United States–imposed embargoes against China in the wake of the Korean War, the oil shocks of the 1970s, and rising protectionism in the West in the 1970s and 1980s – all created conditions that might have warranted more state intervention, yet the laissez-faire nature of the Hong Kong economy remained largely intact. It is plausible, however, that Chinese sovereignty over Hong Kong will test the strength of the laissez-faire system to a greater extent than has been seen thus far.

Embargoes imposed by the United States against China in the 1950s had devastating economic consequences for Hong Kong. Hong Kong's exports to the PRC were valued at HK$1.6 billion in 1952. A year later, they had dropped to HK$520 million, and in 1956 the total was only HK$136 million.[13] In response, the Hong Kong business community took the initiative of shifting from entreprot trade to export manufacturing.

In the 1970s, the successes of East Asian export performance spurred developed countries to take actions to limit exports from the East Asian newly industrialized countries (NICs). These actions proliferated greatly in the 1970s, taking the form of non-tariff barriers against certain goods, many of which happened to come from the East Asian NICs. These ranged from orderly marketing arrangements (OMAs) to voluntary export restraints (VERs). Rising protectionism, plus the worldwide economic slowdown in the wake of oil shocks, created conditions in other East Asian economies for repeated state intervention. The South Korean government, for example, undertook ambitious heavy and chemical industrial drives, while the Singaporean government mandated an across-the-board wage increase of 20 percent in an effort to phase out labor-intensive goods.

In Hong Kong, the business community once again made its own adjustments, this time by moving out of manufacturing and into financial services. In 1971, the manufacturing sector employed about 47 percent of Hong Kong's working population; by 1989, that share had been reduced to 30 percent.[14] Robert Wade argues that Hong Kong's restructuring efforts took a longer time

---

13 John P. Burns, "Hong Kong: Diminishing Laissez-faire," op. cit., pp.108–9.
14 Burns, op. cit., pp. 110–11.

to complete than those of other East Asian economies.[15] Hong Kong's export composition concentrated on low-end products, such as textiles, toys, and clocks for a longer period than elsewhere because the government did not take strong action to steer the economy away from these products.

In the 1980s, the rapid growth of the Chinese economy, its open-door policy, and the impending surrender of sovereignty of Hong Kong from Great Britain provided strong economic and political motives to the Hong Kong business community to "look east." Their adjustments were a combination of locating manufacturing operations across the border – first to sites in Guangdong Province and then to interior provinces – with forming strategic alliances with powerful Chinese corporations in Hong Kong. Both of these forms of economic integration may have had profound implications for business–government relations in Hong Kong.

GOVERNMENT–BUSINESS RELATIONS AFTER 1997

The bedrock of the laissez-faire economy in Hong Kong consists of the rule of law and fair market competition. The economic and political merger of Hong Kong with China naturally raises questions about these two pillars of Hong Kong's economic institutions, for three reasons. First, the economic integration with China introduces to Hong Kong state-owned firms (SOFs) with strong political connections – very different from the kind of firms to which it is accustomed. Second, SOFs are subject to soft-budget constraints and often invest to maximize employment or plant size. They can also acquire Hong Kong firms not for their commercial viability, but for the sake of seeking extraneous policy benefits, such as claiming privileges in China accorded to foreign firms. Third, regulating SOFs may become politically difficult once Hong Kong's regulatory authorities begin taking their instructions from Beijing.

Two unresolved questions are particularly relevant to the future relationship between government and business. The most pertinent question is whether or not the regulatory authorities in Hong Kong can treat Chinese and non-Chinese firms equally in the eyes of the law. Fair competition is the key ingredient in keeping Hong Kong a viable financial center – for Chinese and indigenous capital, and especially for international capital. Another question is whether some Chinese concerns will compete with others from politically privileged positions.

---

15 Wade, op. cit.

Undoubtedly, the vast majority of Chinese firms, although small, compete successfully with other Hong Kong firms under regulatory-neutral conditions, because many Chinese firms are rather small. The Hong Kong Chinese Enterprises Association has some 1,000 members, most of which are not listed on the stock exchange. However, there are concerns about the potential for PRC firms in Hong Kong to compete on the strength of their political and regulatory power rather than on their commercial strength. The PRC government may leverage the sovereignty issue to achieve its policy objectives in Hong Kong. For example, it may strive to reduce the influence of certain firms either on economic or non-economic grounds, while increasing Chinese control in strategic sectors. The harm to Hong Kong's economic institutions would result not so much from the eventual outcome itself as from the fact that in achieving this outcome, the process of regulatory neutrality would be undermined.

In two widely publicized cases, the ideal of regulatory neutrality seems to have been compromised. One case concerns one of the oldest firms in Hong Kong: Jardine Matheson Holding. In 1995, China refused to approve a US$1.6 billion project to construct a container terminal because it objected to Jardine's leading role in the consortium that had been awarded the contract. Some speculated that this was revenge for Jardine's instrumental role in the Opium War as well as its recent support for political reforms advocated by Governor Chris Patten; others speculated that the objection was related to Jardine's decision to delist from Hong Kong's stock exchange and to move its domicile to Bermuda.

The Chinese government is often criticized for taking politics into account when awarding contracts. Of course, this is not a laudable practice, but it is almost unavoidable to some extent. For years, the British colonial administration favored British firms in the colony. However, British favoritism did not prevent Chinese firms from becoming prosperous. As a practical matter, political considerations will diminish in importance in the future because Hong Kong firms eventually will be socialized into political loyalty. More at stake is whether the procedures for awarding contracts should be respected, even if those procedures may produce an outcome at odds with the wishes of political leaders. Even if the motivation underlying Chinese objections to Jardine was legitimate, these objections came after Jardine Matheson had already been awarded the contract. Thus, they constituted ex post facto intervention in normal governmental procedures regarding the awarding of commercial contracts.[16]

---

[16] On the Jardine case, see Edward A. Gargan, "The Humbling of a Heavyweight: In Hong Kong, Change Jolts a Colonial Business Power," *New York Times*, Nov. 30, 1995; David Lindorff, "A

The other case that has garnered considerable press attention concerns the decision by Swire Pacific to sell, apparently at a huge discount, part of its ownership in the lucrative Cathay Pacific Airlines to two Chinese concerns, CITIC Pacific and China Aviation Corporation. In addition, both Swire and Cathay Pacific lost management control over Dragon Airlines.[17] Many countries, including the United States, restrict or ban foreign ownership of their own airlines; however, while it is quite understandable that the Chinese government may want to establish national control over Cathay and Dragon Airlines after 1997, it is its method of acquisition that raises concerns about fair competition. Both CITIC Pacific and China Aviation Corporation are politically powerful firms in China. CITIC Pacific is headed by Larry Yung, the son of Rong Yiren, China's vice president; China Aviation Corporation is the commercial arm of China's regulatory body over the airline industry. Given this background, one may argue that these two firms successfully extracted a political premium from their transactions with Swire Pacific.

The Cathay Pacific case points to a general problem for Hong Kong's regulatory authorities after 1997: how to impose market discipline on a group of Chinese firms which possess assets, employ business methods, and are motivated by considerations that are very different from those in Hong Kong. First, it is quite obvious that many of the PRC firms in Hong Kong possess huge political assets that many other firms simply do not have. Many listed PRC shells have powerful political backgrounds, and questions have arisen as to whether or not China's own regulatory body in the securities industry, the China Securities Regulatory Commission (CSRC), has been able to supervise their activities adequately. If the CSRC already has problems with these firms, the Hong Kong Monetary Authority will have even greater problems after 1997.

Heavy political representation raises questions about the degree to which political power is used to gain commercial advantages. For example, the son-in-law of Deng Xiaoping is the chairman of the board of three listed firms: Silver Grand International Industries, Ltd; Onfem Holdings, Ltd.; and Jin Hua.

Nasty Little Shoving Match in Hong Kong," *Business Week*, Oct. 3, 1994, p. 68; "The Noble Houses Look Forward," *The Economist*, vol. 333, Oct. 1, 1994, pp. 77–78; and "The Taipan and the Dragon," *The Economist*, vol. 335, Apr. 8, 1995, p. 62.

17 See Michael Mecham, "China Expands Stake in Cathay, Dragonair," *Aviation Week & Space Technology*, May 6, 1996, pp. 31–33; Perry Flint, "Farrell's Revenge," *Air Transport World*, June 1996, p. 16; Erik Guyot, "Some Analysts Say CITIC Pacific May Be Real Winner of Airline Deal in Colony," *Asian Wall Street Journal*, May 6, 1996, p. 18; and "China Line," *The Economist*, vol. 339, June 15, 1996, p. 58.

Others – such as Poly Investment Holdings, Ltd.; Hoi Shing Holdings, Ltd.; First Shanghai Investment, Ltd.; and Continental Mariner – have political heavyweights sitting on their boards of directors.[18] Also, the issue of discipline may arise: Once the regulatory authorities in Hong Kong are beholden to political instructions in Beijing, regulating politically connected Chinese firms will be a problem.

In addition, distinctions between the regulatory functions of government and commercial operations of firms are either blurred or practically non-existent in China. Not only is there no fire wall between the regulators and the regulated, but the regulatory agencies of the government often own, and directly profit from, commercial concerns that compete with other firms. The conflict of interest is inherent. The Cathay Pacific case is a good illustration. Swire would have little choice but to discount its ownership sales to China Aviation Corporation because otherwise it would have risked being shut out of China's airline industry by the parent agency of the China Aviation Corporation. In addition to China Aviation Corporation, other Chinese firms in Hong Kong are commercial extensions of the regulatory authorities in Beijing. For example, the China Resources (Holding) Co., Ltd., is the trading arm of the Ministry of Foreign Economic Relations.

Another factor is that Chinese firms, unlike their Hong Kong counterparts, are state-owned enterprises (SOEs). SOEs are known for having huge investment appetites because they are subject only to soft-budget constraints and therefore are not limited by profitability considerations as they apply to private firms. One implication of soft-budget constraints is that the SOEs could outbid Hong Kong firms in their acquisition activities and thus may adopt an overly aggressive investment stance.[19] This problem is complicated by the fact that the SOEs, having a poor record of financial disclosures, lack a well-functioning corporate structure to monitor and supervise their activities.

IMPLICATIONS

There is no question that increasing integration of the Hong Kong economy with that of China has brought enormous benefit to the Hong Kong economy,

[18] Chan Hing Lin, "Chinese Investment in Hong Kong," op. cit.
[19] For a more detailed discussion on the investment appetites of the SOEs, see Huang Yasheng, *Inflation and Investment Controls in China: Political Economy of Central and Local Relations in China in the Reform Era*, op. cit.

and its business community in particular. Hong Kong's GDP was HK$170 billion in 1984 when the Sino-British declaration was signed; it was HK$287.4 billion in 1992. (Both GDP figures are in the 1980 constant prices.) The Hang Seng index, a barometer of Hong Kong's economy, was a mere 871.06 points on its first trading day in 1984; at the end of 1995, it closed at 10,073.39.[20] A fundamental issue, however, is whether in the long run, the costs of eroding the rule of law, regulatory neutrality, and fair market competition can be sufficiently offset by the benefits of closer integration of the Hong Kong economy with a rapidly developing Chinese economy. In the short run, benefits will definitely outweigh costs, but in the long run, when Chinese economic growth eventually slows down, the costs will become more obvious.

Hostage Effect

Some argue that greater integration with the Chinese economy will increase the stability of Hong Kong after 1997 by means of the so-called hostage effect. According to this argument, increasing investments by Chinese firms in Hong Kong will leave China hostage to Hong Kong because Beijing will hurt its own investments if it reneges on the autonomy of Hong Kong and damages its economy in the process.[21]

It is important to note that if Chinese investments should serve as hostage, the effect will be essentially redundant. The Hong Kong economy as a whole has provided a continuous stream of benefits to the Chinese economy as a source of capital, technology, and management expertise.[22] While benefits to China are multiples of the monetary value of Chinese investments in Hong Kong, it is true that Chinese political and policy elites reap a disproportionate share of investment values in Hong Kong. Thus the investment value of Hong Kong is quite concentrated, while the economic value of Hong Kong is diffuse. In this respect, Chinese investments in Hong Kong do enhance the "hostage effect" more than does the contribution made by Hong Kong to the Chinese economy as a whole. Therefore, in order to boost confidence in Hong Kong, the

---

[20] Figures provided by Hong Kong Government Information Services Department. See *Hong Kong 1996*, 1996, Hong Kong Government Printing Department.
[21] See B. Bacher, O. Lorz, & L. Schuknecht, "Chinese Investments: 'Hostages' for Hong Kong," *Journal of Institutional and Theoretical Economics*, no. 123, pp. 645–54.
[22] See Chan Hing Lin, op. cit.

PRC government should form an advisory group on Hong Kong affairs, involving the major Chinese stakeholders in Hong Kong such as Rong Yiren and Ye Xuanping.

Whether the hostage effect comes from the investment or economic values of Hong Kong, it is inconceivable that the PRC government will ever undermine Hong Kong deliberately. The threat to Hong Kong is subtler than that and may come instead from a gradual erosion of the integrity of Hong Kong's economic institutions, and from the inability of the central government to restrain and coordinate numerous and various commercial interests on the part of PRC entities in Hong Kong. Thus in the short run, it is essential for the PRC government to restrict access to Hong Kong by Chinese firms. Over time, this restriction can be relaxed, but only when economic and financial reforms have converted Chinese firms into truly profit-maximizing and politically independent entities.

Deinternationalization

Although Hong Kong is commonly perceived as a gateway to China, it also serves as the base for hundreds of multinational corporations (MNCs) as their Asian regional headquarters. These MNCs service their operations in China as well as in other parts of East Asia and Southeast Asia. Firms may leave Hong Kong if their operations are increasingly crowded out by those Chinese and Hong Kong firms which concentrate increasingly on China in their business portfolio. A good example is the effect of skyrocketing office rentals. Chinese firms are particularly interested in investing in the Hong Kong real estate market, and this pushes up real estate prices as well as making them more volatile. By 1995, Hong Kong was already rated as the most expensive business location in the world. This will make Hong Kong less attractive to those firms which do not derive the main portion of their revenues from China-related businesses or whose China-related revenue is not large enough to offset both the high averages and the high volatility of land prices. This may produce a "deinternationalization effect" – in other words, firms that do not focus on China as their core business may choose to exit from Hong Kong, and the Hong Kong economy becomes merely an extension of the Chinese economy.

Unfair competition, declining market discipline, and regulatory preferences in Hong Kong may also produce a deinternationalization effect. If political connections and regulatory favors become a significant portion of firms' competitive advantage in Hong Kong, then firms lacking the political capital will find themselves in a difficult position. Typically, these firms are non-Chinese, which gives them a comparative disadvantage in operating in an environment where the game is played by opaque rules. Arguably, these firms may have a deeper comparative disadvantage operating in Hong Kong as compared with operating in China itself. In China, these firms, especially Western MNCs, do possess an overwhelming advantage that political capital cannot buy – technology; however, this advantage becomes valuable only in locations with a sizable manufacturing sector.

A good example of deinternationalization could be Western institutional investors in Hong Kong. As previously pointed out, Chinese-controlled firms now account for an increasing share of the Hong Kong Stock Exchange's total market capitalization; thus, government policies in China will exert an increasingly strong influence on the Hong Kong Stock Exchange. However, if the information about policy developments in the PRC is not available to investors other than select Chinese firms in equal amounts and in equal time, confidence in the integrity of the Hong Kong Stock Exchange will decline, and international capital inflow will decline as a result.

Deinternationalization of the Hong Kong economy will, unfortunately, enhance the utility of developing political assets and nurturing particularistic connections as a means of business practice. In essence, this is a variation of "Gresham's law." Firms anchored in Hong Kong become more homogeneous insofar as their core business focuses on China, and, as a result, they adopt the business strategies best suited to the Chinese environment, thereby driving out other firms that are less well suited.

Economic and Social Welfare

The question is not whether the welfare of the Hong Kong tycoons will improve; it definitely will as long as Chinese economic expansion continues to offer lucrative trading and investment opportunities. Rather, the real question concerns the welfare of Hong Kong society as a whole. Under a free market economy, there is ultimate convergence between private and social returns, which is one of the reasons income distribution in Hong Kong compares favorably with economies with avowedly socialist tendencies under laissez-faire conditions. However, if market competition becomes unfair, and if monopolies or oligopolies are unrestricted on account of their political influence, private and social returns will diverge. Small business firms and consumers typically do not have much political clout, and their welfare will be the first to suffer. Politics is always a distributional issue; if politics becomes more intermingled with economics after 1997, there may be some adverse distributional consequences.

Economic and Political Fluctuations

For the foreseeable future, Hong Kong's economy may continue to prosper, but mainly on the strength of the Chinese economy. That Hong Kong is an integral – albeit the most advanced – part of the Chinese economy has both benefits and costs. On the benefits side, Hong Kong is best positioned to take advantage of the Chinese economic takeoff. Because of the speed of Chinese economic growth, the enormous margin for potential improvements in the Chinese economy, and the reversion of sovereignty, the Hong Kong business community already may have calculated that its long-term interests are more aligned with the Chinese economy than with those economic institutions of Hong Kong that have made Hong Kong one of the freest economies of the world. C. H. Tung, Hong Kong shipping tycoon and top vote-getter in the recent nomination for the Hong Kong SAR Chief Executive, has gone out of his way to emphasize Hong Kong's connections with its "Chinese heritage."

In the short run, the economic advantages of being integrated into the Chinese economy may very well outweigh the costs of the deinternationalization of the Hong Kong economy. For example, the infusion of Chinese capital into Hong Kong likely will support the Hang Seng index at a high level, even if some Western institutional investors shift their funds away from Hong Kong.

There are some disadvantages to economic integration, however. For one, Chinese economic growth will not be on a linear path. Its extraordinary performance is due, to a large extent, to the low base of the Chinese economy in the late 1970s. As the margin of improvement decreases, so will the growth rate. Another disadvantage is that Chinese economic performance is highly volatile. Until very recently, the Chinese macroeconomy alternated between high inflation cum high growth and severe economic contractions. Integration into an unstable economy will necessarily inject some economic uncertainty as well as instability into the Hong Kong system.

Political fluctuations will also occur. Remarkably, the economic integration among the three constituents of Greater China is quite deep and has occurred with very little coordination among policy makers in China, Hong Kong, and Taiwan. Again, market forces have led the way, which have profound political/policy implications even though they are not created by political dynamics. However, the absence of government leadership likewise introduces an element of uncertainty in Greater China. Because economic relations among China, Taiwan, and Hong Kong are not governed by well-laid-out economic agreements, investment and trade ties are easily swayed by fluctuations in the geopolitics of the region, as the recent Taiwan Strait crisis demonstrated.

An additional source of fluctuation is that as the PRC share of the Hong Kong economy increases, many political problems affecting the PRC economy will affect the Hong Kong economy in a proportionate manner. An immediate policy implication is the effect of Greater China on the patterns of trade between China and the United States. This has contributed to reexport and reexport markup – with a pronounced impact on trade patterns among China, Hong Kong, and the United States. By one estimate, if U.S. trade data were adjusted for reexport and reexport markups, then its trade deficits with China would be lowered by 35 percent on average.[23] This issue will not disappear after China formally incorporates Hong Kong in 1997; Hong Kong will remain a separate customs territory and a separate member of the WTO.

The concentration of manufacturing locations in China has led to major changes in the direction of trade with the United States, thus complicating the management of the trade deficits within the region. Simply stated, labor-intensive goods that previously came from Taiwan and Hong Kong are now increasingly coming from China. This has produced a widening trade deficit between China and the United States and a dwindling trade deficit between the United States and Hong Kong and Taiwan. Table 4.1 shows that the U.S. trade deficit with China has risen concomitantly with a sharp decline in its deficit with Taiwan and Hong Kong. It is this "deficit shifting" from Hong Kong and Taiwan that has complicated an already fragile political relationship between China and the United States, for rather unnecessary reasons. In fact, the U.S. deficit with "Greater China" has risen by a far smaller margin. While the U.S. deficit with China rose by about sixfold between 1987 and 1992, its deficit with "Greater China" has risen by 9.6 percent. It is difficult to argue that the rise in deficit has been a result of China's import restrictions; the table also shows that China's imports from the United States have grown at a double-digit rate every year except for 1987 and 1990. A more plausible reason for the rising deficit with China is the trade reorientation associated with shifts in industrial locations to East Asia.

[23] K. C. Fung, op. cit.

Yasheng Huang

Table 4.1. *U.S. Trade Deficit (US$ Million) and U.S. Import Growth (%)*

	U.S. deficit with			Annual growth of U.S. imports
	China	Taiwan	Hong Kong	
1987	2,796	17,209	5,871	2.42
1988	3,490	12,585	4,550	37.26
1989	6,235	12,987	3,431	18.58
1990	10,431	11,175	2,805	−16.22
1991	12,691	9,841	1,141	21.56
1992	18,309	9,346	716	11.14
1993	22,806	9,404	703	20.08
1994	29,505	9,597	1,745	30.72

Source: Deficit data are from Nicholas R. Lardy, *China in the World Economy* (Washington, D.C.: Institute for International Economics, 1994), p. 79; U.S. import growth figures are calculated from various issues of *Chinese Statistical Yearbook*.

The United States has shown great interest in seeing a smooth transition of sovereignty from Britain to China. The United States–Hong Kong Policy Act of 1992 becomes effective on July 1, 1997, when the transition of sovereignty is complete. However, the United States needs to understand that the single best protection it can afford to Hong Kong is to keep its markets open to goods from the PRC. Hong Kong capital finances the production of these goods; therefore, if the U.S. market is closed, Hong Kong's prosperity will be severely affected. A less prosperous Hong Kong is also less valuable to the PRC and might thereby undermine the PRC's rationale at least to tolerate political autonomy in Hong Kong.

CONCLUSION

The ultimate irony of the Hong Kong story is that China is both its bane and its boon. On the economic side, closer integration with China has provided solutions to many of the problems that the Hong Kong economy has faced as it matures. The rapid economic growth of China has brought enormous benefits to the Hong Kong business community. Inevitably, however, economic inte-

112

gration with China, in combination with political integration, may also erode Hong Kong's laissez-faire economic institutions. In the short run, the costs of this erosion are not obvious, as they have been masked by the benefits of Chinese economic growth. In the long run, however, these costs will become more significant and more permanent: Economic institutions are easily destroyed and very difficult to rebuild.

5

Hong Kong and Greater China

An Economic Perspective

CHANGQI WU

A long period of division will be followed by integration, and vice versa.
This is the grand circle in the Universe.

Luo Guanzhong, *Romance of the Three Kingdoms (1340–1400)*, p.1

THE trade liberalization movement after the Second World War has led to a rapid growth of trade among nations. In the process of trade expansion and the subsequent internationalization of production, we can observe a number of cases of regional economic integration evolving and running parallel with the global tendency of freer trade. In these regional trade arrangements, such as the European Union and the North American Free Trade Agreement, participating countries more often than not actively promote trade relations among each other, and, sometimes, the integration goes further to include economic policy coordination.

Different from these government-sponsored regional efforts, a close economic relationship among mainland China, Hong Kong, and Taiwan has gradually evolved – despite lack of support from the governments involved. This integration is led not by a bureaucracy but by businesspeople, sometimes against the political will of governments. The convergence is characterized by the rapidly expanding trade and capital flows among these three economies. People use the term "Greater China" to describe this phenomenon.

The growth of Greater China started in 1979 when mainland China initiated its economic reform policy, thereby opening itself to the outside world. In the eighteen years since then, growing trade and capital flows have led to specialization and division of labor in the region. Productivity improves as a result of economic integration. The increasingly close economic ties among Chinese, Taiwanese, and Hong Kong economies have benefited all three. In this period, the economic growth in China in general and in the southern provinces of Guangdong and Fujian in particular reached a level not previously seen in their economic history. New resources in the mainland have become a new engine to regional economic growth. The economies of Hong Kong and, lately, Taiwan, have experienced a fundamental transformation, having been direct beneficiaries of the economic reform and open-door policies of mainland China.

The reversion of Hong Kong to China's sovereignty on July 1, 1997, one of the most significant moments of this century, gives fresh impetus to this process. With imminent transfer of Hong Kong, many people question whether the trend set in the past eighteen years of economic integration and the impressive growth in the region will continue.

The main purpose of this chapter is to explore the implications of the reversion of sovereignty for the future of Greater China. In which direction will the future economic relationship among Hong Kong, Taiwan, and the mainland evolve in the post-1997 era? More specifically, we pose the following questions: What are the driving forces of the convergence of these three distinguishable economies? What roles does each of these economies play in the process of economic integration? What are the implications for such integration processes before and after the reversion of Hong Kong? We address these questions by reviewing the current interdependence of these economies, the consequences of that interdependence, and the factors that contribute to that interdependence.

THE EMERGENCE OF GREATER CHINA

Although the term "Greater China" is not entirely new, it has never been clearly defined and has never been a universally accepted concept. The ambiguity arises for two primary reasons. First, it is unclear whether "Greater China" is simply a way to describe the emergence of the sub-regional economic integration among Hong Kong, Taiwan, and the mainland, or whether the term suggests an institutional dimension that carries political and military implications. The second problem is that even if the focus is on the economic dimension of Greater China, one may still need to specify the geographic scope of the term.[1]

---

[1] A concise review of the origin of the concept and its various meanings and implications can be found in Harry Harding, "The Concept of Greater China: Themes, Variations and Reservations,"

Changqi Wu

Although the first problem is more likely to raise concern among observers of international relations, the second is not free from controversy. In both the popular press and academic journals, several definitions exist for the geographic scope of Greater China. Broadly defined, "Greater China" includes mainland China, Hong Kong, Taiwan, Singapore, and the Chinese population living overseas. However, when closeness is measured not by language and race, but by trade and investment relations, the core of the Greater China economic area is considered to be located in the Guangdong and Fujian provinces of mainland China, Hong Kong, and Taiwan. The term "Southern China Economic Co-operation" has also been used to describe this aspect of subregional integration.

We consider the narrowly defined concept to be more useful because in most circumstances, "Greater China" refers to the economic integration of Hong Kong, Taiwanese, and mainland economies of the past eighteen years. In fact, only part of the mainland has been affected by this integration. Hong Kong and Guangdong Province are already strongly interrelated economies, with Guangdong providing manufacturing facilities and Hong Kong performing service functions including product development, financing, packaging, and marketing. The economies of Taiwan and Fujian Province likewise have become increasingly interdependent, although not on the same scale as Hong Kong and Guangdong. This is for two reasons. First, the process started late: It was not until 1988 that the residents of Taiwan could visit the mainland legally. Second, development has been constrained by the political unwillingness of the Taiwanese government to encourage such developments. Such constraints have increased the cost of economic integration because for now, all transactions must be made via Hong Kong. Nevertheless, "Greater China" is an expanding concept as the economic growth in the four regions generates effects on other Chinese provinces. Following integration of the core of the four regions, closer linkage should occur with other parts of the mainland.

The China Quarterly, 1993, pp. 661–86. Also see Jamie Mackie, "The Risks of 'Greater China' Rhetoric," *Asian Wall Street Journal,* Nov. 7, 1996; Robert F. Ash & Y. Y. Kueh, "Economic Integration within Greater China: Trade and Investment Flowers Between China, Hong Kong and Taiwan," *The China Quarterly,* 1993, pp. 711–45; Pamela Baldinger, "The Birth of Greater China," *The China Business Review,* May–June 1992; Eric Bouteiller, "The Emergence of Greater China as an Economic Force," *Long Range Planning,* vol. 28(1), 1995, pp. 54–60; and June Khanna, *Southern China, Hong Kong, and Taiwan* (Washington, D.C.: Center for Strategic and International Studies, 1995.)

From the point of view of an outsider, mainland China, Hong Kong, and Taiwan are three economies with different structures and at different developmental stages. The important question is how they could have developed such close economic ties in a relatively short time and created such a mutually interdependent growth pattern.

In the late 1970s, all three Chinese economies were at critical stages in the process of economic development, each with its own distinguishing features. At that time, China remained a centrally planned economy. Thirty years of central planning in isolation, and the hostility across the Taiwan Strait, prevented China from developing trade relations that could have benefited all sides. Starting from the 1950s, both Hong Kong and Taiwan experienced rapid economic growth. Hong Kong developed a labor-intensive manufacturing industry with an economy relying on textiles and electronics. Similarly, the Taiwanese economy experienced rapid growth after its government adopted an export-led industrial policy. Export-oriented industry achieved rapid development. As Hong Kong and Taiwan experienced rapid economic growth, wages and land prices increased.

The three Chinese economies were separated by political and ideological barriers. All of them faced different tasks to achieve economic growth, requiring the transformation of each economy. The opening up of mainland China to the outside world marked the start of trade liberalization, and economic integration was driven essentially by private businesses and entrepreneurs in pursuit of new resources and new markets.

In the early 1980s, Hong Kong industry was facing increased competition; it had to find ways to enhance its international competitiveness. Small entrepreneurs in Hong Kong took advantage of China's new polices by starting to invest in the mainland. Cumulative investments from Hong Kong have changed the industrial structure in that city. In the ensuing ten years, Hong Kong's manufacturing industry essentially shifted across the border into Guangdong.

Investments in mainland China also changed the trade patterns of Hong Kong. According to a survey by the Trade Department of the Hong Kong Government, 74 percent of domestic exports to the mainland in 1992 consisted of raw materials and semi-manufactured goods for processing in China. Contractual arrangements stipulated that the resulting processed goods were subsequently to be reimported into Hong Kong. In the same year, 72 percent of imports from China were related to Hong Kong's outward processing. The boom in cross-border processing attests to the fact that China now serves as the manufacturing base for Hong Kong's enterprises. On the other hand, Hong Kong has been assisting China, particularly Southern China, to export its manufactured goods to other countries.[2]

In our study of the determinants for export performance in China's rural industries, we found that the factor most significantly influencing the magnitude of the export ratio in rural China was foreign direct investment. This is not only because foreign investors bring market information and production specifications, but also because their presence enables Chinese businesses to circumvent foreign-trade regulations. In mainland China, domestic firms do not normally have the privilege to export. Instead they must sell their goods to the state-owned foreign-trade companies, and the latter sell the products to the international market. This privilege is, however, granted to joint ventures with foreign investors automatically. Foreign direct investment therefore permits bypassing restrictions on domestic firms' foreign trade.[3]

Hong Kong has benefited tremendously from its direct investments in the mainland. A recent study shows that the repatriated profits from Hong Kong's direct investment in China were US$10.5 billion and US$15.7 billion in 1993 and 1994 respectively, representing a rate of return close to 30 percent. In 1995, Hong Kong earned 9 percent of its gross national product (GNP) in the form of repatriated profit from foreign direct investment abroad, most of it from investments in the mainland.[4]

Economic ties between Taiwan and the mainland did not develop as easily as those between the mainland and Hong Kong. Following a period of sustained economic growth in Taiwan, wages and land prices have risen and exchange rates have moved contrary to its export efforts. Other Asian nations with lower labor costs have become serious competitors for labor-intensive industries. As a result, Taiwan was forced to upgrade its economic structure.

At the same time, the country's exceptional trade surplus and its high savings rate provided the resources to invest abroad. By making overseas investments, Taiwanese companies could combine their competitive advantages in

[2] Chyau Tuan & Linda Fung-yee Ng, "Hong Kong's Outward Investment and Regional Economic Integration with Guangdong: Process and Implications," *Journal of Asian Economics*, vol. 6(3), 1995, pp. 385–405.
[3] Changqi Wu & Leonard K. Cheng, "The Determinant of Export Performance of Township and Village Enterprises in China," Hong Kong University of Science and Technology, Working Paper, 1995.
[4] Rajiv Lall, "The Future of the Hong Kong Dollar: Myth or Reality," in *Investment Research Asia-Pacific*, Morgan Stanley Investment Report, October 1996.

management skills, trading, and technology with the advantages of lower land and labor costs offered in neighboring countries. Mainland China soon became the most favorable investment destination.

The economic relationship between Taiwan and the mainland, unlike that between Hong Kong and the mainland, developed in two stages. The first stage was between 1979 and 1988, when economic relations were defined largely by indirect trade. Only in the second stage – when Taiwanese authorities removed the ban on citizens' travel to the mainland in 1988 – did the mainland begin to receive a steady stream of Taiwanese visitors. Many of the visitors combined private visits with a search for business opportunities. This process led to an influx of Taiwanese capital into mainland China.

Information on indirect trade across the Taiwan Strait can be obtained by examining Hong Kong and mainland official statistics; information on the growth of Taiwan's direct investment in the mainland cannot be obtained directly from Taiwan. In 1991, the Taiwanese government requested that all domestic firms register their mainland investments, including amounts, with the Taiwanese Ministry of Economic Affairs. It is commonly believed that the amounts were underreported. For instance, statistics show that until 1992, the cumulative amount of Taiwan's outward investment in the mainland was only US$754 million, small in proportion to its outward investment in other Asian countries.[5]

It was the large multinational corporations that finally solidified the concept of Greater China. When visiting the regional headquarters of large multinational firms in Hong Kong, one finds that many of them have Greater China units in their organizational charts. This has come about largely because of the evolution of the market and of customers' preferences. The product that sells well in Hong Kong quite likely will be successful in Guangdong. Companies based in Taiwan and Hong Kong may find that, as their customers are now operating in all three places, they now must monitor the changes in three markets that used to be strictly separate. The de facto disappearance of borders between these markets put pressures on corporate leaders to respond by setting up the Greater China units to coordinate cross-border activities. This trend will further deepen the economic integration of the region.

[5] Gee San, "An Estimation of Taiwan's Direct Investment in Mainland China and Its Effect on Both Sides' Export Performance Toward the US Market: The Example of Taiwan's Apparel Industry," *Seoul Journal of Economics*, vol. 8(2), 1995.

Economic integration among the three Chinese economies generated at least three consequences. First, it stimulated economic growth in the region. In the period of 1981 to 1995, the average real gross domestic product (GDP) growth in Taiwan has been maintained at the level of 7.1 percent. Hong Kong's per capita GDP in the same period has grown at the annual rate of 6.1 percent, and its GDP per capita has bypassed that of the United Kingdom by 40 percent. China has grown at breakneck speed with annual real GDP growth rate close to 10 percent. The growth rate in Southern China was even higher.

Second, the integration has led to specialization within the region and has promoted trade with the rest of the world. Hong Kong has turned itself into a highly successful financial, trading, and shipping center in the Asia Pacific region. In 1995, 83 percent of Hong Kong's GDP was in the service sectors, of which 26 percent was in financial services. In the meantime, Hong Kong has moved its labor-intensive manufacturing into southern Chinese provinces, particularly Guangdong.[6]

This process has turned Guangdong into an industrial production base, resulting in the rapid industrialization of Guangdong's economy. Hong Kong's investments in Guangdong have also created employment opportunities. One estimate has suggested that Hong Kong–funded companies employ about 5 million people from the mainland.

The specialization and division of labor between Taiwan and Fujian Province is not as dramatic as that between Guangdong and Hong Kong. Still the process has also greatly changed the landscape of Taiwanese industry. Labor-intensive and high-environmental-cost industries such as textiles and chemicals have been relocated to the mainland, mostly in Fujian Province.

Further evidence of the growing interdependence between the mainland, Hong Kong, and Taiwanese economies is the evolution of the U.S. trade deficit with Greater China. Industry studies show that production facilities formerly located in Hong Kong and Taiwan have now been relocated to the mainland, while keeping the same ownership. The relocation of manufacturing activities is illustrated in Table 5.1, showing the amount of exports from Greater China to the U.S. market.

The third consequence of economic integration is economic transformation and the development of markets in all these places, a consequence of which has

---

[6] Michael Enright, Edith Scott, Jonathan West, & David Dodwell, *The Hong Kong Advantage: A Study of the Competitiveness of the Hong Kong Economy* (Hong Kong: Vision 2047 Foundation, 1996).

Table 5.1. *Measures of Economic Integration*

	1989	1990	1991	1992	1993	1994	1995
Mainland China's trade with Hong Kong (US$ million)							
Export	21,916	26,650	32,137	37,512	22,064	32,365	35,984
Import	12,540	14,258	17,463	20,534	10,473	9,457	8,591
Balance	9,376	12,392	14,674	16,978	11,591	22,908	27,393
Mainland China's trade with Taiwan (US$ million)							
Export	n.a.	n.a.	595	694	1,462	2,242	3,098
Import	n.a.	n.a.	3,639	5,866	12,933	14,085	14,784
Balance			3,044	5,172	11,471	11,843	11,686
Foreign direct investment in mainland China (US$ million)							
From Hong Kong							
	2,078	1,913	2,579	7,706	17,445	19,822	20,185
From Taiwan							
	n.a.	n.a.	472	1,053	3,139	3,391	3,165
National total							
	3,392	3,487	4,366	11,007	27,515	33,767	37,521
% of HK & Taiwan investment in national total							
	61.3%	54.9%	69.9%	79.6%	74.8%	68.7%	62.2%

Note: n.a. = not applicable.
Source: China Statistical Yearbook, various years; China Trade Report.

been to accelerate the expansion of the non-state sector in the mainland. The value-added of the non-state industrial sectors in Guangdong and Fujian provinces in 1994 were 68 percent and 64 percent respectively – substantially higher than the national average of 46 percent.[7] As the governor of Guangdong Province has noted, foreign direct investment in Guangdong has reached a level of US$57 billion in the past few years. The enterprises funded by foreign capital employ over 7 million people in Guangdong. Foreign investors have invested US$7 billion in the infrastructure in Guangdong.[8] In a study of Taiwan's investment in Xiamen, Fujian Province, it is reported that Taiwan investment in

[7] *China Industrial Economic Statistical Yearbook*, 1995, pp. 82–102.
[8] *Hong Kong Economic Daily*, China section, Oct. 16, 1996.

Xiamen has overridden the local government industrial development plans as the determining influence on Xiamen's industrial structure.[9]

Mainland China benefits from expanding relations in terms of capital and markets. In the eighteen-year period starting from 1979, foreign direct investment in China has reached US$135 billion, of which over 60 percent comprises investments from Hong Kong and Taiwan.

THE ROLE OF HONG KONG IN GREATER CHINA

In the process of economic integration, Hong Kong plays a vital role. Hong Kong's geographical location at the heart of the Asia Pacific region is a key advantage. Indeed, Hong Kong's unique location has accelerated the integration of its economy with the economies of the rest of the region, particularly with the mainland.[10] Hong Kong's role can be summarized as follows.

Hong Kong as Financial Center

In the years after the mainland adopted its open-door policy, Hong Kong has been the largest source of foreign capital. Direct investment from Hong Kong accounts for 58 percent of a total of US$153 billion in foreign capital invested in China from 1979 to 1995. In addition to direct investment, Hong Kong provides trade financing and syndicated loans to the mainland in substantial amounts. Hong Kong's financial institutions' debt and liability related to the mainland has been growing at the rate of 30 to 40 percent and it has surpassed US$600 billion.[11]

In addition to providing capital to finance mainland economic growth, Hong Kong plays a role as an offshore financial center. According to some estimates, a substantial amount of foreign direct investment from Hong Kong into the mainland is actually capital from the mainland that is taking advantage of more favorable tax treatment and other privileges reserved exclusively for foreign direct investment. Mainland firms, institutions, and private individuals have

---

[9] Qing Luo & Christopher Howe, "Direct Investment and Economic Integration in the Asia-Pacific: The Case of Taiwanese Investment in Xiamen," *The China Quarterly*, 1993, pp. 746–69.

[10] For earlier development of China–Hong Kong economic relations, see Sung Yun-Wing, *The China-Hong Kong Connection* (Cambridge University Press, 1991).

[11] Zong Hua, "Post-1997 Role of Hong Kong as an International Financial Center," *Hong Kong Economic Report*, vol. 2494, Nov. 4, 1996, pp. 26–28.

used Hong Kong as an offshore center in order to enjoy its benefits indirectly. Hong Kong's social infrastructure, including its legal system and its efficient financial services sector, ensures that investors' interests are protected.

Hong Kong as Transport Center

Hong Kong has one of the largest container ports in the world. In 1995, for instance, it handled over 12.6 million containers. The excellent port facilities and supporting infrastructure make Hong Kong the prime entrepot for China trade. Between 1984 and 1995, Hong Kong's share of the mainland's total exports increased from 34 percent to 53 percent. About 60 percent of these exports were either to or from China in 1995. Hong Kong handles 80 percent of Guangdong's imports and exports.

Both Hong Kong and the mainland have invested heavily in the infrastructure projects that will strengthen Hong Kong's position as the transportation center for China trade. Gordon Wu, jointly with the Guangdong provincial government, developed the Guangdong–Shenzhen superhighway, linking the capital of Guangdong Province to the border with Hong Kong. In just two years, the mainland completed the Beijing–Kowloon Railway, which runs through the hinterland of China and connects the city centers of Beijing and Hong Kong.

Hong Kong as Technology-Transfer Center

As demonstrated in economics literature, a nation's long-term sustainable economic growth requires continuous technological changes. Although Hong Kong has traditionally carried out little research and development, Hong Kong's industries have done a lot to transfer the time-proven, mature manufacturing technologies to Guangdong, where such technologies represent an upgrade in local-production methods. In the 1970s, the majority of Hong Kong's enterprises were small-scale and labor-intensive, producing light industrial and consumer goods. Thus, production facilities set up in Guangdong through joint ventures often utilize simple, mature, and standardized technologies. A considerable amount of capital equipment in Guangdong is second-hand. Very little of the technology can be regarded as advanced and sophisticated. Nevertheless, most of it has been judged as suitable to local conditions.

The technology transfer from Hong Kong to China has been considered successful because it often has been bundled with management, financial, design, and service skills for Chinese companies. Direct investment from Hong Kong in the form of physical capital included technologies that were not available in the mainland. Thus, the technological diffusion inevitably raised the technological level in Southern China.

Hong Kong as Human Resources Center

In the process of economic reform, what the mainland needed most were qualified managers and entrepreneurs. Hong Kong has acted as a source of management expertise and business skills. According to the Census and Statistics Department of the Hong Kong government, over 52,000 Hong Kong residents were working in China in 1992,[12] most of whom were professionals and skilled workers. By the same token, it is estimated that there are about 60,000 people from the mainland working in China-funded companies in Hong Kong. During their stay, they quickly acquire management and business skills. When they return, they bring the business practices of Hong Kong to the mainland.

It has been widely reported that the issue of Hong Kong's reversion to China has created anxiety among Hong Kong residents and that a large number of professionals have left Hong Kong and emigrated to other countries. However, statistics show that emigration levels of Hong Kong residents to some Western countries peaked in the earlier 1990s and then subsided partly, because of the emerging dynamic economies and growth potential in the region. In preparation for the reversion, some Hong Kong residents have obtained foreign citizenship as an insurance policy. Concerns that many foreign and Hong Kong–owned businesses in the territory would lose a large percentage of their middle- and upper-management work force before the reversion have yet to be justified.

Prospects of further economic integration have inspired a large number of overseas Chinese to return to Hong Kong to take advantage of the regional economic boom. Statistics show that, although the total number of emigrants was around 50,000 per year in the last five years, the number of professionals emigrating to other countries represents only a proportion of the total. The number of employment visas issued by the Immigration Department of Hong Kong to foreign citizens increases steadily, not including both British citizens and Hong Kong returnees, who do not need working visas to seek employment in Hong Kong (see Table 5.2). Among many would-be emigrants, it is often the case that, while wives and children live in Canada, the husbands continue to work in

---

[12] "The Report on Hong Kong Residents Working in China," Census and Statistics Department, Hong Kong Government, 1992.

Table 5.2. *Emigration and Immigration in Hong Kong*

	1989	1990	1991	1992	1993	1994	1995
Emigration from HK	42,000	62,000	60,000	66,000	53,000	62,000	43,100
Professionals	n.a.	n.a.	n.a.	23,000	18,000	21,000	15,700
Immigration to HK	76,063	81,335	86,677	95,425	110,500	119,302	114,522
Employment visas issued to foreign professionals	9,854	10,350	10,601	11,900	15,260	17,117	13,759

Note: n.a. = not applicable.
Source: The Immigration Department of Hong Kong.

Changqi Wu

Hong Kong. The brain-drain problem has not been serious enough to curtail Hong Kong's growth.

The influx of professionals from outside Hong Kong traditionally serves Hong Kong well, boosting its efficiency and economic vitality. The technological upgrading of Hong Kong's economy generates demand for a large number of well-trained professionals. Since 1990, Hong Kong employers have been permitted to employ mainland professionals who studied overseas for more than two years, in order to attract more talent to the territory. In the last fifteen years, over 230,000 students from the mainland alone went overseas to pursue advanced studies. Among them, two-thirds went to the United States. However, many have been attracted back to the region by its dynamic economic development, and Hong Kong is the ideal place to realize their market value. Systematically collected statistics do not exist for these groups of professionals in Hong Kong, but their number is estimated at around 2,000. Professionals with PRC citizenship, in addition to their technical training, bring in expertise regarding business operations in the mainland, thereby helping Hong Kong to establish close relations with the mainland. Professionals with citizenship in other countries contribute positively to maintain the international character of Hong Kong.

Hong Kong as Gateway to and from China

Hong Kong constitutes an entry and exit point for 80 percent of mainland-bound tourists. Chinese and Taiwanese tourists also constitute a large proportion of visitors to Hong Kong. The number of visitors arriving in Hong Kong from China is close to 2 million a year, and the number of Hong Kong residents who visited mainland China was 24.8 million in 1995.[13]

ROLES OF MAINLAND CHINA AND TAIWAN

Both mainland and Taiwanese investments have contributed to regional economic integration. Just as Hong Kong is the prime source of capital for the mainland, Hong Kong is also the prime destination for outward investment from China. In 1993, China surpassed Japan in becoming the foremost foreign investor in Hong Kong in terms of cumulative investment, and Chinese capital currently is second only to British capital in Hong Kong.

[13] *Hong Kong Annual Digest of Statistics 1996*, Census and Statistics Department, Hong Kong Government, 1996, tables 7.19 and 7.20.

126

China-funded companies play an increasingly significant role in Hong Kong. According to one recent report from the New China News Agency, the number of companies funded by mainland China capital reached 1,800 in 1996, with combined net assets totaling over US$42.5 billion. Moreover, this number is an underestimate because the report included only companies approved by mainland economic authorities.

At present, mainland China–funded companies are active in the trade, finance, insurance, transport, and properties markets in Hong Kong. China-funded companies accounted for 22 percent of Hong Kong's external trade in 1995, handling 31 percent of the import of Chinese products to Hong Kong and 24 percent of the share of Hong Kong reexported goods to the mainland.[14]

China-controlled companies such as the China Merchant Co. dominate Hong Kong's transport sector. China-related companies own the largest barge fleet and floating harbor and over 10 million deadweight tons of ocean shipping. Annual shipment value takes a quarter of transport volume.

There are over ninety financial institutions from China operating in Hong Kong for which the Bank of China is the note-issuing bank. The assets of the Bank of China Group constitute a 12 percent share of the total assets for the Hong Kong banking industry. Deposit market share is 25 percent and lending market share, 7.8 percent.

In the capital market, over fifty listed companies are controlled by Chinese companies with market capitalization of over US$20 billion, which accounts for 6 percent of total capitalization for all shares listed on the Hong Kong Stock Exchange. (This number excludes the state-owned enterprises from China listed in the Hong Kong Stock Exchange – so-called H shares.)[15]

It is hard to gauge the magnitude of Taiwanese capital in the mainland. It is estimated that over 30,000 Taiwanese firms are investing and operating on the mainland, and in some sectors the whole production process, from the supply of raw materials to final production, has been shifted to the mainland. According to the Taipei Stock Exchange, over 83 firms among 364 listed companies have invested, including many blue-chip companies, with a total investment in excess of US$1.4 billion. The latter contrasts sharply with the situation at the end of 1994, when cumulative Taiwanese investment in the mainland totaled only US$180 million.[16]

---

[14] Interview of Qian Guoan, deputy of economy division, Xinhua News Agency, Hong Kong Branch, in *AsiaWeek*, Sept. 8, 1996, pp. 56–57.

[15] See "The Stock Exchange of Hong Kong," *The Hong Kong Securities Journal*, November 1996.

[16] Special Report, "Lee Teng-Hui Made a U Turn," *AsiaWeek*, Sept. 1, 1996, pp. 23–26.

Published statistics from the mainland show that in the last five years, Taiwanese investment on average amounted to about 10 percent of total utilized foreign direct investment. Of this amount, about 65 percent was concentrated in Fujian Province.

While many businesspeople believe that Taiwan's economic future lies in achieving closer commercial ties to the mainland, the government, of course, has its political considerations, and these promise that the road will be bumpy. Even if these political considerations are put aside, differences in levels of development and social systems may impede closer economic integration.

FACTORS CONTRIBUTING TO ECONOMIC INTEGRATION

The economic reforms that took place in mainland China in 1979 began a new process that fundamentally changed the economic relationship between Hong Kong, Taiwan, and mainland China, shaping the path of regional economic development for the ensuing eighteen years. An economy can grow in essentially three ways. One is to accumulate and to mobilize its resources; the second is to put these resources to better use through improved allocation; the third is to make technological advances in order to produce more output with the same input. Trade in goods and services, capital flow, and technology transfer all allow production to be organized in a more efficient way and across larger areas.

Looking at the three Chinese economies within geographic proximity, one can see clearly the factors that have contributed to the rapid development in trade and economic relations in the past eighteen years and, in turn, the process of regional economic integration. First of all, the opportunity for integration lies in complementary productive factors. The differences in the endowment of natural resources, the supply and demand of labor, the availability of capital and technology, and the inclusion of management skills together form the basis for economic linkage.

The mainland provides a seemingly unlimited number of skilled and semi-skilled laborers who earn a fraction of the wages prevailing in Hong Kong and Taiwan. According to an estimate by Morgan Stanley investment bank, hourly labor costs for the manufacturing sectors in Hong Kong, Taiwan, and the mainland were US$2.30, US$1.70, and US$0.19, respectively, in 1985. Ten years later, such gaps had grown even larger.[17] Additionally, the abundant natural

[17] *The Economist*, Nov. 2, 1996, p. 95.

resources in mainland China, especially land, provided room for Hong Kong and Taiwan's businesspeople to maintain their international competitiveness by shifting their labor-intensive production to the mainland. As for Hong Kong and Taiwan, they provide capital, technology, and management expertise. Hong Kong also supplies value-added services such as packaging and transportation.

In addition to their different endowments, these three economies have different comparative advantages. Hong Kong's well-developed legal and social infrastructure, coupled with its preponderance of marketing skills, makes it the natural choice for the region's business center. Mainland China, with its abundance of low-wage labor and presence of basic technology, is ideal as a base for labor-intensive manufacturing. Taiwan, in the process of its industrialization, has accumulated many intangible assets, such as production organization, production skills, and manufacturing technology. Although the differences in the endowment of productive factors among the three economies provide the foundation for trade and investment flows, business transactions do not take place in a vacuum but depend on the social and legal infrastructure and policy environment. In this respect, the region offers a number of unrivaled benefits, over and above geographical proximity, such as common linguistic and cultural factors, to facilitate the development of close economic ties.

An investor entering new territory must rely on local social and legal infrastructures. The lack of a well-developed legal system in the mainland offers further comparative advantages to Hong Kong and Taiwanese entrepreneurs. When business contracts cannot be clarified and implemented on the mainland because of its underdeveloped legal environment, kinship and connections offer an alternative institutional arrangement. Business relations in Greater China need to be based on mutual interest and mutual trust because of the insufficient legal protection for invested capital and the lack of guarantees for mutual cooperation. In other words, kinship plays a crucial role in business transactions between China, Taiwan, and Hong Kong because of the weakness and underdevelopment of the Chinese legal system. This explains, in part, why the lion's share of foreign capital investment in China is from Hong Kong and Taiwan.[18]

In addition, the impact of the mainland's economic policy on the economic integration of Greater China is obvious. From a very early stage of economic reform, mainland economic policy has shown more favorable treatment toward

---

[18] Chu-chia Steve Lin & Ivan P. L. Png, "Kinship, Control, and Incentives," Hong Kong University of Science and Technology, Working Paper, 1995.

Hong Kong and Taiwanese businesses. For instance, in order to encourage trade between the mainland and Taiwan, the Ministry of Commerce of the People's Republic of China (PRC) issued a circular in June 1980 indicating that products made in Taiwan should be treated as domestic trade, therefore free of import tariffs. The same document went on to urge that Taiwanese businesses purchasing mainland products be granted a 20 percent discount. Partly because of that policy, indirect trade between Taiwan and the mainland increased three-fold in just three years. Although the tariff-free import policy was recently abolished, products made in Taiwan can still enter the mainland market at tariff concessions of about 10 percent. Such policies did stimulate much indirect trade between the mainland and Taiwan.[19]

Despite the extensive trade and investment relations among the three economies, there remain substantial institutional barriers to further integration of these economies. The reversion may lead to a more efficient coordination mechanism between Hong Kong and the mainland, but economic relations between Taiwan and the mainland are expected to be bumpy. Moreover, the intertwining of these three economies makes each of them vulnerable to external shocks. When China experiences the transformation of its economy, the policies are subject to changes that are accompanied by uncertainties in the business environment.

IMPLICATIONS OF THE REVERSION

After the reversion of Hong Kong to China's sovereignty, Hong Kong will become the Special Administrative Region (SAR) of the PRC. This change will have little significant impact on the process of integration among these three economies. We do not see any significant changes in the economics of Greater China, mainly because the "Greater China" concept does not represent a political identity. Moreover, all sides appear to be reluctant to pursue complete economic integration at this stage. They all have incentives to keep the current status quo and take full advantage of it.

First, the reversion does not change Hong Kong's system in any fundamental way. Both Hong Kong and the mainland authorities realize that they have common interests in maintaining the situation both before and after the reversion. A good example is the status of Hong Kong in the World Trade Organization (WTO). Because Hong Kong will retain its status as a separate contract-

---

[19] Li Fei, *The Economic and Trade Relations over the Taiwan Strait* (Beijing: The Foreign Trade Education Publishing House, 1994).

ing party of the WTO, the reversion of sovereignty should not produce significant effects on trade. The factors that drove the economic growth of Hong Kong
and Greater China will remain largely intact. They will continue to contribute
to the growth of the region.

Second, the reversion may provide a good opportunity for Hong Kong in the
sense that it will have stronger influence on the level of economic integration
after reversion. After 1997, the influence of Hong Kong on mainland China
may increase because of direct and more effective communication channels to
Beijing. Hong Kong can negotiate greater access for Hong Kong–based services and investments on the mainland, and it will be in a better position to
coordinate with the mainland and participate in the development of infrastructure projects in the Greater China region. Hong Kong can also strengthen its
position as China's gateway between the region and the outside world. Nevertheless, the transition poses a degree of uncertainty that needs to be handled
with care.

As the neighboring provinces in Southern China have increased their dependence on Hong Kong's infrastructure, the dependence of China's northern
provinces on Hong Kong has actually decreased. Indeed, coastal cities farther
north, including Shanghai and Dalian, are improving their competitiveness by
expanding their own port facilities and improving other infrastructure. A growing share of China's overall trade volume is generated by non-southern
provinces, for which the natural transport corridor is in the north, not Hong
Kong. The increasing foreign trade of the mainland has become large enough
to sustain the business centers that specialize in serving regional needs.[20]

By the same token, China will become less attractive to Hong Kong's capital for two reasons. First, the favorable tax and tariff treatments toward Hong
Kong will be gradually phased out. Second, improvements in the mainland's
legal system will make the comparative advantage of Hong Kong and Taiwan
less obvious. In order to sustain the competitive edge of Hong Kong's economy, Hong Kong must raise its technological level by developing high
tech–based service industries. Hong Kong has capital but lacks the expertise
and experience to implement high technology. Both Taiwan and the mainland
can contribute positively in this regard.

Policy makers in Taiwan are worried that economic interdependence with
the mainland may provide the mainland with political leverage. Taiwanese

---

[20] See Wu Changqi & Song Yanxia, "Hold the Hong Kong Obituary, Fortune," *Asian Wall Street
Journal*, July 1, 1995.

authorities have recently signaled that they would not be willing to see further deepening in the economic relations between the mainland and Taiwan. For instance, Taiwanese authorities do not want to see Taiwanese banks set up branches in the mainland; instead, they believe, these banks should use their third-country subsidiaries to enter the mainland market indirectly. Such measures can only add to the cost of doing business and weaken the competitive position of Taiwanese firms not only in the region but also globally. In realizing the consequences, Taiwanese authorities are developing contingency plans for direct capital flows, as well as making shipping and aviation arrangements.

Such barriers to closer economic integration will not disappear in the foreseeable future. The mainland still has a long way to go to liberalize its international trade. First, it must face the daunting task of reforming its economy. Different technical levels for industry and market structures prevent mainland firms from competing directly in the international market. In addition, mainland China is not a member of the WTO, and its currency is still not convertible. All these factors constitute barriers to future economic integration despite the reversion of sovereignty of Hong Kong to China.

SUMMARY

"Greater China" is not a well-defined concept and is often used in different contexts to refer to different things. In our view, Greater China should be used to describe the developing economic relationship between Hong Kong, Taiwan, and Southern China. The integration of the Southern Chinese, Hong Kong, and Taiwanese economies is the result of a process that has been evolving over the past eighteen years, reflecting the compatibility of the resources each of these three economies offers. By utilizing their comparative advantages, these three Chinese economies have achieved continuous and sustained economic growth.

The underdeveloped legal system in China makes ownership rights difficult to enforce. Family ties have proved to be the best institution to guarantee the implementation of business transactions to take advantage of policies adopted by the mainland.

Hong Kong has played a vital role in the process of the emergence of Greater China. The reversion of sovereignty will not change the fundamental incentives for a close economic relationship to develop. On the contrary, the reversion provides Hong Kong with new opportunities to strengthen its position as the most important business center in the Greater China region.

132

6

One Country, Two Currencies

Monetary Relations between Hong Kong and China

EDGARDO BARANDIARAN AND TSANG SHU-KI[1]

INTRODUCTION

IN the past fifteen years, the economic integration of Hong Kong and China has been impressive. The transformation of Hong Kong into a service economy and the opening of the Chinese economy have been interrelated processes, although each process alone is much broader and larger than its interrelation with the other. Moreover, each process is far from over, and a closer integration may follow.

Given that economic integration, many observers suspect that Hong Kong's reunification with China in 1997 will do little to strengthen it – and much to weaken it. Low expectations concerning the potential for strengthening and fears of reversal are the result partly of political considerations but mainly of misunderstandings about the two economic systems and how they have been evolving. By focusing only on the present differences between the two systems, the debate ignores the underlying transformation processes in the two economies.

In particular, the threat of change to Hong Kong's monetary system has been a source of concern. Notwithstanding the Chinese government's repeated assurances about the maintenance of the existing monetary regimes based on the Hong Kong dollar (HK$) and the Renminbi (RMB), there lies the presumption that some change is inevitable, because of either political considerations or economic reasons.

[1] Edgardo Barandiaran is senior economist, World Bank Resident Mission in China; Tsang Shu-ki is professor, Department of Economics, Hong Kong Baptist University.

In this chapter, we analyze the economic rationale for the coexistence of the present monetary systems after reunification. Indeed, this amounts to addressing the rationale of monetary unification, the alternative to the coexistence of the two currencies. Not surprisingly, this is a unique experience. It cannot be compared directly with Europe's ongoing economic integration and monetary unification because of the differences in the political systems. Indeed, in Europe, monetary unification has been advanced as an instrument of political integration. Nor can it be compared directly with the reunification of Germany, where the two economic systems were hardly related before the collapse of communism in Eastern Europe, and monetary unification was a prerequisite for absorbing East Germany rapidly into the West German economic entity.

In the following two sections, we discuss the Hong Kong and Chinese monetary systems separately. Both have been changing, especially the Chinese system. We try to emphasize the similarities without ignoring the differences, and to assess the direction in which they have been evolving independently of the prospect of reunification. As shown by the recent experiences of many other countries, especially developing countries and transitional economies, the main challenge of any monetary authority is to build a reputation as an organization fully committed to price stability in a world of closely integrated financial markets. The presumption underlying our discussion of the two monetary systems is that both monetary authorities are committed to price stability, although the Chinese authority is still struggling with some legacies of the old system.

Next, we analyze first the economic rationale for monetary unification and then the ways in which the two currencies could continue to coexist. Because of the political reality, a system of one currency could only mean the elimination of the HK$. We find that there is no sound economic argument for unifying the two currencies and that unification would entail high economic costs for Hong Kong. Concerning the coexistence of the two currencies, we characterize the present situation as one of spontaneous competition, that is, one in which only the RMB is legal tender in China but – at least in some areas of the country – Chinese residents use both currencies spontaneously for domestic transactions and the HK$ in most transactions with Hong Kong residents (and perhaps with other non-residents). On the other hand, residents in Hong Kong use mainly the HK$ but all other foreign currencies may be used for some transactions, especially with non-residents. Given this spontaneous competition, should the Chinese government encourage it or limit it? We analyze the possibility of using the HK$ as legal tender in some limited areas of China, and touch upon the issue of enforcing strictly the prohibition of circulating the HK$ and foreign currencies in China because of its impracticality.

In Hong Kong, historically, bank notes are issued by a few designated commercial banks. The territory followed China in adopting the silver standard before its collapse in the 1930s. In 1935, Hong Kong moved to a "currency board" system. However, *no currency board actually existed.* Instead, an "Exchange Fund" was created and controlled by the Colonial Treasurer, and it acted as the ultimate backing for the notes issued by three designated note-issuing banks (NIBs). In issuing HK$ bank notes, the three NIBs had to deposit sterling at a fixed rate with the Exchange Fund, receiving in exchange certificates of indebtedness (CIs), with which the NIBs could issue equivalent amounts of notes.[2]

After a short period (1974–1983) in which the HK$ was floated, the currency was pegged to the U.S. dollar (US$) at the rate of HK$7.80/US$ under "the linked exchange rate system," commonly called "the link." The link was in fact a rescue measure in a crisis caused by the dispute between China and Great Britain over the future of the territory. Because of heightening tension, the HK$ plunged in September 1983, touching a low of HK$9.60/US$. The authorities had to resort to a fixed exchange-rate system again, with the rate pegged at HK$7.80/US$. The link is still in effect today.

The link is in essence a resurrection of the "currency board" scheme adopted in the territory from 1935 to 1972, with modifications. While the Hong Kong currency board is not completely independent, it contrasts with practices in Argentina, Estonia, and Lithuania (AEL), where notes and coins are issued by a "currency board" as a unit within the central bank. Moreover, the AEL central bank is required to retain full backing not only for notes and coins but also for member banks' balances, i.e., for the monetary base – indeed, all are the central bank's financial liabilities.[3] In all three countries, market exchange rates have been quoted very narrowly *around* the official rate despite various shocks

---

[2] John Nugée, "A Brief History of the Exchange Fund," *Quarterly Bulletin*, Hong Kong Monetary Authority [hereafter, "HKMA"], May 1995, pp. 1–17.

[3] See Anthony Latter, "The Currency Board Approach to Monetary Policy: from Africa to Argentina and Estonia, via Hong Kong," in HKMA, *Monetary Management in Hong Kong*, Proceedings of Seminar on Monetary Management, Oct. 18–19, 1993; and Tsang Shu-ki, *A Study of the Linked Exchange Rate System and Policy Options for Hong Kong*, 1996, a report commissioned by the Hong Kong Policy Research Institute.

in the past two years. In Hong Kong's idiosyncratic system, the market exchange rate has not been as close to the official rate. On average, a 1 percent deviation has been observed on either side of the peg.

In 1988, the Hong Kong government proceeded to establish a parallel central banking system to support the linked exchange-rate system. The process was consummated with the inauguration of the Hong Kong Monetary Authority (HKMA) in 1993. In addition to defending the link, the HKMA is charged with the functions of regulating and supervising financial institutions and markets, managing government reserves, and serving as the lender of last resort to the banking system. Some regard these developments as a violation of classical currency board principles.

The Currency Supply Process

The core of Hong Kong's "currency board" system is a note-issuing and withdrawal mechanism (NIWM) which has two tiers. The NIBs must deposit with the Exchange Fund an equivalent amount of US$ at the 7.80 rate to obtain CIs for issuing HK$ bank notes. Conversely, the NIBs can withdraw bank notes from circulation by returning the CIs to the Exchange Fund and reclaim the US$ deposit.

The arrangement for the other banks in Hong Kong to obtain (return) bank notes from (to) the NIBs was similar up to 1994. These banks had to place a non–interest-bearing US$ deposit at the 7.80 rate with the NIBs to obtain HK$ notes; the US$ deposit was returned to them upon the surrender of the notes. In the early 1990s, however, the market exchange rate was persistently on the strong side of 7.80, and banks incurred an exchange loss in receiving cash deposits from customers and redeeming them with the NIBs. To rectify the situation, the HKMA modified the system in February 1994 to allow banks to obtain (return) HK$ bank notes from (to) the NIBs by placing with (receiving from) them HK$ deposits.

Outside this two-tier NIWM exists the wider foreign-exchange market. The mechanism whereby the "market" rate of these activities would converge toward the "linked" rate for note issuance and withdrawal is ostensibly based on two factors:

1. *Arbitrage:* Any deviation of the market rate from 7.80 will generate a profitable arbitrage opportunity. For example, if the market rate is HK$7.90/US$, any party with access to the NIWM described above

could put forward HK$7.80 in cash to obtain US$1, then sell the US$1
to obtain HK$7.90 from the market, thereby fetching a profit of
HK$0.10 for every US$, assuming that there are no transaction costs.

2. *Competition:* Since access to the NIWM is not universal, arbitrage
efficiency is not guaranteed. However, since all banks have access to
the NIWM, a retail customer presumably can approach any bank, pay
a fee, and connect with the NIWM. The more competitive the banking
system, the lower the access cost to the NIWM for any non-bank
party. Thus competition should increase the efficiency of arbitrage.

In theory, the amount of bank notes circulating in Hong Kong under the link
is determined by the demand for these notes. To cater to the need for more HK$
notes, the NIBs must surrender US$ reserves to the Exchange Fund. This could
be easily satisfied by a portfolio shift on the part of the Hong Kong residents
who hold a large amount of foreign-currency assets. In the unusual situation
where residents do not have enough foreign exchange, the demand for more
notes will materialize along with a balance-of-payments surplus.

Because of the key position of the NIBs in the NIWM, it is very unlikely that
there will be an excess supply of HK$ notes. That would happen only if the
NIBs overestimate the actual demand for notes, with the result that they proceed to issue notes using their foreign-currency reserves. For example, an unexpected inflow of foreign capital does not necessarily lead to an increase in the
supply of HK$ notes; the residents or the NIBs may choose to invest the funds
in interest-bearing assets without any need to convert these funds into HK$
notes through the Exchange Fund.

Hong Kong Dollar Convertibility

In the pre-1972 period, Hong Kong, as a member of the Sterling Area, was
under foreign-exchange control empowered by the United Kingdom's Defense
(Finance) Regulations of 1939. There was an Exchange Controller in the territory, whose Exchange Control Office (ECO) oversaw the implementation of
controls. "Authorized exchange banks" were allowed to participate in the foreign-exchange market, provided they acted as agents of the ECO to administer
the exchange control regulations. At the time of its strictest application, such
control required a permit for every transaction. After 1959, however, scrutiny
was concentrated on capital movements and the authorized exchange banks
could themselves approve current account payments, which eventually became

a routine matter. When sterling was floated in June 1972, foreign-exchange controls applicable to the Sterling Area were quickly dismantled.[4]

From then on, despite the change in the exchange-rate regime in October 1983 (from the floating to the linked rate system), the HK$ has been a freely convertible currency, in the sense that foreign-exchange market participants have the right to engage in unrestricted exchange of HK$ into foreign moneys and vice versa. The Hong Kong authorities do not impose any controls on current-account or capital-account transactions.

The Credibility of the Link and the HKMA

In all monetary systems with well-defined rules, including currency boards, there is always an "escape clause" to cope with extraordinary events. For example, in the currency boards of Argentina and Estonia, there is an escape clause stating that the peg rate can be revalued but not devalued. Without an escape clause, pure economic rationality will not justify the existence of the home currency if its exchange rate is fixed against a foreign currency. The foreign currency may well be used as the legal tender.

Under the Hong Kong link, there is no explicit escape clause, not even one concerning revaluation. Nevertheless, the adoption of the US$ as the legal tender in post-1997 Hong Kong is politically unthinkable. Given the historical background of its evolution (as a crisis response), the credibility of the monetary system in Hong Kong is closely tied to the continued viability of the link. Commitment to the link has become a prime objective of the HKMA, so much so that even revaluation is excluded from official discourse.

The link has remained relatively stable in the face of major political and economic shocks since its inception – for example, in 1984, 1987, and 1989. However, the deviation of the market rate from the official parity of HK$7.80/US$ was up to 3 percent (at one very brief point) in the 1980s and about 1 percent in the 1990s. In the past six years, the market rate has been persistently on the strong side of 7.80. The key factor is that since arbitrage is cash-based in the two-tier NIWM, it will create problems in optimal cash balances for banks if they actively participate in such an activity[5] – hence the persistence of devia-

---

[4] Y. C. Jao, *Banking and Currency in Hong Kong: A Study of Postwar Financial Development* (London: Macmillan, 1974).

[5] John Greenwood & Daniel L. Gressel, "How to Tighten the Linked Rate Mechanism," *Asian Monetary Monitor*, Jan.–Feb. 1988, pp. 2–13.

tions. Because of the "inconvertibility" between HK$ cash and deposits for banks (not for customers), problems of "cash flood" or "cash drain" will arise if banks actively engage in arbitrage. Understandably, they have not been keen to perform any such activity despite the persistent deviation of the market exchange rate from the official parity.[6]

The Hong Kong government was aware of these problems in the indirect NIWM. Instead of changing the NIWM fundamentally, since 1988 it has proceeded to establish a central banking system alongside the currency board scheme to strengthen the link. After taking several steps to push through "new accounting arrangements" with the clearing bank (the Hong Kong and Shanghai Banking Corporation – HSBC), issuing "Exchange Fund Bills and Notes" to facilitate open-market operations, and setting up a "liquidity adjustment facility" (LAF) to serve as the "the discount window," the HKMA was formally established on April 1, 1993.[7]

The idea of a currency board is praised by economists such as Steve Hanke and Kurt Schuler precisely because it does away with the necessity of having a central bank which might damage the economy by pursuing "independent" but ultimately unworkable monetary policies.[8] Since the existence of a currency board implies that the money supply is determined by demand, the establishment of a parallel central bank in Hong Kong was regarded by some as the betrayal of "automaticity" inherent in a currency board system.[9] However, top

---

[6] If, for example, the market rate is on the strong side of 7.80 – say, 7.70 – an NIB can sell a deposit of HK$770 in the interbank market to acquire US$100, which it then transfers to the Exchange Fund to obtain HK$780 in cash, fetching a profit of HK$10. Unlike the non-bank customers, however, the NIB cannot convert the noninterest bearing cash into deposit, *other than by reversing the transactions that it has just performed*! The NIB can eliminate the cash balance by redeeming it at the rate of 7.80 with the Exchange Fund and recover US$100; however, its arbitrage profit of HK$10 will then disappear (as it exchanges the US$100 for an interbank deposit of HK$770 at the market rate of 7.70)!

Conversely if the market rate of the HK$ weakens to above 7.80 – say, 7.90 – the NIB could sell US$100 in the market for HK$790 in the form of interbank deposit. However, then it will have difficulties in converting the amount into cash, which theoretically it could transfer to the Exchange Fund for US$101.28 (790/780), hence fetching a profit of US$1.28. It can, of course, use its own vault cash to do the arbitrage. However, then it will find itself with a cash/deposit ratio lower than the prudential level.

[7] HKMA, *The Practice of Central Banking in Hong Kong,* 1994.

[8] Steve H. Hanke & Kurt Schuler, *Currency Boards for Developing Countries* (San Francisco: International Center for Economic Research, 1994).

[9] John Greenwood, "Hong Kong: Intervention Replaces Arbitrage – The July Package of Monetary Measures," *Asian Monetary Monitor*, July–Aug. 1988.

monetary officials[10] have emphasized time and again that the HKMA has a paramount objective: "to regulate the value of the currency."[11] After all, there is no "Central Bank Charter" in Hong Kong, and the HKMA was legalized only by the Exchange Fund (amendment) Ordinance of December 1992. The institution of mechanisms for open-market operation, adjustment of interbank liquidity, and short-term interest rates are all for "the purpose of ensuring exchange rate stability,"[12] rather than to fine-tune aggregate demand or to target money supply, which is still the *raison d'être* of many central banks in the world.

The LAF is also a discount window, which serves as the "lender of last resort" (LOLR) function, at least on an overnight basis. A typical currency board is not supposed to undertake such a responsibility. In modern currency boards, the Argentine system is more activist than the Estonian one.[13] As Gerald Gaprio and his associates put it, a currency board that both guarantees convertibility and implements the LOLR function faces the dilemma of achieving "two objectives with one instrument, namely, reserves."[14] In any case, even before the establishment of the HKMA, the Exchange Fund actually undertook large-scale rescue operations during the crisis of 1985 to 1986, providing funding for the government to take over two banks and giving financial assistance for third parties to restructure four other banks.[15]

The Exchange Fund's huge reserves are an important factor in defending the HK$ as a fully convertible currency. At the end of June 1996, the ratio of international reserves to currency in circulation was 537 percent, much higher than the 100 percent requirement of a typical currency board.[16] In Argentina, Estonia, and Lithuania, where notes are issued by the "currency board" as a unit in the central bank, gathering sufficient international reserves to back up the cur-

---

[10] See Joseph Yam, "Monetary Developments in Hong Kong," in HKMA, *Monetary Management in Hong Kong*, Proceedings of Seminar on Monetary Management, Oct. 18–19, 1993; Andrew Sheng, "The Tools of Monetary Management," reprinted from *The Practice of Central Banking in Hong Kong*, HKMA, May 1994, pp. 54–61; and John Nugée, "A Brief History of the Exchange Fund," *Quarterly Bulletin*, HKMA, May 1995, pp. 1–17.

[11] HKMA, *Money and Banking in Hong Kong*, 1995.

[12] Joseph Yam, "Monetary Developments in China and Implications for Hong Kong," in HKMA, *The Practice of Central Banking in Hong Kong*, 1994.

[13] Tsang Shu-ki, *A Study of the Linked Exchange Rate System and Policy Options for Hong Kong*, a report commissioned by the Hong Kong Policy Research Institute, 1996.

[14] Gerald Gaprio, Jr., Michael Dooley, Danny Leipziger, and Carl Walsh, "The Lender of Last Resort Function Under a Currency Board: The Case of Argentina," Policy Research Working Paper, no. 1648 (The World Bank, 1996).

[15] See John Nugée, "A Brief History," op. cit.

[16] See *Monthly Statistical Bulletin*, HKMA, July 1996.

rency issuance has been problematic.[17] No such problems have ever been noted in Hong Kong.

The Hong Kong government has, since 1976, transferred its fiscal reserves to the Exchange Fund, in return for an agreed annual interest payment. A stricter definition of Hong Kong's foreign-exchange reserves may focus on only two items: CIs and accumulated earnings of the Exchange Fund. According to this narrower definition, the ratio of reserves to currency in circulation was still a comfortable 291 percent at the end of June 1996.

A related issue is the credibility of the three NIBs: the Hong Kong Bank, the Standard Chartered Bank, and the Hong Kong Branch of the Bank of China. The first two have been NIBs since the nineteenth century. The parent of the Hong Kong Bank, HSBC Holdings, now ranks first in the world in terms of tier-one capital, and thirteenth in terms of total assets, whereas the Bank of China is one of four state banks in China.[18] Although official figures are not available directly, it is widely estimated that the three banking groups (including Hang Seng Bank, a subsidiary of the Hong Kong Bank, and the thirteen sister banks in the Bank of China Group in Hong Kong) have a total market share of over 70 percent in HK$ deposits. This oligopolistic market structure is seen as beneficial to the stability of the link, as the NIBs have a direct stake in maintaining the worth of their HK$ assets and liabilities.

Prospects

As a variation of the currency board system, the Hong Kong link is neither a classical version nor a "modern" one like that in Argentina and Estonia, where a centralized clearing and reserves system is operated by the central bank, which deals with each commercial bank directly. The idiosyncrasies of Hong Kong's two-tier NIWM have been augmented by an emerging central bank committed to the fixed exchange rate of 7.80.

The HKMA is introducing a real-time gross settlement (RTGS) system, soon to be operated by the Hong Kong Interbank Clearing Ltd. (HKIC), which will replace the functions of the present clearing bank (the Hong Kong Bank) and provide the fundamental hardware and software for centralized clearing. It can be used to solve the problem of the inconvertibility between HK$ cash and deposits for banks: HK$ cash may be admitted for interbank settlement, and

---

[17] See Tsang Shu-ki, op. cit.
[18] See *The Banker*, July 1996.

banks with surplus positions may demand HK$ cash from the HKIC.[19] Efficiency of cash-based arbitrage will be enhanced. Alternatively, the RTGS scheme can be turned into a reserves system whereby each bank in Hong Kong keeps reserve deposits with the HKMA, which would be the case if the HKMA chooses to follow the example of Argentina and Estonia. Arbitrage will then be largely implicit, or even unnecessary.[20] This development will, however, move Hong Kong further away from having the traditional currency board.

THE CHINESE MONETARY SYSTEM

Since the early 1980s, People's Bank of China (PBC) has been transforming into a modern central bank. By late 1996, its four main functions – the supply of money, the regulation and supervision of foreign-exchange transactions, the regulation and supervision of financial intermediation and markets, and the provision of payments services – had become remarkably more sophisticated. In the next ten years, the ongoing and planned investments in human resources, equipment, and organization, jointly with the reform of China's legal system, should set the foundation for PBC to perform all four functions at levels similar to those of its counterparts in developed countries.

Prior to 1984, PBC's main responsibility was the mobilization of domestic savings to finance the state sector; it also performed a variety of other functions, resembling the "monobank" system found in other socialist economies. Between 1984 and 1993, the most important reform was the transfer of the function of financial intermediation to specialized state banks, with PBC taking responsibility for monitoring the implementation of the credit plan and funding the plan when the banks failed to mobilize enough deposits. After July 1993, the control of strong inflationary pressures became a high priority, and PBC's transformation accelerated greatly. In March 1995, the Central Bank Law set the legal framework for PBC to be a modern central bank. Although the credit plan remains an instrument of government policy, its relevance is now limited, and it may soon be abandoned altogether.

The Currency Supply Process

The monetary liabilities of modern central banks consist of currency in circulation and all bank reserves with the central bank which are official substitutes

---

[19] See Greenwood & Gressel, op. cit.; see also Tsang Shu-ki, op. cit.
[20] See Tsang Shu-ki, op. cit.

for currency. These two liabilities define the base to which all other monetary aggregates are related. In China, however, it is still appropriate to focus only on currency in circulation because the reserve requirements are a mechanism for taxing bank intermediation rather than for assisting banks with their liquidity. The reform of the system of reserve requirements, under consideration for some time and expected to be announced soon, will eventually justify the conventional reliance on the whole monetary base as a reflection of the monetary stance of the central bank.

Inherent in all monetary systems is the possibility of an excess supply of or demand for money. How this imbalance is eliminated depends on the system. In China, after the reforms of the past three years, the relevant question is whether the currency supply is determined by its own demand, or whether it continues to be determined by PBC's financing of government-mandated expenditures, or whether it has become a policy variable controlled by PBC, or some combination of these three alternatives. If it is demand-determined, then an excess supply (demand) will be eliminated by a decrease (increase) in supply rather than by changes in the determinants of demand (that is, by fluctuations in interest rates, prices, or income levels). There is, as yet, no answer to this question because the process through which currency is fed into the economy is still evolving; increasingly, however, the money supply has become determined by demand.

As a result of reforms in the past three years, the currency supply process now – with expected further changes – resembles that of a currency board. As a source of monetary expansion, the increase in net foreign assets – at the expense of a decline in the net credit to deposit banks – becomes important in the backing of currency. For example, by June 1996, the value of PBC's net foreign assets reached RMB 841 billion, exceeding the value of currency in circulation, RMB 767 billion.[21] The sharp increase reflects an increase in PBC's foreign-exchange reserves. China has fulfilled – probably unintentionally – the requirement of a currency board that the issuance of currency be fully backed by equivalent foreign-exchange reserves.

These achievements have been possible because of the high level of household savings relative to gross national product (GNP) channeled as deposits into the banking system – between 15 and 18 percent of GNP, of which PBC receives over 18 percent as bank reserves – and the growing inflow of foreign exchange from exports and investments. To give an idea of how these forces line up in

---

[21] For additional information, see PBC, *Quarterly Statistical Bulletin*, 1993–1996.

order of magnitude, without any changes, foreign-exchange reserves would double the value of currency in circulation some time in 1999, with no pressure on the exchange rate between the RMB and the US$. Given such factors as the size of the Chinese economy, the high level of currency in circulation, and the level of foreign-exchange reserves reached at the end of June 1996, the accumulation of reserves needed to double the value of currency would be around US$90 billion. Despite those achievements, PBC is not a currency board because it is not committed to a fixed exchange rate. Moreover, it has not announced any well-defined rule for pegging the RMB to any foreign currency.

Simultaneous with the accumulation of foreign-exchange reserves, PBC has gained control of its domestic-credit operations. Since July 1993, the State Council has been protecting PBC's autonomy from all other state agencies, including local governments. Although the State Council continues to instruct PBC to finance some expenditures (e.g., the operations of the Agricultural Development Bank, one of the three policy-lending banks established in 1994), other agencies can no longer rely on PBC credit to finance their expenditures. Until July 1993, it was accurate to describe the expansion of PBC's domestic credit as a direct transfer to finance government-mandated expenditures. Regardless of how the transfers were accounted for in PBC's books, PBC's revenue from money creation (the increase in currency in circulation relative to gross domestic product, or GDP) was used to finance state expenditures directly. PBC is currently changing to a system of domestic credit based on open-market operations with securities (that is, tradable financial assets) and a rediscount window based on commercial paper. Both types of transactions are expected to become important instruments to fine-tune the aggregate demand for domestic output. The effectiveness of these transactions will depend largely on PBC's ability to put them to use.

RMB Convertibility

In comparison with other transitional economies, China has made slower progress in increasing the convertibility of the RMB. Only in the past two years have many of the controls on current-account transactions been eliminated, and capital controls are still pervasive. The elimination of current-account controls has led to a parallel increase in the convertibility of the RMB: in June 1996, PBC issued "Regulations on the Sale and Purchase of and Payment in Foreign Exchange" with the declared purpose of achieving the convertibility of the RMB for current-account transactions. The new regulations do not imply, however, that restrictions to current-account transactions have been eliminated; they signify, rather, that there are no exchange restrictions in addition to some trade controls on these transactions. Conversely, capital-account transactions are still subject to exchange restrictions and capital controls.

For unrestricted transactions, a convertible RMB means the right to exchange it into foreign currency *at the going* exchange rate. Whereas a currency board is committed to converting its currency into the foreign currency *at a given* rate of exchange, PBC has not assumed a similar commitment and does not intend to do so. However, PBC does not intend to let the exchange rate float freely either. More likely, as long as there is no fundamental change in China's external environment, PBC will continue its cautious managed floating of the exchange rate between the RMB and the US$ within a narrow band.

The higher convertibility of the RMB and the stability of its exchange value are strengthening the demand-determined process of currency supply by increasing the speed at which an excess supply (demand) is eliminated. Undoubtedly, both achievements have been facilitated greatly by the increase in the supply of foreign exchange. The decision to reform the foreign-exchange regime was taken in response to China's growing popularity among foreign investors: Most notably, in January 1994 the RMB was devalued and the foreign exchange certificates (FECs), used by foreigners for domestic transactions, were eliminated. Further progress in increasing the convertibility of the RMB will depend, however, on government decisions concerning the remaining controls on capital-account transactions.

PBC's Performance and Reputation

While PBC's foreign-exchange transactions allow the passive adjustment of the currency supply to its demand, PBC expects its domestic-credit operations to become an instrument for fine-tuning the aggregate demand for domestic output. To this end, PBC has been trying first to stop financing government-mandated expenditures and second to set the foundations for managing the money supply through market exchanges of securities (government bonds and commercial paper). Since early 1995, domestic-credit operations have not been significant – a signal of progress in ending the financing of government-mandated expenditures – but the continuation of these transfers highlights PBC's dependence on the State Council.

The development of a new relationship between PBC and the State Council is an institutional problem that will take some time to resolve. Although past and present reliance on PBC's financing of government-mandated expenditures may have been a matter of expediency, the fact remains that until July 1993, PBC's monetary revenue was used largely to finance government-mandated expenditures. The first step toward developing a new relationship is to terminate PBC's financing of these expenditures, a step which could take place subsequent to reforming the system of reserve requirements. If deposit-taking institutions are to mobilize funds to finance the state sector, the funds can go directly to the financial agency responsible for monitoring their use (as is now the case with the State Development Bank, created in 1994 and China's largest policy-lending bank). Another important step is the appropriate and timely disclosure of information about PBC's domestic-credit operations. Despite the progress in preparing and reporting statistics, it is not yet possible to identify which domestic-credit operations are transfers to finance expenditures, and which are the result of market exchanges. Finally, although the Central Bank Law enacted in March 1995 has formalized PBC's dependency on the State Council, its nature and extent are likely to change. At present, it can be assumed that all important policy and regulatory decisions are initiated by PBC but always ratified by the State Council, which likewise monitors PBC's performance closely.

In the long run, the effectiveness of PBC as a modern central bank will depend on its ability to cultivate a reputation as an institution that is both legally responsible for and technically capable of providing China with a stable money supply. To establish this reputation, PBC (and the State Council) must deliver monetary stability over time and must disclose, in an accurate and timely manner, the information on which its policy decisions are based. Notwithstanding the institutional reforms implemented in the past three years – already reflected in PBC's behavior and performance – many still believe that PBC is simply a means to finance government-mandated expenditures and to control the allocation of bank credit.

Prospects

Efforts to transform PBC into a modern central bank are slowly paying off. Our analysis has focused only on the progress made to transform its money-supply function; however, progress has also been made in transforming its other three main functions, especially the regulation and supervision of foreign-exchange transactions. Recent reforms of the money supply process have succeeded in introducing elements of a demand-determined process; the full implementation of the reforms of domestic-credit operations should end PBC's financing of

146

government-mandated expenditures, thereby providing PBC with market-based instruments to fine-tune the aggregate demand for domestic output. The anticipated reform of the system of reserve requirements, along with the formal abandonment of the credit plan, should further strengthen PBC's control of its own monetary liabilities.

A stable RMB will depend on the effective implementation of the new rules governing PBC's money supply process as well as PBC's ability to use its discretionary power wisely. Both will take years to become reality. Although the general principles underlying the new rules may be sound, only their implementation will make their consequences clear to all interested parties, at a time when they, too, are struggling to reform their own activities and organization.

COEXISTENCE OF THE TWO SYSTEMS

Under the framework of "one country, two systems," the future Hong Kong Special Administrative Region (SAR) is to decide its own monetary policies. Post-1997 monetary relations between mainland China and Hong Kong have come to be officially defined as, in the words of Joseph Yam, Chief Executive of the HKMA, "one country, two currencies, two monetary systems and two monetary authorities which are mutually independent."[22] Such a characterization has been endorsed by Chen Yuan, a deputy governor of the PBC. Chen emphasizes that "The Hong Kong dollar and the Renminbi will circulate as legal tender in Hong Kong and the mainland respectively. The HK$ will be treated as a foreign currency in the mainland. Likewise, the Renminbi will be treated as a foreign currency in Hong Kong."[23]

Of course, such remarks reflect only the official stance, which may or may not be subject to modification. Whether this stance is consistent with economic reality is another story. In this section, we explore the rationality of different scenarios after 1997.

Unification or Coexistence

A possible case for unifying the two currencies is largely political in nature. Of course, the RMB will replace the HK$ and PBC will eliminate the HKMA,

[22] Joseph Yam, "Hong Kong's Monetary Scene: Myths and Realities," speech delivered at Bank of England Seminar on "Hong Kong Monetary Arrangements through 1997," London, Sept. 10, 1996.
[23] Yuan Chen, "Monetary Relations between China and Hong Kong," speech delivered at Bank of England Seminar on "Hong Kong Monetary Arrangements through 1997," London, Sept. 10, 1996.

rather than the other way around. Independent of political considerations, a more pertinent issue is whether there is any *economic* rationale for unification.

The benefits of unification are related primarily to (1) the transaction costs of currencies and (2) the risk posed by exchange-rate variations. In the case of China and Hong Kong, unification will reduce the transaction costs and the risk of exchange-rate variations *only between the HK$ and the RMB, not between the RMB and other currencies.* (The transaction costs and risk of variation between the HK$ and other currencies are generally perceived to be relatively small.) For China, the value of these benefits will be determined mainly by the relative importance of trade and capital flows between China and Hong Kong, which, while rather high, is not overwhelming. For Hong Kong, however, their value will depend mainly on the impact on trade and capital flows between Hong Kong and countries other than China, which in turn will depend on perceptions about the quality of the RMB: *There will be no impact only if the RMB is a perfect substitute for the HK$.* This is unlikely to be the case in the short run.

Studies of other countries have shown that transaction costs of organized exchange markets are low. Hong Kong has a well-developed foreign-exchange market, which is linked to important international trading centers. According to the Bank for International Settlement, the daily average foreign-exchange turnover in Hong Kong in April 1995 was US$91 billion, representing 6 percent of the world total and placing Hong Kong in fifth position, after the United Kingdom, the United States, Japan, and Singapore. In comparison, China has a rudimentary interbank foreign-exchange market, which came into being only in 1994. This market has been making rapid progress, but it will take a long time before it matches the scale and status of its Hong Kong counterpart.

The risk of exchange-rate variation depends on the nature of the exchange-rate regimes of the two monetary authorities. The HK$ has been pegged to the US$ according to the rules of a currency board, but the RMB has not been pegged to the US$ despite the recent stability of its performance against the US$. Unification will eliminate the exchange risk between the HK$ and the RMB; however, from the viewpoint of Hong Kong's trade and capital flows, the unification can be a source of exchange-rate risk with the US$ and other currencies. Therefore, the reduction of exchange risk brought about by unification will have a positive impact only on the trade and capital flows between Hong Kong and China, and even if this impact is significant, it can be offset and exceeded by the negative impact of increased exchange risk for Hong Kong's trade and capital flows with other countries. Only if PBC commits itself to well-defined rules for pegging the RMB to the US$ will the latter effect be minimal. Having said this, we have to point out that the experiences of other countries do not support the hypothesis that exchange risk is a significant deterrent to trade and investment.

The costs of unification will also depend on Hong Kong's ability to cope with the loss of a policy instrument to adjust its macroeconomy to shocks and to fine-tune aggregate demand. The specific conditions under which monetary policy may become an effective instrument are still the focus of debate. First, for the costs to be high, one must show first that Hong Kong is (almost) an optimal currency area. It can be argued that the so-called Pearl River Delta (consisting of Hong Kong, Macau, and southern Guangdong), rather than Hong Kong alone, more closely approximates the notion of an optimal currency area because of the high degree of integration of output and factor markets, as well as similarities in the flexibility of prices and wages. Second, one must show that in Hong Kong, monetary policy has been the best instrument to adjust the macroeconomy to shocks and to fine-tune aggregate demand. However, by definition, a currency board has abandoned the idea of relying on monetary policy to cope with shocks. The HKMA stresses that it employs various instruments for the purpose of maintaining exchange-rate stability. Therefore, the costs of unification will hardly be high.

In conclusion, both the economic benefits and costs of unification are likely to be low. Moreover, at least for Hong Kong, the net benefit could turn out to be negative. While there is no sound economic argument for unifying the two currencies, questions remain concerning how they may coexist and what the Chinese government can do to facilitate any particular form of coexistence. Three forms of coexistence are distinguished: spontaneous competition, legal competition, and monopoly. The first two forms imply that both currencies *may* be used by residents of the same geographical areas for their domestic transactions. Specifically, in the discussion that ensues, "spontaneous competition" refers to the situation where only the RMB is legal tender but, *at least in some areas of China*, the Chinese spontaneously use both currencies for their domestic transactions and also use the HK$ in their transactions with Hong Kong residents (as well as, perhaps, with other non-residents). "Legal competition" means that both currencies are legal tender at least in some areas of China, and the Chinese can use them freely in transactions of all kinds. "Monopoly" assumes the strict enforcement of the prohibition of the HK$ (and any foreign currency) to circulate in China; however, it is omitted from the following dis-

Edgardo Barandiaran and Tsang Shu-ki

cussion because it would be too difficult to implement. Efforts to enforce such prohibition would, at most, limit the range of transactions in which the two currencies could compete.

Spontaneous Competition

Given two neighboring countries or territories, each with its own currency, two forces are conditioning the extent to which the two currencies are used and demanded in both areas. First, the degree of market integration between the two economies conditions the transaction demand for the currencies (i.e., their demands as means of payment). Second, if the two economies are closely integrated, the differences in the quality of the two currencies as determined by the stability of their values and their convertibility into other foreign currencies condition the asset demand for the currencies (i.e., the demand for real cash balances).

In the case of a large country, close integration with neighboring countries is often limited to its bordering areas. This tends to be the case independent of the degree of economic development of the two countries or territories. In these bordering areas, as long as the two currencies are stable and the transaction costs of formal and informal exchange markets are low, residents on both sides of the border may be indifferent about which currency to use in the transactions between themselves. In the past twenty years, the elimination of restrictions on the use of foreign currencies in most countries has facilitated greatly this type of monetary integration in bordering areas everywhere.

The degree of economic integration between China and Hong Kong is very high in the Pearl River Delta, but declines rapidly as one moves away from it. Actually, the delta may be developing into an optimal currency area, that is, an area with a high degree of factor mobility and closely integrated markets for goods and services. As with many other world experiences of integrated bordering areas, the process has been accompanied by an increased use of the HK$ and the RMB as means of payment, at least between residents and non-residents. If the HK$ has taken a dominant position as a means of payment, it is largely because of the relative instability of the RMB and the reluctant acceptance of foreign-exchange markets in China until the reforms of early 1994.

As in some Latin American countries, spontaneous competition and currency substitution are two closely related phenomena. Although in many instances the close integration of areas bordering on some Latin American countries has brought about significant transaction demands for the currency of the neighboring country (for example, between Brazil and Paraguay in the area of Foz

150

de Iguazu), the process of currency substitution observed in several Latin American countries in the past twenty years is very much related to high inflation and the associated decline in quality of their national currencies. The US$, rather than other Latin American currencies, substituted for the national currencies when inflation became high and chronic. Indeed, Argentina is an extreme example of the consequences of substituting of the US$ for an unstable national currency: Only by introducing a currency board based on a very high degree of convertibility of the Argentine peso (perhaps the highest degree possible in today's world) has the latter been able to survive.

The unexpected change in the relative quality of the HK$ and the RMB appears to have played a major role in the substitution of the former for the latter during the Chinese inflationary episode of 1992 to 1994. Reports at that time indicated a sudden increase in the use and holding of HK$ by residents of the Pearl River Delta. The ratio of currency in circulation relative to GDP in Hong Kong also shot up significantly above the normal declining trend. Part of the HK$ was circulating in Southern China. The phenomenon persisted even after the Chinese government legally prohibited the circulation of foreign currencies in the country at the end of 1993. It is well known that during these two years, both the inflation differential between China and Hong Kong and the differential between parallel and official exchange rates for the RMB increased sharply.

By 1995, the increasing stability of the internal and external values of the RMB appeared to have halted the substitution of the HK$ for the RMB. Although quantitative analyses of demands for both currencies needed to confirm this hypothesis are lacking, the behavior of relevant variables is consistent with it. In particular, the differential between inflation rates in Hong Kong and China has been substantially reduced, and the differential between parallel and official exchange rates of the RMB has almost disappeared. Even if the use of HK$ notes and coins in the Pearl River Delta continues to increase, the demand for holding HK$ will increase very little, so long as the value of the RMB remains stable.

Not surprisingly, the rapid substitution of HK$ for the RMB in 1992 to 1993 raised concern about the implications for monetary policy. Indeed, this substitution reduced the base on which PBC could raise revenue in the form of seignorage and inflation tax; it has also made demand for the domestic currency more unstable. Both effects were of little significance, however, because they were limited to a small area of the country. Indeed, it would have been a mistake to attempt to suppress the symptoms artificially without addressing the cause of the substitution process.

Edgardo Barandiaran and Tsang Shu-ki

Legal Competition

The circulation of two or more currencies in the same geographical area can be governed by three different rules: only one currency is legal tender and all other currencies are prohibited to circulate; only one currency is legal tender but the others are allowed to circulate; and two or more currencies are legal tender and others are allowed to circulate. In this subsection we look at the third alternative; we assume that both the HK$ and the RMB are legal tender in some restricted area of China.

Actually, competition between two or more legal tenders in one country or territory is rare. Today each country or territory is expected to have its own currency, the only legal tender, as a symbol of its sovereignty. A few countries or territories have opted to use as legal tender another country's currency (for example, Panama); however, none has yet opted for more than one legal tender. Even when foreign currencies are allowed to circulate in a country or territory, the national currency has an advantage because it is legal tender: Buyers and debtors can legally discharge their obligations by paying with that currency, even if the original contract provided that payment should be made in kind or with another country's currency. More important, in practice, the government may force its use in its own domestic transactions with residents and non-residents alike.

Until the end of 1993, the coexistence of the RMB and the FEC was an example of two legal tenders in the same geographic area. They were, however, used for two different sets of transactions. The RMB was used for transactions involving only residents, while the FEC was used for transactions between authorized and non-authorized residents. This system was used to enforce the inconvertibility of the RMB, which, in turn, was a natural consequence of the old policy of strictly controlling the exchange of goods and services between residents and non-residents. This two-currency system is now only a historical curiosity, providing little guidance as to how to approach the coexistence of the RMB and the HK$, or the convertibility of the RMB.

Given the size of the Chinese economy and the different degree of integration of some areas of China within the world economy, the question arises as to whether the Chinese government should consider a special legal status for a foreign currency in some restricted areas. Such a policy would be consistent with the government's strategy of establishing special legal frameworks for the promotion of some economic activities in well-defined geographical areas. This type of preferential policy toward a geographical area would be appropri-

152

ate when the ultimate purpose of the government's action is to promote the financial integration of this area with international markets. The Chinese government has been encouraging this type of integration only in the area of Shanghai, including Pudong. Thus, the acceptance of the HK$ as legal tender in Shanghai could be an instrument for promoting the transformation of Shanghai into an international financial center. This transformation assumes the elimination of most controls on international capital transactions, including restrictions on the convertibility of the RMB for these transactions. In other words, by accepting the HK$ as legal tender in Shanghai, the government could separate this area from the rest of the country for the specific purpose of promoting Shanghai's financial integration with international markets. Indeed, the value of this option depends heavily on the government's interest in rapidly achieving this particular integration.

The cost of allowing the HK$ to become legal tender in Shanghai would be a loss in PBC's power to control the money supply. The loss would be significant only if this action were to lead to a large substitution of the HK$ for the RMB, and if the PBC were interested in having a significant discretionary authority on the money supply. The enhanced legal status of the HK$ would likely lead to a final change in the composition of real cash balances in Shanghai, followed by a change in the composition of the flow demand for these balances. These changes would make demand for RMB less stable, which would in turn make it harder to predict the behavior of demand for RMB.

CONCLUSIONS

The discussion of any policy issue is very much shaped by the initial conditions and the end-states toward which the current reality is supposed to evolve. In the case of China and Hong Kong, the most important initial conditions are the fact that (1) two currencies, and therefore two systems to supply them, have existed for a long time, and (2) the HK$ is perceived as a stable, convertible currency whereas the RMB has yet to be perceived as such. The projected end-states are that the HK$ will stay as it is and that the RMB will eventually become a stable, convertible currency in the international arena.

Because of the size of the Chinese economy relative to that of Hong Kong and the growing linkage between the two economies, the possibility of a net economic benefit from eliminating the HK$ cannot be ignored. In the near future, however, the net benefit of unification hardly looks positive. Moreover, there is no reason to believe that it will become significant because the benefits of unifying two or more *stable* currencies are few. This, of course, presupposes that the RMB will fulfill the Chinese government's announced objective of becoming a stable, fully convertible currency.

Indeed, the unification of two currencies of different qualities will produce a net benefit only if the "inferior currency" is eliminated. This is why, in a multi-currency situation, the German mark (the "best currency") is always seen as the model for the unified European money. In the case of China and Hong Kong, however, it is unlikely that the RMB would be regarded as an "inferior" cur- rency to be eliminated.

Thus, the relevant policy issue is whether the Chinese government should do something to *regulate* the coexistence of the two systems, that is, to move from spontaneous competition to some form of legal competition or to a strict enforcement of the prohibition of using currencies other than the only legal tender in each area. While legal competition does not appear to be an option of any nationwide significance, spontaneous competition is still a fact of life, at least in the Pearl River Delta, even after the explicit prohibition of foreign currency circulation in the 1994 reform. PBC does not seem to insist on its total elimination. Until the RMB becomes a fully convertible currency, the HK$ is bound to persist as a convenient substitute in areas where trade and capital flows with Hong Kong continue to grow. The experience of 1992 to 1996 shows that such competition will heighten (decline) if the stability and convertibility of the RMB deteriorates (improves).

The HKMA and PBC may be converging into a broadly similar type of central bank (the dominant type of central bank emerging in many developing countries). This type is characterized by:

1. A 100 percent backing of the central bank's monetary liabilities in the form of foreign assets
2. Limited autonomy to undertake market operations with domestic securities
3. A limited and well-defined function to serve as lender of last resort to deposit-taking institutions
4. A clear commitment to exchange-rate stability, including a rule that pegs the domestic currency to a foreign currency or a basket of foreign currencies

The two institutions will continue to show important differences in how each rule is implemented, however. As long as the Chinese government is committed to transforming PBC into a modern central bank, the similarities will become more obvious and dominant over time.

7

Political Participation in Hong Kong

Trends in the Mid-1990s[1]

JOSEPH Y. S. CHENG

IN this chapter "political participation" refers to any act on the part of the people of Hong Kong to influence policy making in the territory. The author conducted a series of in-depth interviews in the second half of 1995. The hundred or so interviewees included senior government officials; political party leaders; members of the Legislative Council, Urban/Regional Council, and District Boards; leaders of various types of interest groups and grassroots organizations; some members of the Preliminary Working Committee (PWC) of the Preparatory Committee for the Hong Kong Special Administrative Region (HKSAR), Hong Kong Affairs Advisors, and District Affairs Advisors; executives and journalists of the territory's media; and a few academics interested in the subject. A follow-up series of in-depth interviews was conducted in the third quarter of 1996 to update the information and analysis. It covered about one quarter of those interviewed earlier.

The purpose of this research project is to study the political mood of the people of Hong Kong, including how they attempt to articulate their interests, how they assess the performance of the British administration, the political parties, interest groups, and grassroots organizations, and how they define and exercise their options in protecting and promoting their interests. No attempt has been made to quantify the findings of the interviews, although quantitative analysis will be the likely objective in a later stage of the project. Wherever it is possible and relevant, available opinion surveys are used. Since the vast majority of the people of Hong Kong are politically quiescent, surveys help to find those

[1] This chapter is an adaptation of a paper with the same title presented at the Conference on the 1995 Legislative Council Election, May 17–18, 1996, organized by the Hong Kong Institute of Asia-Pacific Studies, The Chinese University of Hong Kong.

155

who would otherwise be inactive. Admittedly, the views articulated are not very strong and clear.[2] At this stage, the author is satisfied with the detection and identification of the present trends of political participation in the territory, as well as preliminary attempts to explain such trends.

In the first half of the 1980s, political participation in the territory picked up momentum significantly, spurred by the Sino-British negotiations on Hong Kong's future and the Chinese authorities' promise of *gangren zhigang* (self-administration) to the people of Hong Kong.[3] In the mid-1990s, a number of conflicting indicators appeared, making the work of identifying the trends of political participation much more complicated and fascinating.

THE POLITICAL AND ECONOMIC ENVIRONMENT

With the approach of 1997, the Chinese authorities' influence on Hong Kong has become increasingly significant. At the end of December 1995, membership of the Preparatory Committee for the HKSAR was announced, and it now has a formal office in the territory. According to Chen Zhiying, deputy head of the State Council's Hong Kong and Macau Affairs Office, the recovery of China's sovereignty over Hong Kong has entered the stage of concrete work.[4] In December 1996, the first Chief Executive, Mr. C. H. Tung, was nominated by the Selection Committee for the First Government of the HKSAR established by the Preparatory Committee for the HKSAR.[5] Later in the month, the Selection Committee also elected the provisional legislature. In February 1997, the team of top civil servants will be announced. Both the Chief Executive and the provisional legislature will have started working after their elections.

It is significant that the people of Hong Kong had no input in these processes. Moreover, the community did not appear to be concerned about their exclusion. Few people were interested in the issues, and the media merely speculat-

---

[2] Sidney Verba, "The Citizen as Respondent: Sample Surveys and American Democracy," *American Political Science Review*, vol. 90(1), March 1996, pp. 1–7.

[3] Joseph Y. S. Cheng, "Hong Kong: The Pressure to Converge," *International Affairs* (London), vol. 63(2), Spring 1987, pp. 271–83.

[4] *Ming Pao* [a Chinese newspaper in Hong Kong], June 25, 1995.

[5] See "Decision of the National People's Congress on the Method for the Formation of the First Government and the First Legislative Council of the Hong Kong Special Administrative Region," adopted by the Seventh National People's Congress at its third session on Apr. 4, 1990, in *The Basic Law of the Hong Kong Special Administrative Region of the People's Republic of China* (Hong Kong: One Country Two Systems Economic Research Institute Ltd., 1992), pp. 67–69.

ed on the chances of the potential candidates to fill the post of the first Chief Executive. In September and October of 1996, the media offered many profiles of the declared candidates. The media's orientation meant that the pro-democracy camp did not have many opportunities to criticize Chinese authorities. Indeed, the pro-democracy political groups did not treat such issues as an important part of their political platforms in the Legislative Council elections in September 1995.

The people of Hong Kong were predictably more dissatisfied with the British administration, and Governor Chris Patten became their target. According to opinion surveys, the community's support for the Governor's annual policy speeches dropped steadily from 67.82 percent in 1992, to 61.40 percent in 1993, to 57.48 percent in 1994, to 52.06 percent in 1995.[6] In response to Chris Patten's final policy speech, delivered on October 2, 1996, a survey indicated that 30.2 percent of the respondents thought that the territory had declined as a result of his years as Governor, 24.9 percent thought that it had gained in stature, and 42.2 percent thought that it had maintained its stature. The same survey population gave Chris Patten a score of 56.9 percent for increasing · democracy in Hong Kong, 55.1 percent for improving social welfare, 41 percent for enforcing the Basic Law, and 36.8 percent for forging good relations between Hong Kong and China. Significantly, only 15.2 percent of the respondents believed that the Governor's popularity would increase during that month, and 37.6 percent thought that his popularity would decrease.[7]

Another series of polls likewise indicated that the people's evaluations of Chris Patten were becoming increasingly negative. Approval ratings for his competence fell from 68.77 percent in July 1992 to 60.36 percent in June 1996; approval ratings for his trustworthiness declined from 64.69 percent to 54.40 percent over the same period.[8] More damaging still, in an opinion survey taken in May 1995, 48 percent of respondents said that the territory would be better served if the Governor were to leave two years early and be replaced by a council of local people.[9] It appears that the Governor had absorbed the blame for the deterioration in Sino-British relations over Hong Kong. In a series of opinion polls on the replacement of the Governor, the proportion of respondents favoring his departure reached a peak of 26.3 percent in January 1994, decreasing to

---

[6] *Ming Pao*, Oct. 12, 1995.

[7] *South China Morning Post* [an English newspaper in Hong Kong; hereafter, *SCMP*] Oct. 7, 1996.

[8] *Ming Pao*, July 8, 1996.

[9] *SCMP*, May 29, 1995.

18.5 percent in July 1995, when Sino-British relations improved somewhat as a result of an agreement on the Court of Final Appeal.[10]

While the Hong Kong community expressed its increasing frustration with the British administration, its assessment of the Chinese authorities was only slightly better. The community's evaluations of Zhou Nan and Zhang Junsheng, authorities at the local branch of New China News Agency, have been relatively stable at a low level. Approval ratings for their competence improved from 52.45 percent in July 1992 to 54.32 percent in June 1996; approval ratings for their trustworthiness increased slightly from 46.34 percent to 47.52 percent in the same period.[11] Zhou Nan and Zhang Junsheng trailed the Governor, but the gap was narrowing.

By mid-1995, the Hong Kong community's confidence in the "one country, two systems" arrangement seemed to have risen slightly. An opinion survey in mid-July showed that 44 percent of the respondents indicated confidence in "one country, two systems"; with an increase of three percentage points, it reached the level recorded in early 1993. At the same time, 38 percent of the respondents revealed no confidence in "one country, two systems."[12] There remains a reluctance to accept the eventual return of Hong Kong to China, but it seems to be in decline as July 1997 approaches. A survey in mid-1995 indicated that 52 percent of the respondents still preferred independence or remaining under the British administration to becoming a Special Administrative Region under Chinese sovereignty. This proportion did not differ significantly from that of early 1993, when about 42-44 percent of the respondents hoped to see the return of Hong Kong to China.[13] In February 1996, another poll in the same series showed that 46 percent of the respondents wanted Hong Kong to become part of China; the proportion of those who wanted Hong Kong to be independent fell from 25 percent in 1993 to 14 percent in early 1996.[14]

The trend became more significant later in the year. In May 1996, a survey showed that 55 percent of the respondents indicated confidence in the future of Hong Kong, while only 15.3 percent indicated a lack of confidence. This was the first time that over half of the respondents in an opinion poll demonstrated

---

[10] *Ming Pao*, July 10, 1995. For the Sino-British agreement on the Court of Final Appeal, see *Hong Kong Economic Journal* [a Chinese newspaper in Hong Kong], June 10, 1995.

[11] *Ming Pao*, July 8, 1996.

[12] *Ming Pao*, Aug. 3, 1995.

[13] *Ming Pao*, July 15, 1995.

[14] *SCMP*, Feb. 17, 1996.

confidence in the territory's future.[15] Similarly, 59 percent of the respondents in a survey in November 1996 said that they would feel happy at midnight on June 30, 1997, while 20 percent said that they would feel sad at the critical moment.[16]

In the second half of 1995, the people of Hong Kong expressed their frustration with the territory's political, economic, and social environment. An opinion survey revealed that 36.8 percent of the respondents believed that the political environment had deteriorated when compared with that of 1992; only 24.2 percent believed it had improved. Similarly, 69.3 percent thought that the economic environment had worsened, while only 17.2 percent thought it had improved; 46.4 percent considered that the social environment had deteriorated, while 29.4 percent considered that it had improved.[17] In assessing the future, the same survey showed considerable pessimism: 32.5 percent of respondents believed that the political environment would worsen in the coming three years, while 14.9 percent believed that it would improve. Similarly, 35.5 percent thought that the economic environment would decline further, while 19.7 percent thought that it would gain strength; 34.6 percent expected the social environment to deteriorate, while 19.4 percent expected to see improvement. The approach of 1997 has brought about a vague sense of unease.

More specifically, Hong Kong residents are concerned with the spread of corruption. About 72 percent of the respondents in a poll taken in October 1995 believed that the 1997 changeover would lead to an increase in corruption.[18] In March 1996, the commissioner of the Independent Commission Against Corruption (ICAC) noted that the number of police officers convicted of corruption had increased from 23 in 1994 to 58 in 1995. He acknowledged that the uncertainty surrounding 1997 prompted many people to make "quick money."[19] Journalists, as expected, are disturbed by the phenomenon of self-censorship: A series of surveys of the profession from the end of 1993 to 1995 revealed that about 90 percent of the respondents assumed that self-censorship existed. About 60 percent indicated that self-censorship existed where they worked, and over 50 percent said self-censorship came from pressure from their superiors.[20]

[15] *Ming Pao*, May 28, 1996.
[16] *SCMP*, Nov. 25, 1996.
[17] *Ming Pao*, Aug. 10, 1995.
[18] *Ming Pao*, Oct. 14, 1995.
[19] *Ming Pao*, Mar. 16, 1996.
[20] *Ming Pao*, Aug. 5, 1995.

Less than 10 percent of those surveyed expected to work until retirement. In June 1996, it was reported that about 60 percent of the staff of Radio Television Hong Kong worried that they would lose their editorial independence after 1997.[21]

Reports from various sectors have shown that senior police officers, senior staff members of the ICAC, and teachers were the professions hit hardest by emigration. A study conducted by the Royal Hong Kong Police reported that 18 percent of those who held the rank of police inspector and above planned to leave; of this percentage, 40 percent were chief superintendents and senior superintendents.[22] It was confirmed in June 1996 that forty-four local police officers, with ranks ranging from senior superintendent to senior assistant commissioner of police, had asked to leave by July of 1997.[23] Similarly, the ICAC determined that, among its fourteen directorate-grade officials, about one half would depart before the end of 1996. Some legislative councilors expressed serious concern that Hong Kong's ability to combat corruption might be adversely affected by such trends.[24] In the education sector, the Education Department released a survey of teachers in March 1995 showing that more than 1,100 teachers and principals had emigrated from 1992 to 1994.[25] This emigration flow was expected to peak in 1996. The main reason for this trend appears to have been that teachers and principals in the primary and secondary schools were worried about their superannuation funds, and therefore opted for early retirement to claim payments before 1997. (Middle-class teachers between 40 and 50 years old are qualified to emigrate to Canada, Australia, and New Zealand.)

The most striking feature of the public mood since the summer of 1995 has been the "feel bad factor." An editorial in the *South China Morning Post* made the following observation: "One of the year's most curious phenomena has been how growing pessimism about Hong Kong's economy, among all sectors of society, has remained so sharply at odds with official statistics – which continue to predict healthy growth."[26] The economy grew by 4.6 percent in 1995. Unemployment was at a ten-year high; however, it reached only 3.5 percent in the third quarter of the year. Exports were strong, and massive infrastructure

[21] *Ming Pao*, June 13, 1996.
[22] *Ming Pao*, July 29, 1995.
[23] *SCMP*, June 6, 1996.
[24] *Ming Pao*, July 13, 1995.
[25] Ibid.
[26] "Feel Bad Factor," editorial, *SCMP*, Aug. 9, 1995.

projects continued to stimulate the economy. However, a survey in October 1995 indicated that about 30 percent of employees were concerned about losing their jobs; 8 percent of them were very worried.[27] Employees could still vividly remember that in the early 1990s, employers were quick to offer improvements in remuneration and promotions to retain staff. At the same time, private consumption has been declining.[28]

Most analysts concluded that this "feel bad factor" was largely psychological and related to the approach of 1997. The rise in unemployment was primarily due to long-term structural changes in the economy. As labor costs rose, manufacturers in the territory moved their operations to the Pearl River Delta in China and Southeast Asia. The process began in the early 1980s and picked up momentum in the second half of the decade. Until the past two years, the rapid expansion of the service sector was able to absorb the surplus labor while maintaining the wage level. In the mid-1990s, growth rates began to decline, and even some labor-intensive service industries had moved to China to cut costs – data-processing was a prime example. Under these circumstances, the unemployment rate climbed slowly. Admittedly, some jobs – for example, in the construction industry – could not attract enough local laborers.

Private consumption has been declining among employees in the low-income brackets as a consequence of stagnation in wages. In the past two years, restraint has spread to the middle class; their propensity to spend has been eroded by the retreat in the real estate and stock markets since early 1994. Many middle-class families have had the extra financial burden of supporting family members living abroad; a high proportion of them also sent their children to study overseas. With the approach of 1997, there emerged a deliberate attempt to enhance savings in preparation for the uncertainty ahead. Apparently, the real estate companies and the airlines had absorbed much middle-class consumption power at the expense of restaurants and department stores.

By mid-1996, the economic situation seemed to have improved; the economic confidence indicator recovered after two years of continuous decline. It rose from 73 points to 76 points in January 1996, and further increased to 84

---

[27] Ibid.; *Ming Pao*, Oct. 22, 1995.

[28] In the second quarter of 1995, private consumption grew by only 1.4 percent on an annual basis. In the following November, retailers were warning that consumer demand was still weak, with the latest monthly figures registering the seventh month of successive decline. Car sales had dropped by 20 percent, while people continued to shun costly consumer durables. See *SCMP*, Nov. 7, 1995.

points in April and 87 points in October.[29] Then the unemployment rate gradually dropped to 2.8 percent in June–August 1996.[30] Both the stock market and the real estate market performed well, too.

Trade unions and laborers were not impressed, however. The Hong Kong Confederation of Trade Unions complained that 1.5 million employees suffered a decline in real wages in 1996, as was the case in 1995.[31] Trade unions also refused to accept the explanation that the fall in unemployment rate represented an upturn in Hong Kong's economy, as some workers had been forced to accept considerable cuts in wages after being unemployed for a certain period of time. A survey of laborers in September 1996 revealed that 51.3 percent of the respondents believed that wage levels would deteriorate after 1997, and only 8.3 percent believed that they would improve; 52 percent thought that the unemployment situation would deteriorate after 1997, and only 18.6 percent thought that it would improve; further, 45.6 percent of the respondents believed that social welfare would deteriorate after 1997, and only 8.3 percent believed that it would improve.[32] Middle-class families, too, reveal some concern about the decline in real income and the job situation, especially employment opportunities for their children. Notably, in late August of 1996, the Hong Kong government reduced its forecast for economic growth for 1996 from 5 percent to 4.7 percent.[33]

ELECTIONS AND THE DEVELOPMENT OF POLITICAL PARTIES

With the development of the representative system of government, elections have become an increasingly important factor in the political process in the territory. Since the Legislative Council elections in September 1991, the British administration can no longer be assured of stable majority support in the legislature. Endorsement of its legislative programs and requests for appropriations depend on strenuous lobbying of the legislators by senior government officials, who must also attempt to secure public support. With the removal of the remaining three official members and eighteen appointed members in the new Legisla-

[29] *Ming Pao*, Apr. 29, 1996; *SCMP*, Oct. 28, 1996.
[30] *Ming Pao*, Sept. 17, 1996.
[31] *Ming Pao*, Sept. 12, 1996.
[32] *Ming Pao*, Sept. 15, 1996.
[33] *SCMP*, Aug. 31, 1996.

tive Council in October 1995, the British administration has found it even more difficult to lobby for majority support in the wholly elected legislature.[34]

The Chinese authorities, too, recognized that they had a serious stake in the elections despite the rejection of "through train" arrangements for the District Boards, Urban/Regional Council, and Legislative Council in 1997. They would like to prevent the pro-democracy groups from winning a majority in the legislature, and they would like to secure a majority which would at least respect China's vital interests. The Democratic Alliance for the Betterment of Hong Kong (DAB), the key pro-Beijing political group, would be responsible for coordination within this majority. Since the Sino-British negotiations on the territory's future, the Chinese authorities have been expending considerable resources in establishing a pro-Beijing united front. Certainly, this united front had to demonstrate its mobilization power in the 1995 Legislative Council elections. From an orthodox ideological point of view, it had to develop itself and expand through campaigns while testing the caliber and loyalty of its supporters. From an organizational point of view, it had to cultivate candidates, consolidate and expand its grassroots networks, and refine its campaign strategies and tactics.

The conservative political groups finally came to realize that they had to prove themselves in elections; otherwise, they risked losing their clout and ceasing to be a significant political force. The creation of nine new functional constituencies and the electoral college provided them with important opportunities, too. On the other hand, the pro-democracy groups certainly wanted to maintain the lead they had achieved in the 1991 elections, when they did not encounter serious contest opposition.

It is not the intention of this chapter to analyze the results of the 1995 Legislative Council elections. This section focuses only on the features believed to be significant in terms of political participation and the development of political parties.

Over 920,000 voters participated in the 1995 Legislative Council elections, surpassing by about 170,000 the turnout seen in 1991. The voter turnout rate, however, was 35.79 percent, more than three percentage points lower than in

---

[34] The composition of the new Legislative Council after the 1995 elections is as follows: thirty seats elected by functional constituencies, ten elected by an electoral college, and twenty directly elected. For background information, see the author's "Hong Kong's Legislative Council Elections: Review of 1991 and Planning for 1995," in Benjamin K. P. Leung & Teresa Y. C. Wong (eds.), *25 Years of Social and Economic Development in Hong Kong* (Hong Kong: Centre of Asian Studies, the University of Hong Kong, 1994), pp. 291–313.

1991.[35] The number of registered voters increased from 1.9 million in 1991 to 2.57 million in 1995; therefore, it would have been unrealistic to expect an improvement in the voter turnout rate. In general, with the exception of young voters who had recently qualified to vote, those who registered in later rounds were less enthusiastic political participants than those who had registered in the initial rounds. Rough estimates indicated that registered voters constituted 60 percent of the qualified voters, which meant that actual voters consisted of only 21 or 22 percent of those qualified.

The voter turnout rate reflected the community's political apathy. The people of Hong Kong realized that most major decisions were made by Beijing or on the basis of Sino-British agreements; such perceptions reinforced their sense of political impotence. They, too, understood that the Legislative Council elections would have a limited impact on the livelihood issues which most concerned them, especially economic growth and unemployment. Admittedly, many Hong Kong residents had not established a habit of participating in elections. Most of them voted in order to fulfill a civic obligation, rather than to exercise their political right to elect a government. The increase in the number of voters was partially due to the mobilization power of pro-Beijing groups and the lowering of the voting age from 21 to 18. These factors suggest that it will be increasingly difficult to improve voter turnout.

Given the Sino-British quarrels over the elections, the low voter turnout rate easily prompted claims that the elections lacked representativeness. An electoral system, however, gives the people the right to elect their own representatives, and it requires those representatives to be accountable to the electorate. As long as the elections are genuinely open and fair, low turnout rates can be attributed to the political culture; it cannot be assumed that elections with low turnouts are unrepresentative.

The most noteworthy result of the recent Hong Kong elections was the outstanding performance by pro-democracy groups. According to various estimates – based on assessments of the political inclinations of some independents and the Hong Kong Association for Democracy and Peoples Livelihood (HKADPL) – such groups and their allies controlled twenty-seven to thirty-one seats in the legislature. On issues ranging from the further development of representative government and Sino-British negotiations on Hong Kong, to the expansion of social services, the pro-democracy alliance commands a majori-

---

[35] See all major newspapers in Hong Kong on Sept. 18, 1995.

ty and can therefore oppose positions taken by Beijing, by London, or by the two regimes jointly.

The electoral victory of the pro-democracy groups was obviously embarrassing for the Chinese authorities: Voters had supported Beijing's critics. It was natural for the electorate to expect that criticisms and strict monitoring would create checks and balances on those in power, and their feeling was that Beijing's power over Hong Kong exceeded that of the British administration. This should not be interpreted to mean that Hong Kong people wanted to confront the Chinese authorities. In the elections in the 1980s, the electorate similarly supported harsh critics of the territory's British administration; even so, most people at that time trusted the Hong Kong government and were satisfied with its performance.

A vast majority of the people of Hong Kong would like to give the "one country, two systems" arrangement the benefit of the doubt; nonetheless, they have some vague fears and worries concerning 1997. It is generally believed that if the Chinese authorities' policy toward Hong Kong had become more tolerant and flexible, the pro-Beijing groups would have been able to secure more electoral support, and vice versa. On the eve of the elections, incidents such as the behavior of the Chinese public security personnel in the Fourth World Women's Conference, the denial of labor activist Han Dongfang's return to China by the local New China News Agency, and the latter's reaffirmation that there would be no "through train" arrangement for the Legislative Council in 1997 damaged the chances of pro-Beijing candidates.

Some surveys taken before the elections indicated that people were most concerned with the economy and with unemployment and public housing issues. The candidates' attitudes toward China as well as their positions on the Tiananmen incident had become less significant. One possible explanation was that, although voters paid closest attention to issues affecting their livelihood, candidates had not responded to these concerns. Rather, they presented similar platforms, with the result that voters did not expect the elections to have much impact on issues of concern to them.[36]

The development of political parties in Hong Kong has been highly dependent on the evolution of the electoral system. Indeed, similar to their Western counterparts, local political parties exist largely to provide the machinery for

---

[36] See the author's analysis of the Legislative Council elections in September 1995 in "A Relaxed and Tolerant Policy is the Only Way to Ensure a Stable Transition [in Chinese]," *Ming Pao*, Sept. 26, 1995.

Joseph Y. S. Cheng

winning elections; reflecting this, their electoral performance provides an accurate indicator of their growth and strength.

Despite their spectacular electoral victories in 1991, pro-democracy groups have failed to expand their membership significantly. The Democratic Party (DP) probably does not have more than 200 to 300 active members, nor does it plan to develop into a mass party – hence, its heavy dependence on the media to maintain an attractive image in the community. Image-building usually dominates the tactical considerations of DP leadership. The DP has been successful in establishing itself as a staunch critic of both the Chinese authorities and the British administration, and as the most important group fighting for the freedoms and rights of the people of Hong Kong. Its efforts have been rewarded at the elections.

The DP, however, encounters severe challenges that it has not been able to overcome. In the first place, its concern for publicity often alienates it from grassroots pressure groups. Such groups are issue-oriented; they want concrete solutions to problems. The DP can certainly help by raising issues espoused by grassroots groups in the Legislative Council or with senior government officials, thus exerting pressure on the British administration to come up with solutions. However, the party's high profile and hunger for publicity often result in failure to compromise and delay in achieving settlements. Many grassroots pressure groups worry about being used in this way and therefore prefer to act without the involvement of political parties.

To attract the media's attention, the DP legislators usually dramatize their gestures and statements. A harsh criticism of Beijing obviously has a better chance of making newspaper headlines than a balanced statement. The DP's success with the media, however, makes it very difficult for its leaders to establish a dialogue of mutual trust with senior civil servants. This success has also provided Chinese officials with a convenient excuse for rejecting any contact with the party. Such political posturing also has had a negative impact on party support among the intelligentsia. However, as July 1997 approaches, the middle class in the territory has been overly willing to compromise.

Chinese authorities regard the Hong Kong Alliance in Support of the Patriotic Democratic Movement in China, which emerged in the wake of the Tiananmen incident, as a "subversive" organization. Most of the leaders of the alliance are also leading members of the DP. The Chinese authorities have officially ruled out contact with the DP not only on that basis, but also on the basis of the DP's refusal to support the Basic Law and its opposition to the provisional legislature.

166

In 1996, however, the Chinese authorities began to soften their stance. When Lu Ping, director of the State Council's Hong Kong and Macau Affairs Office, visited the territory in April 1996 to consult with the local community on the work of the Preparatory Committee, attempts were made to invite leaders of the Hong Kong Professional Teachers' Union (PTU) to take part in the consultative sessions. Two important leaders of the PTU, Szeto Wah and Cheung Man-kwong, were also DP leaders and Legislative Councilors. A formal dialogue between Lu Ping and the PTU leaders therefore could be interpreted as a breakthrough. Subsequently, the PTU leaders made some uncompromising statements, and their invitations were withdrawn. It was generally assumed that different views existed among the Chinese authorities on the resumption of a dialogue with pro-democracy groups in Hong Kong.

The following August, Vice-Premier Qian Qichen, head of the Preparatory Committee, indicated in its fourth plenary session in Beijing that the Chinese authorities were willing to discuss Hong Kong–related issues with people who held varying views on democracy. This was seen as an olive branch from Beijing to the DP, perhaps with a view to involve the DP in the Selection Committee soon to be established. The DP refused to alter its stance, and again, Beijing's gesture did not lead to breakthrough. It is significant that opinion surveys run by several local newspapers, as well as a DP poll of its own membership, uniformly indicated majority support for DP members' participation in the Selection Committee, and for DP's changing its stand on the provisional legislature in return for a dialogue with Beijing.[37]

The DP leadership believed that participation in the Selection Committee would give it no influence in the process of setting up the first HKSAR government. It was concerned with the united front offensive from Beijing and its divisive tactics. It also feared that softening its position would lead to severe challenges from The Frontier, a new political group founded by radical legislators such as Emily Lau, Lau Chin-shek, and Lee Cheuk-yan. The general public obviously welcomes a dialogue between Beijing and the DP, as it would contribute to the territory's political stability. The author also believes that it would be beneficial for the DP to alter its relationship with the Chinese authorities from one of conflict to one of civil discourse. Securing official recognition to engage in legitimate political struggles would be an important achievement, given the differing views among the Chinese authorities. The DP should try to operate both within and outside the Establishment.

[37] *SCMP*, Aug. 21, 1996.

From the DP's point of view, it must now map out its strategy for the post-1997 era. At this stage, it has no choice but to prepare to survive as the opposition in the political wilderness. Its impact on the HKSAR government's decision-making process will be limited, and its influence will very much depend on the extent of freedom enjoyed by the mass media. This new position will require considerable adjustment on the part of the DP leaders. Their electoral successes in 1991 and especially 1995 have enabled them to play a key role in the legislature. In many ways they have become part of the political establishment, and their influence is felt through constitutional channels. Does the post-1997 era demand a return to the pressure-group role of the late 1970s? Will some DP legislators opt to stay within the formal political structure, and, if so, will they be absorbed by the pro-Beijing united front?

Meanwhile, the formation of The Frontier will mean that at least three pro-democracy groups will compete among themselves.[38] The Frontier will adopt a staunchly anti-communist stand, while the HKADPL will be keen to maintain a dialogue with Beijing and to operate within the Establishment. The Frontier was founded in anticipation of the transformation of the electoral system into one of proportional representation in direct elections. The radical independents must group together in order to carve their share of the votes from the DP. There is speculation that the Chinese authorities are pleased with the emergence of The Frontier.[39]

The pro-Beijing groups did not perform well in the 1995 Legislative Council elections in terms of seats won. However, they secured 34 percent of the vote, and their mobilizing power was impressive in a number of ways. In the Hong Kong Island East constituency, a relatively unknown candidate representing the pro-Beijing Hong Kong Progressive Alliance competed against Martin Lee, leader of the DP, and received almost 30 percent of the vote. This performance indicated the power of the grassroots network underlying pro-Beijing organizations. Most significantly, public opinion revealed great sympathy for the DAB leaders who lost to the candidates of the pro-democracy groups. Many Hong Kong residents felt that the former had been doing a good job in serving the public, and their presence in the legislature would have contributed to the well-being of the community and the development of representative government. If the existing simple majority, single-seat constituency system is

---

[38] For a brief introduction to The Frontier, see *SCMP*, July 30, 1996.
[39] *Ming Pao*, Aug. 27, 1996.

replaced by a proportional representation system or the single-vote, medium-size, multi-seat constituency system recently abandoned by Japan, the DAB and its allies will be able to secure six or seven seats out of twenty in the direct elections on the basis of their share of the votes in 1995. The indications are that the Chinese authorities will likely change the electoral system after 1997, and the Hong Kong community may not be strongly against that change.

The DAB's performance in the elections showed that in the long run, the community service offered by pro-Beijing groups will be rewarded. Given their financial resources, they will be able to expand their grassroots network gradually. Moreover, the pro-Beijing united front can also reward its supporters with honors such as memberships in the National People's Congress, the Chinese People's Political Consultative Conference, and the provincial counterparts of these two bodies, as well as appointments to the Preparatory Committee for the HKSAR, Hong Kong Affairs Advisors, and District Affairs Advisors. By the mid-1990s, the Chinese authorities had established their system of honors for the Hong Kong community. Such efforts and resources have laid a strong foundation for pro-Beijing political groups. With a more favorable electoral system and the support of the pro-business groups, the Chinese authorities can hope to secure reliable majority support in the legislature after 1997. Willingness to accept elections will support the Chinese authorities' attempts to seek legitimacy for the HKSAR government and encourage them to be responsive to public opinion in the territory.

The DAB also demonstrated, however, that in order to win elections, it could not afford to toe the Beijing line closely at all times. The Chinese leaders' insecurity regarding Hong Kong since the Tiananmen incident and the Sino-British confrontation has not allowed the DAB much room to maneuver. Signs of disagreements between the DAB and the Chinese officials responsible for Hong Kong are apparent. In the appointments to the Preparatory Committee for the HKSAR announced at the end of 1995, the DAB received four seats, while other pro-Beijing groups – which had been far less effective in elections but which had been faithful in supporting the Beijing line – were more handsomely rewarded.

In contrast to the Legislative Council elections in 1991, the Liberal Party had to fight for its survival in 1995. Its leader, Allen Lee, won a seat in the New Territories Northeast constituency, and it did well in the old functional constituencies and in the nine newly created functional constituencies. Anticipated changes to the electoral system after 1997 will favor the Liberal Party, which will likely remain a formidable force in the legislature. The development of representative government has convinced some business leaders that competing in elections will safeguard their business interests.

In the District Board elections in September 1994, the Urban/Regional Council elections in March 1995, and the Legislative Council elections in September 1995, the major political groups all demonstrated sophisticated campaign strategies and skills.[40] With perhaps the exception of the DAB and the Hong Kong Federation of Trade Unions, most political groups were severely limited by their relatively small work force and shortage of funds. Consequently, they had to deploy their resources very efficiently. All political groups have been skillful in attracting media attention and in using opinion surveys. The pro-democracy groups no longer have the edge they enjoyed in the previous decade.

By the standard of developing democracies, Hong Kong's elections have been remarkably clean. One can argue that the interests at stake are limited, but the political culture obviously detests "money politics," and the purchase of votes is unthinkable. Minor violations of electoral rules are common: They usually take the form of disobeying the regulations concerning the display of publicity materials, underreporting of campaign expenditures, and so forth. Violence is virtually non-existent.[41]

THE CHINESE AUTHORITIES' POSITION
ON REPRESENTATIVE GOVERNMENT

In the course of drafting the Basic Law, it became clear that the Chinese authorities often wanted to retain final control, especially in matters relating to the autonomy of the political system.[42] Their decisions regarding the concept of "residual power" and the amendment and interpretation of the Basic Law are significant examples. Within the HKSAR political system, the fact that appointees are designated by the Central People's Government of the Chief Executive and principal officials implies that they are accountable to the Cen-

---

[40] See Chi-keung Choi, Sai-leung Lau, & Pak-kwan Chow, *Politics of Elections and Legislature* [in Chinese] (Hong Kong: Hong Kong Humanities Press, November 1995).
[41] The discussions above are based on my interviews of leaders of political parties, political scientists following the elections, and journalists in the two weeks before and after the Legislative Council elections in September 1995.
[42] See Joseph Y. S. Cheng, "The Basic Law: Messages for Hong Kong People," in Richard Y. C. Wong and Joseph Y. S. Cheng (eds.), *The Other Hong Kong Report 1990* (Hong Kong: The Chinese University Press, 1990), pp. 29–63.

tral People's Government. Hong Kong residents realized that the Chief Executive needed to be someone acceptable to the Chinese authorities; in the mid-1990s, this criterion apparently also applied to the principal officials.

The gist of Chris Patten's political reform proposals announced in October 1992 was that the pro-democracy groups would have a chance to secure a majority in the Legislative Council and thus control the legislature. This was certainly antithetical to the original plan of the Chinese authorities to ensure a majority in the legislature that was acceptable to Beijing.[43] It is expected that in the Legislative Council elections in 1998, the nine new functional constituencies will be redefined and the composition of the Election Committee, which will return ten legislators, will strictly follow the Basic Law. In short, the Chinese authorities want an electoral system which will guarantee reliable majority support for their Hong Kong policy and the HKSAR government.

Since the conclusion of the Sino-British Joint Declaration in 1984, the Chinese leaders have been according top priority to the cultivation of the business community in the territory. Their rationale is simple and straightforward. Hong Kong must remain attractive to investors. If investors stay, the stability and prosperity of the territory will be maintained. In both the Basic Law Drafting Committee and that of the Preparatory Committee for the HKSAR, business leaders dominate the membership.[44] The business community in return has been firmly supporting the Chinese government in the Sino-British conflict. It has confidence in China's economic reforms and its openness to the outside world. Such momentum picked up soon after the Tiananmen crackdown. Businesspeople believe that the trend is irreversible; consequently, they have been bullish about the economic future of China and Hong Kong's role in China's development.[45] Seen in this context, the Sino-British confrontation is a temporary phenomenon which will become increasingly irrelevant as July 1997 approaches. Such business confidence explains the continuing boom in the real estate and stock markets in the past years, though mild adjustments have taken place in the property market since the second quarter of 1994 and in the stock market since the beginning of the year. Undeniably, a great deal of money has

---

[43] See Joseph Y. S. Cheng, "Sino-British Negotiations on Hong Kong During Chris Patten's Governorship," *Australian Journal of International Affairs*, vol. 48(2), Nov. 1994, pp. 233–34.

[44] For an analysis of the membership list of the Preparatory Committee for the HKSAR, see *Ming Pao*, Dec. 27–28, 1995.

[45] See, for example, Bruce Gilley, "Red Flag Over Hong Kong," *Far Eastern Economic Review*, vol. 158(49), Dec. 7, 1995, pp. 72–78.

flowed from China into the markets too. It is not surprising that the business community has been most critical of Chris Patten's China policy.

In terms of political participation, local business leaders enjoy access to the very top Chinese leaders. When the latter visit Guangdong, they typically arrange to see the richest dozen or so of Hong Kong's tycoons. Local business leaders believe that the future HKSAR government will respect their interests, and they consider that the best way to articulate those interests is to cultivate and maintain good relations with the Chinese leadership. The most effective means of achieving this end appears to be major investments in China and generous donations. Local business leaders tend to believe that support for pro-business political parties is unimportant; in fact, it may even be troublesome. They prefer instead to donate to the Better Hong Kong Foundation or similar projects, which, they think, are apolitical.

The present political system, despite the implementation of Chris Patten's political reform proposals, continues to favor the business community. The functional constituencies provide more than a dozen seats for business interests in the legislature, and businesspeople dominate the major advisory committees. Most important, the political philosophy of the British administration is in accord with that of business interests. However, local business leaders do oppose the Governor's handling of relations with Beijing and his political reforms.

A group of second-generation business leaders felt compelled to mobilize in order to counter the labor groups in the 1995 Legislative Council elections. They were the leaders of the Liberal Party, and they worked hard to win seats in the nine new functional constituencies.[46] After the 1995 elections, the pro-democracy groups plus the pro-Beijing labor unions have commanded a clear majority in the legislature. Their positions on issues such as labor importation schemes and a mandatory pension fund are not acceptable to the business community, yet the government must meet their demands. The business community has expressed its uneasiness with the situation; however, it is relatively powerless. Business leaders seem resigned to the fact that the present legislature is to be replaced by a provisional legislature by 1997, elected by the Selection Committee for the First Government of the HKSAR, established by the Preparatory Committee for the HKSAR.

An important task of the Preparatory Committee was to form a 400-member Selection Committee, whose membership was announced in early November

[46] See Chi-keung Choi, Sai-leung Lau, & Pak-kwan Chow, op. cit., pp. 211–22.

1996. The first Chief Executive and the provisional legislature were chosen by the Selection Committee in December. The most significant functions of the Preparatory Committee were to serve Beijing's "united front" strategy and to legitimize the formation of the first government of the HKSAR. Establishment of the Selection Committee was another major offensive in Beijing's united front strategy following the appointments to the Preliminary Working Committee and the Preparatory Committee, and those of Hong Kong Affairs Advisors and District Affairs Advisors. Besides individual community leaders, the targets included the important interest groups in the territory such as business organizations, professional associations, political parties, and grassroots groups.

In 1985, when the Basic Law Consultative Committee was formed, the Chinese authorities invited most of the important groups in Hong Kong to recommend members, and their recommendations were respected. However, the Chinese authorities ensured their own safe majority within the Basic Law Consultative Committee by appointing a proportion of the members.[47] It appeared that the tasks of selecting the first Chief Executive and the provisional legislature of the HKSAR were more significant than the consultative work relating to the Basic Law, and that, because of the deterioration of Sino-British relations in the past eleven years, the Chinese officials concerned could not allow more than a modicum of error. From the beginning, the Preparatory Committee adopted the principles of confidentiality and collective responsibility. Those who had hoped to see a larger share of democracy and transparency in Preparatory Committee operations relative to those of the Preliminary Working Committee must have been sorely disappointed.

An opinion survey taken in June 1996 showed that 56.3 percent of the respondents had no confidence in the Preparatory Committee; 26.9 percent and 11.7 percent of the respondents had, respectively, "extremely low" and "low" confidence in the Preparatory Committee.[48] This level of confidence was even lower than that expressed in the Preliminary Working Committee. Professor Lau Siu-kai, a member of both committees, admitted that people were disappointed when the Preparatory Committee failed to consult the people of Hong Kong actively.[49]

[47] See Kit-fung Cheung, Kin-hing Yeung, Wing-hung Lo, & Lo-sai Chan, *No Change, 50 Years? – The Sino-British Hong Kong Contest Concerning the Basic Law* [in Chinese] (Hong Kong: Long Chiu Publisher, 1991), chap. 3, pp. 45–53, 73–83.
[48] *SCMP*, June 24, 1996.
[49] Ibid.

Joseph Y. S. Cheng

On the basis of the Preparatory Committee's membership, it seems that the Chinese authorities plan to cultivate a number of pro-Beijing groups and avoid dependence on one single political organization. One Country Two Systems Economic Research Institute received eight seats, New Hong Kong Alliance seven, Hong Kong Progressive Alliance five, and Liberal Democratic Federation five.[50] These political groups do not have much popular support, and their performance in recent elections has been far from satisfactory. In comparison, the DAB secured only four seats, despite the fact that it has established a solid grassroots network and was able to pose a serious challenge to the DP in the elections that took place in 1994 to 1995. This may well be a sign that the Chinese officials responsible for Hong Kong want to strengthen control of the united front, and to prevent the emergence of possible checks and balances as well as the further development of political parties with strong mass support.

In both the election of the first Chief Executive and that of the provisional legislature, the Chinese authorities wanted to ensure that nothing could go wrong. The formation of the Selection Committee had been critical, and the process well demonstrated the style of "election with Chinese characteristics." The Preparatory Committee rejected the proposal that various important interest groups in the territory be allowed to nominate a number of representatives to the Selection Committee. Instead, people who wanted to join the Selection Committee would take part on an individual basis; therefore, they would not be accountable to the organizations to which they belonged. In drawing up the final list of candidates, the Preparatory Committee's presidium had ample discretionary power. Finally, in the voting process, it is assumed that the fifty-six mainland China members of the Preparatory Committee voted alike, influencing decisively the outcome of the elections.

The Chinese authorities therefore expected no surprises from the Selection Committee, and the question of whether the Chinese leadership had designated a candidate for the post of the first Chief Executive was insignificant. Similarly, in the election of the provisional legislature, when Qian Qichen appealed for support for those candidates with experience in legislative affairs, the Selection Committee understood and returned thirty-three incumbent Legislative Councilors plus eight former Legislative Councilors. Among the sixty members of the provisional legislature, fifty-one were members of the Selection Committee; thirty-three were members of both the Selection Committee and pro-Bei-

[50] See footnote 43.

174

jing political groups. Only six were neither members of the Selection Commit-tee nor pro-Beijing. Lau Siu-kai, a Preparatory Committee member heavily involved in designing the political system of the HKSAR, observed that the Chinese authorities were satisfied with the outcome of the provisional legisla-ture election. He noted that since no political party could dominate the provi-sional legislature, the Chief Executive would not be restrained by the provi-sional legislature.

As a result of the Sino-British confrontation, the British administration has found it increasingly difficult to co-opt respectable community leaders into the consultative system. This has weakened the appeal of the administration. At the same time, senior civil servants have been tempted to appoint more compliant figures on their advisory committees. This has made their jobs easier, as they must spend more time on the Legislative Council and in the media. Members of many advisory committees also complain about an absence of important papers to discuss, reflecting the lack of initiatives and the difficulties of the senior civil servants at the final stage of the transition. Serious members – who are often severe critics – in some advisory committees may feel that they have little to con-tribute, and a few have resigned in frustration. To a large extent, advisory com-mittees cannot compete with the Legislative Council for the limelight.

The British administration had an earlier strategy: to choose a group of prominent non-politicians – businesspeople, professionals, and academics – to fill the advisory committees so that they can offer the civil servants valuable advice and support. Apparently, the emphasis has been too much on support. As a result, while the system of advisory committees has not been problemat-ic for the Hong Kong government, it has gradually lost its important function. It is likely that the first HKSAR government will place an equal emphasis on support, given the pattern of Beijing's present united front strategy. Further, community leaders today have already displayed an overeagerness to please the Chinese authorities, which has resulted in severe criticism.

Since members of the Preparatory Committee are largely business leaders, they do not have much time for the work of the Preparatory Committee. As in the case of the drafting of the Basic Law, the secretariat of the Preparatory Com-mittee assumes a heavy responsibility. The secretariat is based in Beijing and relies on cadres located there. Participation by Hong Kong experts is limited. One Country Two Systems Economic Research Institute, a think tank funded by a group of important Preparatory Committee members, also may play a role in policy research. Another think tank of a similar nature, Hong Kong Policy

Research Institute, has become active in recent years. How these institutes will develop and what role they will assume after 1997 is worth monitoring.

With the approach of July 1997, different interest groups must respond to the new challenges and devise strategies to ensure their effective articulation. For instance, the Hong Kong General Chamber of Commerce must shed its image of enjoying special status under British administration, its leadership having been dominated by the British *hongs*. In recent years, the chamber has elected leaders who can communicate well with the Chinese authorities, and their recognition has been affirmed by appointments to the Preliminary Working Committee and Preparatory Committee. In 1995, for the first time, the chamber joined other established business groups in the celebration of the National Day of the People's Republic of China.

Similar changes have taken place within a number of important professional associations. Access to Chinese authorities has been considered an important factor in their competition among the leaders of these associations, while expatriates, voluntarily or involuntarily, are adopting lower profiles. Most professional associations would like to persuade the Chinese authorities to allow them to retain their role in determining their respective professional qualifications in the territory. With the rapid expansion of economic exchanges between Hong Kong and China since the late 1970s, professional firms with an early start in the China market tend to do well, their status and influence rising correspondingly. Heads of these firms often receive appointments and honors from the Chinese authorities, which obviously gives them a vested interest in maintaining good relations with Beijing.

The Chinese united front's emphasis on individuals, however, has complicated the decision-making process for business and professional groups. An even more significant challenge has been the development of representative government in the territory. Ever since the British administration lost its safe majority in the Legislative Council in 1991, business and professional groups have had to lobby the legislature as well as the Hong Kong government. Their relationship with the legislature has been frustrating. While they can normally count on the support of the pro-business Liberal Party and the legislators from their own functional constituencies, these groups often need to secure the votes of legislators from pro-democracy parties to ensure majority support from the Legislative Council.

In general, the dialogue between business groups and pro-democracy political parties in the 1990s has not been fruitful. Rather, it has served to expose the discrepancy in values between the two camps. There is little incentive on both sides to engage in a give-and-take bargaining process. Usually, pro-democracy parties are only too eager to champion the causes of the lower social strata, and they fear that compromises with business groups will be perceived as betrayals of their supporters and violations of their party platforms. The business groups do not have much to offer to induce the pro-democracy parties to cooperate, and they cannot effectively challenge the pro-democracy parties in elections. They therefore choose to concentrate on lobbying the government.

As the Hong Kong government increasingly must play a balancing role in the legislature, it cannot afford to endorse the policy positions of pro-Establishment interest groups consistently, even when it shares their concerns and values. Such groups, in their frustration, believe that it may be more rewarding to lobby the Chinese authorities, at least with regard to post-1997 scenarios. The Chinese authorities respect business interests and are keen to maintain an executive-led system of government after 1997, which would diminish the legislature's role in the policy-making process.[51] In recent years, political parties have become much more skillful in parliamentary tactics. Given the number of votes it controls, the pro-democracy camp has become quite effective in extracting concessions from the Hong Kong government.[52] It remains to be seen how the provisional legislature and its successor will revamp the parliamentary procedures and conventions established in the early-1990s in anticipation of the need to readjust the balance between executive and legislature after 1997. Ideology aside, both business and professional groups demand efficient government, and they refuse to accept the price of democracy in the form of time-consuming debates and delays. For example, none of the eighteen proposals put forward by the Legislative Councilors in 1995 came to fruition in January 1996, and only one had a date set for its first reading.[53]

Despite the development of representative government, a significant segment of the Hong Kong community and grassroots pressure groups treat political parties and politicians with suspicion, and are of the opinion that they are interested only in publicity. Grassroots pressure groups are usually issue-oriented; their supporters are interested in concrete results. Consequently, they are

---

[51] See Joseph Y. S. Cheng, "The Political System," in Peter Wesley-Smith & Albert Chen (eds.), *The Basic Law and Hong Kong's Future* (Hong Kong: Butterworths, 1988), pp. 141–71.

[52] See Section 2 of Chi-keung Choi, Sai-leung Lau, & Pak-kwan Chow, op. cit.

[53] *Sunday Morning Post*, Jan. 7, 1996.

Joseph Y. S. Cheng

often reluctant to enlist the support of political parties, including those from the pro-democracy camp. They appreciate the publicity secured by political parties, as well as the opportunities this affords to raise their concerns with top government officials and legislators; however, they fear that this publicity might overpoliticize these concerns, thus reducing the chances of exacting prompt concessions from the government departments concerned.

Because of its limited resources and its concentration on parliamentary work in recent years, the DP has neglected the cultivation of grassroots pressure groups, thus further alienating some groups. This neglect has sparked initiatives among groups of radical social workers. Some social workers and grassroots activists are disappointed with the lack of progress in the democratization process. Consequently, they have become confrontational, resulting in further polarization. In recent years, many small radical groups have emerged to protest Chinese authority.

Many interest groups outside the Establishment are wrestling with the divisive issue of how to prepare for the approach of July 1997. For example, in mid-1996 arguments and differences of viewpoint became apparent in the territory's Christian community.[54] The Catholic Church wanted to serve as "the conscience of society," but it ran a large number of schools, hospitals, and charities which depended very heavily on government funding; Catholic Church leaders appreciated the need to maintain a good relationship with the incoming HKSAR government. Other Christian groups quarreled over the issue of church commemoration of China's National Day. Apparently, Lutherans and Methodists were most amenable to cooperating with the Chinese authorities. Some of their leaders argued that "Hong Kong is returning not only to China but to the People's Republic of China." On the other hand, local evangelical churches, which have strong links to China's secret "house churches," began moving underground.[55]

The Chinese authorities began publicly building their community network and influence in the territory in 1985, when the local New China News Agency opened three district offices in Hong Kong Island, Kowloon, and the New Territories. Pro-Beijing political forces mounted a campaign to block the introduction of direct elections to the Legislative Council in 1988. They mobilized their supporters, identified candidates for support, and attacked political oppo-

---

[54] See Melana K. Zyla, "Devil of a Dilemma – Churches Ponder How Close to Get to Beijing," *Far Eastern Economic Review*, vol. 159(31), Aug. 1, 1996, p. 17.
[55] Ibid.; *Hong Kong Economic Journal*, June 15, 1996.

178

nents in subsequent elections. The local New China News Agency has been active in cultivating the district-based community leaders, voluntary bodies, and interest groups. It normally sends high-ranking officials to attend the latter's functions, most of whom are experts in united front tactics.

The Hong Kong government apparently does not see this as a threat; it reduced funding for the Home Affairs Branch (previously known as the City and New Territories Administration) in the early 1990s. Since the latter half of the 1980s, people have often complained about District Officers as well – that they are too young and immature, that they are unable to speak Cantonese well, and that they are insensitive to local traditions and customs. Because they remain in their posts for only two to three years, they do not have time to establish strong ties with community leaders in their respective districts.

In the 1991 Legislative Council elections, many district-based pro-Beijing groups emerged. Their development was hindered by the Tiananmen incident, but it has been regaining momentum with the approach of July 1997. Examples of such groups are the Kwun Tong Manchung Friendship Promotion Association and Hong Kong Eastern District Community Association. While they do not seem to be very active, their names appear increasingly in advertisements and posters supporting the work of the Preparatory Committee. Funding for these groups comes mainly from pro-Beijing businesspeople, and their leaders and activists are often honored with appointments by the Chinese authorities. At this stage, such groups tend to concentrate on social activities. From the united front's point of view, however, they should develop into organizations with effective mobilization power and the ability to reach ordinary people at a neighborhood level.

The mobilization power of pro-Beijing groups is mixed at best, despite the financial and political resources at their disposal. In the 1995 Legislative Council elections, Choy So-yuk of the Hong Kong Progressive Alliance challenged Martin Lee, leader of the DP, in the Hong Kong Island East constituency. Few voters had heard of Choy, who had no significant service record at the district level. Yet she won almost 30 percent of the votes. In contrast, Fung Chi-kin of the DAB competed in the Financing, Insurance, Real Estate and Business Services functional constituency and lost badly to the DP candidate, Cheng Karfoo. Fung was assumed to have the firm endorsement of all the Chinese enterprises and their friends in these sectors; his failure indicated that many employees of Chinese enterprises refused to deliver the votes as directed by their superiors.

CONCLUSION

By early 1997, both Chinese leaders and the people of Hong Kong have exhibited more confidence in the notion of a stable transfer of power compared with, say, seven years ago. Even the leadership succession of Beijing does not seem to pose a threat, as people accept that the post-Deng era has already begun. This improvement in confidence stems from a number of causes. Hong Kong residents realize that Chinese leaders value the territory, and have been working hard to retain investors – an important indicator being the composition of the Preparatory Committee. It is obvious that China's economic reforms and openness to the outside world are irreversible.

Given the choice of being unemployed in Canada or Australia, or obtaining a job comparable to their own in Shenzhen, most Hong Kong professionals would opt for the latter. Worry over 1997 has been much reduced by the realization that there are no greener pastures outside the territory. The return flow of former emigrants has indeed been expanding as Hong Kong approaches July 1997. It was reported that for every 100 emigrants leaving Hong Kong in 1995, 60 former emigrants returned to the territory from overseas. The corresponding proportions in previous years were 27.9 percent in 1994, 29.1 percent in 1993, 16.2 percent in 1992, 7.7 percent in 1991, and 7.2 percent in 1990.[56] The people of Hong Kong, however, have also lowered their expectations of the future. Few support a high degree of autonomy for the HKSAR. They now accept the stationing of the People's Liberation Army in the urban areas. They no longer demand a say in the selection of the first Chief Executive. In sum, they accept stability and prosperity as the substitute for democracy and autonomy. Slackening economic growth and unemployment are now the Hong Kong community's foremost concern.

Increasingly, Hong Kong residents have come to believe that since Hong Kong has become the focus of much international media attention, and given Chinese leaders' concern with appearances, all will go well in 1997. These may, however, be pragmatic rationalizations to suppress fears for the time being. They indicate that worries of a major upheaval occurring by 1997 have been diluted to concerns that the rule of law, the freedoms now enjoyed, and, indeed, the way of life in Hong Kong will slowly erode. These rationalizations also mean that the Chinese authorities have gained time. They have been given

[56] *Ming Pao*, Sept. 11, 1996.

the benefit of the doubt to make "one country, two systems" work. They have also been given a vote of confidence by local and international investors. Less reassuringly, however, a recent study estimated that 700,000 members of the local population hold foreign passports, and that probably another 500,000 possess the right of abode in a foreign country.[57] It is believed that they are largely well-educated, middle-class families who have adopted a "wait-and-see" attitude.

Respect for the rule of law and freedom of the media is perhaps the best way to win the hearts of the Hong Kong community. Operations of the Preparatory Committee are the most significant starting point. While the people of Hong Kong understand that the Preparatory Committee is not accountable to them, they will closely monitor its performance to assess whether it justifies their benefit of the doubt. The needs for transparency and due process cannot be overemphasized, and shortcomings will not escape notice.

The author's interviews with Preparatory Committee members in early October 1996 revealed that the Chinese authorities were largely satisfied with the situation. They were especially encouraged by the fact that approximately 6,000 people had applied to join the 400-seat Selection Committee. With the exception of the pro-democracy camp, applicants represented the elites from all sectors of the community. Many retired politicians and former senior civil servants also applied, apparently in an attempt to show their support for the Chinese authorities. In the competition for the post of Chief Executive of the first HKSAR government, a small number of candidates considered acceptable to the Hong Kong community competed vigorously. In an opinion survey in early October 1996, the two front runners, Sir Ti-liang Yang and Che-hwa Tung, received approval ratings of 73 percent and 56 percent, respectively; their disapproval ratings were 14.1 percent and 26.9 percent, respectively.[58] The competition reduced the suspicion that the Chinese authorities completely controlled the process. In general, the election of the first Chief Executive went smoothly; however, election of the provisional legislature did not.

The Chinese authorities were particularly pleased with the pragmatism of Hong Kong residents, who typically prefer to avoid confrontation with Beijing.

---

[57] See a report prepared by Hong Kong Policy Research Institute; a version of this report appears as Jane C. Y. Lee & Ng Chi-sum, "The Nationality and Right of Abode Policy for Hong Kong Residents – Political or Pragmatic Consideration?" *Hong Kong Journal of Social Sciences* [in Chinese], no. 7, Apr. 1996, pp. 192–211.

[58] *Sunday Morning Post*, Oct. 6, 1996.

In his final policy speech, Governor Chris Patten strongly defended his political reform package and argued for non-cooperation with the provisional legislature.[59] An opinion survey held soon afterward revealed that 78.1 percent of the respondents believed that the Hong Kong government should help the provisional legislature if it operated from early 1997; even among those who did not support the provisional legislature, the percentage was as high as 71.1 percent.[60]

Various opinion surveys gauged the public selection of the first Chief Executive. The present Chief Secretary, Anson Chan Fang On-sang, was consistently the most popular choice; she consistently secured 50 to 60 percent of the respondents' support. As her chances declined in the autumn of 1996, however, support among respondents also dropped to 39.6 percent in October. Martin Lee, leader of the DP, did not appear to be a popular choice. He received the support of 16.2 percent of the respondents in December 1995, a level that gradually decreased to 4.8 percent in October 1996.[61] The people of Hong Kong apparently preferred to see a senior civil servant assume this post; this would represent continuity and maintenance of the administration by civil servants. They did not believe that pro-democracy leaders would be ideal candidates, since they wanted to avoid confrontation with Beijing. However, they did want pro-democracy leaders to remain in the legislature as critics of Beijing and the local government; pro-democracy leaders have remained very popular among the Hong Kong populace.

Political development in the postwar era in Hong Kong has been a process of promoting citizens' demands and rights, or those of a segment of the community, through the combination of public opinion, legal means, and pressure group activities within the existing political system.[62] Inherent to this process is an implicit negation of the "winners take all" model, with all parties accepting that political strategies should consist of long-term negotiation, bargaining, cooperation, and conflict resolution.[63] Such a system is most likely an important model for China at this stage of its political development.

The spirit of bargaining and negation of "winners take all" permeates every level of Hong Kong politics. At the highest level, before the Sino-British Joint

[59] For the text of the policy speech, see all major newspapers in Hong Kong on Oct. 3, 1996.
[60] *SCMP*, Oct. 8, 1996.
[61] *Sunday Morning Post*, Oct. 6, 1996.
[62] See Joseph Y. S. Cheng, "Political Modernization in Hong Kong," *The Journal of Commonwealth and Comparative Politics*, vol. 27(3), Nov. 1989, pp. 294–320.
[63] See Tsou Tang, *Twentieth Century Chinese Politics* [in Chinese] (Hong Kong: Oxford University Press, 1994).

Declaration in 1984, neither the colonial government nor the Hong Kong community desired a fundamental change of the political system as it might attract interference from Beijing. Since 1984, the people of Hong Kong have understood that their option is either to accept the "one country, two systems" arrangement or to emigrate. At the grassroots level, petitions and protest rallies in the territory are usually peaceful and orderly; protesters and the police are willing to cooperate to avoid clashes. Hong Kong residents generally shun confrontation and violence.

In the process of drafting the Basic Law, for example, political groups and the concerned public seriously debated every controversial clause in the document. Though many in Hong Kong had doubts concerning the binding power of the Basic Law on the Chinese authorities, there was general acceptance that securing a Basic Law acceptable to the community was almost the only option available. The hope was also expressed that the serious debates would have an educational effect on all parties concerned.

The people of Hong Kong have adopted a utilitarian attitude toward democracy: They view it as a means to realize practical, concrete objectives. Few actually practice democracy as a way of life. For example, many vote in elections in order to fulfill a civic obligation. Many vote for the candidates of the pro-democracy camp who are severe critics of the Hong Kong government and the Chinese authorities because they hope to achieve a certain degree of checks and balances. They neither expect nor desire the pro-democracy camp to capture the government. Since the Hong Kong community treats democracy as a means to an end, they are prudent in the calculation of the cost of political participation. While they perceive democracy as an important means to guarantee their freedoms, their lifestyles, and their living standards, they also consider that their own individual efforts are more significant – more liable to improve their own lives. Such attitudes and orientations continue to define political participation in Hong Kong in the mid-1990s.

8

Strategic and Military Implications of Hong Kong Reversion[1]

RONALD N. MONTAPERTO

INTRODUCTION

ON July 1, 1997, the British Crown Colony of Hong Kong will revert from British to Chinese rule. For the leaders of the People's Republic of China (PRC), Hong Kong reversion and the creation of the Hong Kong Special Administrative Region (SAR) are a potent symbol of the end of nearly two centuries of maltreatment by exploitative foreign powers. For Beijing, regaining sovereignty over Hong Kong is a major step toward completing the reunification of China, a process that began with the proclamation of the PRC in 1949 and will be completed only after Macao and Taiwan are returned to the embrace of the motherland.

The reversion of Hong Kong is also a moral issue for Beijing: The British used coercive military force to establish their ownership of the territory. Although all Chinese governments since the 1840s have grudgingly accepted the reality of British control, and even profited by it, none has accepted the legal or moral basis for the British presence. (Leaders in Beijing and Taipei find common ground in their respective evaluations of the status of Hong Kong.) For Chinese Communists and Chinese Nationalists alike, reversion amounts to a correction of the historical record, or the resolution of an historical anomaly. The restoration of Chinese sovereignty is to be viewed as a moral act.

[1] This chapter is based upon information gathered in interviews conducted in Hong Kong, China, Japan, and Washington during the period of June–December 1996. The author particularly acknowledges the assistance of Mr. Alick Longhurst and LTC Dennis Blasko of the United States. The conclusions and judgments contained herein are those of the author, who bears sole responsibility for any errors. Similarly, the views expressed here do not necessarily represent those of the National Defense University or the Department of Defense.

It is precisely for this reason that the stationing of members of the Chinese People's Liberation Army (PLA) in Hong Kong is an issue of transcendent importance for China's leaders. For Beijing, the PLA presence is more than a matter of defending the territory against any external threat. Nor are PLA deployments viewed primarily as a means of enhancing China's military or strategic capabilities within the Asia Pacific region, although, as will be seen, such deployments have some relevance for Chinese strategic thinking.

Rather, for Beijing, the PLA presence in Hong Kong is an outward and visible symbol of the restoration of Chinese sovereignty over territories extorted from a succession of weak governments by militarily stronger Western powers. The PLA presence in Hong Kong symbolizes Beijing's determination to redress the wrongs of the past and is yet another manifestation of Chinese determination to assume the status of a strong, modern state that is able to pursue its interests effectively.

How one assesses the strategic and military implications of Hong Kong's reversion is very much a function of one's individual priorities and preconceptions. For those who view China primarily as a new and increasingly aggressive Great Power, the implications of the reversion can be very disturbing. According to this view, the acquisition of Hong Kong's wealth, intellectual capabilities, and productive capacity will provide Beijing with powerful weapons for use in its determined march to achieve regional preeminence. Hong Kong will provide yet another platform from which Beijing will spread its influence throughout the region.

Others who may acknowledge the challenge inherent in the emergence of a China as a "rich country with a strong army," but who also consider the impact of growing economic interdependence, have different sets of concerns. These analysts tend to emphasize the ways in which bearing responsibility for Hong Kong will impose constraints on Beijing's behavior within the international community. Overall, they judge that Hong Kong's reversion will serve to moderate Chinese behavior by involving Beijing more deeply in the web of the global economy. For them, the challenge is mainly political, diplomatic, and managerial.

Discrete populations exhibit a similarly wide variety of viewpoints. For example, for the people of Hong Kong, the impact of reversion on Beijing's strategic position in the region is not a matter of great salience. They remain primarily concerned with the impact of reversion on their own livelihoods and lifestyles. With respect to the Chinese military, as might be expected, members of the PLA tend to downplay the impact of Hong Kong's reversion on China's

185

overall regional strategic/military position. Interestingly, so, too, do members of the U.S. military establishment. On the other hand, military officers in Japan, Korea, Southeast Asia, and Taiwan tend to exhibit a higher level of concern about a potential Chinese military challenge in the future.

Each of these assessments probably has some basis in fact. Moreover, to the extent that perceptions affect actions, there may be some danger that these different assessments will produce a series of conflicting self-fulfilling prophecies.

Clarity might, however, be enhanced if two general propositions are kept in mind. First, the leaders of the Chinese Communist Party (CCP) will not awaken on the morning of July 1, 1997, and suddenly find themselves masters of a nation that is noticeably stronger or richer than it was on the evening of June 30. China will remain a developing country with yet another pocket of modernity that will have to be accommodated within the national political framework. This will increase the burden on a leadership that is already struggling to redefine the relationship between the center in Beijing and China's unevenly developing provinces and regions.

Second, China's domestic and foreign policy priorities will not change. At home, the leadership will continue to focus on maintaining internal stability, achieving disciplined economic development, privatizing the state sector of the economy, and consolidating the leadership transition.

At the same time, foreign and national security policies will continue to focus on the tasks of arresting Taiwan's perceived movement toward independence, managing ties with the United States (a nation that is perceived to be determined to thwart or contain China's progress), responding to a redefined U.S. security alliance with Japan, and safeguarding its position in the South China Sea. Moreover, the Chinese must do all these things in ways that do not threaten the regional peace and stability necessary for continued economic development.

In some respects, control of Hong Kong could eventually aid Beijing's efforts to meet these challenges and thereby enhance China's strategic position. In the near term, however, Beijing needs to demonstrate to the people of Hong Kong, to the people of Taiwan, and to the hopeful but skeptical regional powers that two very different political, economic, and social systems can coexist within one nation (that is, that the concept of "one country, two systems" can work), and this will constrain its freedom of action. To the extent that this is so, Hong Kong's reversion will be a liability in the military/strategic sense.

This will be most apparent during the five years or so immediately following the official transfer of power, until about mid-2002. During this period, the entire world will be monitoring Beijing's actions very closely. Also during this period, the possibility of some untoward incident occurring will be quite high. If Beijing and the SAR government were to judge it necessary to use the PLA to control the populace, and if the PLA were to act in a manner that recalls the events of Tiananmen Square in June 1989, the Chinese leadership would be vulnerable to an array of charges ranging from perfidy to incompetence. The "one country, two systems" concept will be judged to have failed, and the worst fears of a skeptical regional community will have been confirmed. However, if they are able to negotiate this transition period successfully, China's leaders will gain a high measure of confidence and credit. If that happens, Hong Kong's reversion will indeed increase Beijing's ability to extend Chinese influence throughout the region. Let us see how this is so.

THE MILITARY DIMENSION I: HONG KONG'S REVERSION AND BEIJING'S
REGIONAL MILITARY POSITION

Gaining control of Hong Kong will not have any major impact on China's military position within the Asia Pacific region. Hong Kong's harbor and its associated military and air facilities will not increase the ability of the PLA to concentrate force in any of the areas of greatest concern to Beijing: the Taiwan Strait, the South China Sea, or along the border with Vietnam. Several considerations uphold this assessment.

The PLA has little need or incentive to utilize Hong Kong facilities for taking military actions in any of these areas. Since 1949, the Chinese have constructed and developed facilities on Hainan Island, at Zhanjiang , and of course along the Fujian coast opposite Taiwan. Hainan and Zhanjiang are closer to the Spratly Archipelago in the South China Sea and to Vietnam than is Hong Kong. Similarly, the PLA's facilities in Fujian provide better direct access to Taiwan than would Hong Kong. Owing to Hong Kong's location, its facilities are not directly relevant to the axes of military effort, lines of communication, and supporting logistical grids that would need to come into play in the event of conflict.

Nor is there any incentive to mount a major effort to improve Hong Kong's military facilities for future use. Such a program would be extremely costly. It would divert scarce resources from other, more pressing areas and mission requirements, such as modernizing the nuclear force and developing a next-generation fighter aircraft; also, it would not increase substantially the PLA's ability to concentrate military force in the areas most requiring such concentrations.

There are also compelling political and diplomatic reasons for further discounting the military utility of Hong Kong to China. Even if conflict were to occur in the Taiwan Strait or in the South China Sea, it is most unlikely that the Chinese would wish to use Hong Kong as a major staging area, except as a last resort. To fight a local war from Hong Kong, or even to involve Hong Kong very directly in such a conflict, would be extremely disruptive to the economic life of the SAR.

Also, factors such as Hong Kong's large foreign population, the porous quality of its borders, and the doubtful loyalty of the Hong Kong community to the Beijing government mean that military activities need to be conducted from a base that would be far less than adequately secure. All in all, it is most unlikely that Hong Kong would figure very prominently in any plausible conflict scenario. On the contrary, political, diplomatic, and military considerations all provide Beijing with powerful incentives to downplay any Hong Kong connections with the PLA and to reduce the scope of Hong Kong's involvement in future conflicts in the region.

This reflects the fact that, owing to the political and economic circumstances surrounding its existence, Hong Kong has never loomed very large in Chinese military thinking. As noted elsewhere in this volume, since 1949, Beijing has found it in its interest to accord far more value to Hong Kong's economic and political roles than to military functions. Indeed, part of the unspoken bargain on maintaining Hong Kong's colonial status consisted of the understanding that the territory would not be used for sensitive purposes, especially that of projecting military force. The political and economic importance of Hong Kong has caused the territory to be insulated in a military/strategic sense. It is clearly in the Chinese interest to preserve this insulation.

In a strictly military sense, the reassertion of Chinese sovereignty probably causes Beijing to lose more than it gains. As noted, Hong Kong's reversion brings little or no benefit to the PLA in terms of increasing its military capabilities in either the short or longer terms. Although, in theory, Hong Kong gains a number of additional points from which to mount military operations, the economic and political costs of bringing these up to a useful operational standard are not worth the military benefit.

In fact, Hong Kong's reversion means that the PLA will acquire a new mission of helping Hong Kong's other disciplined services maintain internal order and stability, a mission that is fraught with political and, therefore, strategic risks. Also, the PLA is now responsible for conducting the military defense of a territory that history shows is notoriously difficult to defend. Overall, Hong Kong is a military liability for China.

THE MILITARY DIMENSION II: THE IMPACT OF REVERSION ON THE U.S. POSITION IN THE ASIA PACIFIC REGION

Does reversion in any way weaken the U.S. military/strategic position in the Asia Pacific region? If so, what should Washington do in order to compensate for its losses?

Hong Kong has never been a major factor in the U.S. military calculus. Since 1949, Washington has been an active participant in the unspoken bargain that called for all concerned parties to avoid any action that might threaten the status of Hong Kong as a free port and entrepot, and later as a manufacturing and financial center.

The United States always had strong incentives for participating in this bargain. By adopting a relatively unobtrusive stance in Hong Kong, Washington was able to support its ally, the United Kingdom – particularly in the 1950s, a period during which Britain was sorely pressed. Similarly, even though the United States did not have diplomatic relations with China, Washington saw economic and other benefits in maintaining an environment in which Hong Kong was not a point of contention. For its part, Beijing derived great, and well-documented, benefits from the colonial status of Hong Kong.

In these circumstances, and especially because the U.S. military had access to excellent bases and facilities elsewhere in the region, Washington deliberately refrained from defining Hong Kong as a focal point of its strategic posture. Hong Kong was of value to the U.S. military as a window into China and a recreation center for military personnel. The British Crown Colony had little or no importance as a staging or basing facility for U.S. military activities within the region. The reversion of Hong Kong to Chinese control does not remove the essence of the unspoken bargain. China and the United States have a continuing interest in maintaining the spirit of the status quo.

For the United States, the major questions concerning the future are as follows. First, what will be the post-reversion status of the United States Consulate General and its associated United States Defense Liaison Office (USDLO), which together manage U.S. military and military intelligence interests in Hong Kong? Second, will the U.S. Navy have continued access to Hong Kong as a recreation area?

At this writing, both of these questions have yet to be resolved. Although it seems probable that the United States Consulate General will remain in some form, the continued existence of the USDLO and the accessibility of the SAR to U.S. naval vessels remain to be decided. Despite the hopes of the Clinton administration, the first round of discussions held purposely to address such questions proved inconclusive. However, if the promise of improved bilateral relations between Washington and Beijing is fulfilled, the possibility of a continued U.S. military presence in Hong Kong will increase.

However, even if the U.S. military were to be denied access to Hong Kong, the consequences for the U.S. regional position would not be grave. The loss of access to Hong Kong would produce some inconvenience, as Navy ships would have to call at other ports. This, in turn, might require expanding or negotiating new agreements with other regional governments such as Singapore, Australia, the Philippines, and Thailand. Although this would produce temporary delays and necessitate some adjustments, it would not affect the ability of the U.S. Navy to operate effectively within the region.

On the other hand, even if the USDLO remains open, the U.S. military intelligence effort in Hong Kong is bound to suffer some degradation, at least temporarily. Although its importance has declined in recent years, Hong Kong remains a useful window into Southern China. Regardless of whether the USDLO remains, adjustments will be required.

There are two views about the future status of the U.S. military in Hong Kong. The optimistic view is that economic and political imperatives will motivate the Chinese government to accept the continued existence of both the Consulate General and the Defense Liaison Office. In this scenario, the staffs and many of the functions of both units would be reduced; the number of ship visits each year would decline from the present level of approximately fifty, to approximately thirty-five. The optimists also see the possibility of an increase in the number of visits to prereversion levels after two or three years. The more pessimistic view holds that the USDLO will cease to exist and that U.S. naval port calls will become a thing of the past. If U.S. relations with China continue to improve, the more optimistic assessment is likely to become reality; however, neither outcome – it is important to note – will have a significant impact upon the U.S. strategic position or its military capabilities within the region.

There is, however, one respect in which the reversion may impose some additional burden on the U.S. military. Should it become necessary to evacuate U.S. and other foreign nationals from Hong Kong, success will require a high degree of coordination between the U.S. and other concerned nations. It will also require the cooperation of the Chinese government. The United States would undoubtedly have to use naval assets based in Japan, while Japan would probably be expected to provide logistical support, possibly including vessels of the Maritime Self-Defense Force. Thus, any such operation or operations would directly test the recently redefined U.S.-Japan Security Alliance, Japan's relations with China, and China's relations with the United States. A non-combatant evacuation operation (NEO) would have serious, and potentially destabilizing, implications for the entire region.

THE BROAD STRATEGIC DIMENSION

Analyzing the impact of Hong Kong's reversion on China's military position within the region is a relatively straightforward task. However, the military dimension is but one aspect of the larger whole that is subsumed within the term "strategic."

Hong Kong's position within the global economic system, as well as China's recent history, guarantees that reversion to Chinese sovereignty will have a direct impact on how China is viewed within the region. If the reversion is smooth and successful, esteem for China within Asia Pacific will grow and Beijing's strategic position will be strengthened overall. If, on the other hand, the reversion is marked by stress and conflict, China's strategic position will be diminished. Ultimately, therefore, analysis of the strategic impact of Hong Kong's reversion must consider "soft" questions related to perceptions, intentions, and points of leverage arising from a wide variety of sometimes elusive economic, political, historical – and, in the case of Hong Kong, moral – sources.

THE BROAD STRATEGIC DIMENSION I: THE IMPACT OF HONG KONG'S REVERSION ON THE SITUATION IN THE TAIWAN STRAIT

China's President Jiang Zemin has made it clear that the reassertion of Chinese sovereignty over Hong Kong is but one step on the road to complete national reunification. In 1999, Beijing's attention will turn to Macao and then to the real prize, Taiwan.

Regaining sovereignty over Hong Kong will not increase Beijing's ability to influence cross-strait relations by bringing military pressure to bear against Taiwan. The dynamics of the military situation in the Taiwan Strait originate in Beijing, Taipei, and, to a lesser extent, Washington – they should not be greatly or directly influenced in the short term by what transpires in Hong Kong. Similarly, political and economic considerations will discourage Beijing from using Hong Kong as a major base for military operations against Taiwan. However, in a broader strategic sense, Hong Kong's reversion will almost certainly have an impact on the pattern of cross-strait political relations and on the atmosphere in which they are conducted.

The events of July 1, 1997, will give concrete form to, and establish a momentum for, the national reunification process outlined by Jiang in general terms. This, in turn, should enable Beijing to move from its present reactive policies toward regaining some initiative in the cross-strait relationship. For example, reversion will mean that Taiwan's trade with Hong Kong will de facto become direct trade with China. Taiwan will also be forced to amend its present policy of no direct contacts with China and deal directly with the mainland in other respects, including mail, shipping, and individual travel. Beijing has sought direct contact for many years, and now it will become reality. Direct contacts between Taipei and Hong Kong will provide China with certain new leverages in forging cross-strait links. All in all, the Taiwan leadership will face the challenge of responding to a new set of circumstances in which Beijing has more leverage than has thus far been the case.

Moreover, the pressure for Taipei to respond, one way or another, should increase with the passage of time. If the transition is smooth, then Beijing should be able to claim that the "one country, two systems" formula works, and Taipei will obviously face increased pressure from China (and from the regional powers) to enter into some form of cross-strait interaction designed to achieve integration in the future. If, on the other hand, the transition is marked by conflict, Taiwan's resistance to reintegration with China is likely to intensify, and Taipei will try, albeit only with great difficulty and risk, to move in a direction of its own.

More likely than not, Hong Kong's reversion will have a negative impact on relations between China and Taiwan, at least in the short run. This is because, in Taipei's view, Beijing's "one country, two systems" formulation really means two economic systems but only one political system. The political reality is that Taipei does not believe that the present Chinese government is willing or able to tolerate a democratic political system. Moreover, in Taiwan (as in Hong Kong), China's willingness to accept a different economic system is regarded as being beside the point because there is, in actuality, very little difference between the two sides on economic questions.

Rather, the differences arise as a result of divergent views on the best form of political and social organization. Taiwan sees itself as a pluralist, civil society and judges that China is years away from achieving a similar state of development. As a result, there is little incentive in Taiwan to compromise with China, or even to enter into a long-term dialogue designed to produce a formula for reunification.

Therefore, in the short term Taipei is likely to continue to stonewall and make only the most essential and formal concessions in response to increased Chinese and other external pressures. Although Beijing is in no hurry to achieve reunification, the leadership remains deeply concerned about what they perceive to be an increasingly dominant tendency toward independence among the island's people. China's leaders are, accordingly, determined to arrest this perceived drift. In a corollary manner, they also appear to be growing less willing to accept a situation in which there is no movement at all. Taiwan will find it extremely difficult to maintain a strategy of stalling.

Hong Kong's reversion, therefore, will not only give Beijing an improved platform from which to approach cross-strait relations, it will also provide the Chinese with a wider range of economic and political instruments. Chinese and other external pressures on Taipei to achieve some compromise or accommodation with Beijing will increase; internal resistance to such compromise is also likely to rise. This contradiction has the potential to increase the volatility of ties between Beijing and Taipei. It also raises the already better-than-even odds of another crisis erupting in the Taiwan Strait.

THE BROAD STRATEGIC DIMENSION II: HONG KONG'S REVERSION AND
CHINA'S STATUS IN THE ASIA PACIFIC REGION

The reversion of Hong Kong will produce a number of advantages and disadvantages for China, all of which bear directly on China's status within the Asia Pacific region. Overall, the reversion will help to confirm and validate within the region the notion of a China that is making deliberate and steady progress toward achieving its national reunification goals. Reversion will also be interpreted as yet another indicator of China's rise to the status of a major power; thus it could influence the flow of regional political currents. Although analysts in the various capitals of the region may disagree about the desirability of this latest confirmation of a rising China, all will agree that it is impossible to check Beijing's momentum.

Ronald N. Montaperto

Regional leaders as a whole give their counterparts in Beijing high marks for their efforts to date in conducting and managing negotiations with Britain. If, as seems likely, the approach to July 1, 1997, proceeds peacefully, Beijing will receive even more credit for managing the preliminary stages of the reversion process in an efficient and responsible manner. Moreover, regional leaders believe that Beijing not only shares their hope for a smooth transition that will enable the Hong Kong pattern of economic life to continue, but also is prepared to work actively to achieve that goal.

It is also likely that, at least in the short term, regaining sovereignty over Hong Kong will help partially to offset regional concerns about China's political unity and stability. The reversion seems likely to reinforce the position of the Jiang Zemin leadership. Jiang will be able to claim with some justification that he has completed a major step in the process of national reunification, as a result of which Beijing is now well positioned to deal with Macao, and especially Taiwan, with greater credibility.

If the current upward trajectory in U.S.–China relations continues, and if the transition in Hong Kong does in fact proceed smoothly, Jiang will approach the Fifteenth National Congress of the Chinese Communist Party, scheduled for October/November 1997, with well-burnished credentials as an effective leader who is able to guide China successfully into the post–Deng Xiaoping era. This will do much to allay fears outside of China about instability at the highest levels of political leadership. It will also calm regional concerns that political instability in China might also produce negative economic and political consequences for the region. This, too, will contribute to China's regional status and prestige.

By the same token, China's regional status could also be adversely affected if difficulties arise in the future. As other contributors to this volume have noted, Beijing must complete the integration of Hong Kong politically as well as economically. Much could go wrong in Beijing as the leadership attempts to integrate the SAR into China's increasingly fragile national political/administrative framework. Much can also go wrong in Hong Kong as the SAR government continues to interact with Beijing in the context of Hong Kong's different political and social systems.

Beijing judges that the key to containing discontent in Hong Kong, as with its own population, lies in maintaining the pace and scale of Hong Kong's economic dynamism. This judgment may prove to be incorrect. It may be that, by placing overwhelming emphasis on economic matters and concerns, China's leaders have in fact underestimated the importance of political values and ideas

194

to the people of Hong Kong. However, even if demonstrations do occur, it does not necessarily follow that China's relations with the other powers of the region will suffer significant damage. This is because Beijing also appears to believe that, for the regional powers, the litmus test of its future dealings with Hong Kong will reside in the perception of how well Hong Kong's economic system is maintained rather than in how well Beijing and the SAR respond to political currents within Hong Kong. This has certainly been the focus of Beijing's efforts to date, and the trend is likely to continue.

In fact, the Chinese appear to be taking a gamble that Hong Kong's economic importance within the region will help to offset any tendencies by the regional powers to diminish their ties with China as a result of mistakes Beijing makes in the political arena. If reactions to China in the wake of the PLA suppression of the Tiananmen demonstrations are a reliable indicator, the judgment may well prove to be correct. If so, China's strategic position within the region will suffer little more than a temporary decline. Only in the United States and Taiwan do memories of the Tiananmen repression continue to be of political relevance.

Even so, some vulnerability remains. If, as many Hong Kong residents and analysts anticipate, reversion results in the slow decay of Hong Kong's commercial, manufacturing, legal, and social service infrastructures, and if this decay produces a decline in Hong Kong's economic life and a commensurate loss of external commercial and financial presence, then China will have to accept responsibility and its strategic position will diminish accordingly. Years will pass before the final verdict is rendered.

THE BROAD STRATEGIC DIMENSION III: THE IMPACT OF REVERSION ON U.S. RELATIONS WITH CHINA

No discussion of the military/strategic implications of Hong Kong's reversion can be complete without some reference to how the reversion process might affect relations between Washington and Beijing. Although the broad outlines of any possible impact have already been suggested both here and elsewhere in this volume, some additional comments are in order.

The issue of U.S. commercial and military access to Hong Kong is likely to be merely the bellwether of U.S. relations with China rather than a major determinant of the pattern of those relations. If bilateral ties are sound in other respects, the U.S. position in Hong Kong will also be sound.

However, even if U.S.–China relations continue to reflect the cyclical pattern of the years since 1989, the Chinese are likely to think very carefully indeed about treating the U.S. position in the SAR as a point of leverage in managing bilateral ties. Doing so would undermine the confidence of the foreign business community in their ability to operate within the SAR. Many might simply transfer their operations to other locations. It is doubtful that Beijing would allow the requirements of dealing with Washington to have an adverse impact on Hong Kong's overall economic position.

Nonetheless, in the short to mid-term, the reversion of Hong Kong will almost certainly become an irritant in U.S.–China relations. Powerful political interests in the United States will examine the evolution of the reversion process with critical eyes. These interests will focus on human rights, and will scrutinize closely the responses of Beijing and the SAR government to political currents in Hong Kong.

It is reasonable to expect that the next few years will witness an increase in the number of critical studies and reports on Hong Kong issued by various think tanks, non-governmental organizations, and the U.S. Congress. The congressional practice of producing resolutions and legislation designed to deal with one aspect or another of the reversion process is also likely to continue. This line of critical commentary and activity, however muted, is bound to complicate relations between Washington and Beijing. As with similar U.S. actions with respect to Taiwan and the South China Sea, Beijing will treat them as unjustifiable intrusions into Chinese internal affairs.

A similar level of irritation might emerge if the Hong Kong infrastructure does in fact decay in the face of China's different approach to administrative, legal, and financial management. Businesspeople accustomed to doing business according to the traditional Hong Kong pattern are likely to ask their governments to intercede. Considering Chinese responses to U.S. initiatives on intellectual property issues, efforts by any U.S. administration will probably also receive a cold shoulder. It is probably impossible to prevent the rise of such tensions from these and other sources. Both sides will be challenged to accept them as irritants and to ensure that they are not allowed to affect other aspects of bilateral relations.

In conclusion, there is probably only one set of circumstances under which Hong Kong's reversion could cause major damage to U.S. relations with China. If Beijing were to authorize the use of the PLA to suppress a mass demonstration, and if such PLA activities were to result in the loss of human life, the U.S. government would, as in 1989, face the strongest possible pressure to react by restricting bilateral ties. The Taiwan factor would also come into play. A

Tiananmen-like event would undoubtedly stiffen Taiwan resistance to reunification with the mainland while simultaneously increasing pressures on the U.S. government to expand support for the island. Either action by a U.S. administration would seriously damage ties between Washington and Beijing.

9

Hong Kong and China's Integration into the International Community[1]

MICHAEL YAHUDA

THE way in which the Chinese authorities manage the return of Hong Kong will greatly affect the next stage of China's integration into the international community. China is already a major player in international politics and in the international economy. However, its domestic political and economic structures and practices are not yet fully congruent with those of the international community. Hong Kong, by contrast, is in many ways regarded as a model of good practice according to the conventions and ideals espoused by the leading institutions of the international economy. Although Hong Kong, as a British colony, has not been an assertive political entity on the world stage, it has nevertheless been of political importance. In part, that importance has flowed from its role both as an international financial center of major regional significance and as a meeting point between different Chinese communities.

If the return of Hong Kong is managed well – so that its autonomy as a separate system follows in practice the outline of the Sino-British agreement and the Basic Law – the beneficial consequences for China will inevitably serve to accelerate and deepen its integration into the international community. This will enable the Chinese Communist authorities to demonstrate a capacity to encompass, within the sovereignty of the People's Republic of China (PRC), an enclave that follows laissez-faire capitalism under the rule of law, with an independent judiciary, a freely and fairly elected legislature, and an autonomous executive guided by a politically neutral and efficient civil service that allows its people basic freedoms. Under such conditions, Hong Kong's position will be enhanced; it will be more self-governing than it ever was as a British colony.

[1] This chapter draws heavily on my book *Hong Kong: China's Challenge* (London & New York: Routledge, 1996).

Hong Kong, China, and the International Community

Under these circumstances, Beijing will feel more confident about its policies toward Taiwan, and many of the anxieties of people on the island will diminish; this will lead to a general relaxation of tensions, which in turn will ease Beijing's relations with Washington and Tokyo. Farther afield, many of the Chinese communities in Southeast Asia will be less doubtful about the durability and continued adaptability of reformist tendencies in China.[2] The governments of Southeast Asian countries, too, will feel more positive about their dealings with China and will find even greater merit in their policies of constructive engagement with Beijing. Japan will become more confident not only concerning the significant investments it has directed toward Hong Kong but, more important, concerning its prospects for cooperative, as opposed to conflictual, relations with China as a rising power. Similar reactions will occur in the United States, where closer attention is being paid not only to the economic welfare of Hong Kong but also – and perhaps even more important – to the continuity of the political structures and liberties of the territory. A China that can manage the return of Hong Kong will find that many of its perennial problems with the United States will diminish. Clearly, a Chinese government that demonstrates respect for the Hong Kong system, and that allows the territory to continue to flourish as an international financial center with its own international personality, will find that its path of entry to remaining international economic institutions, notably the World Trade Organization (WTO), will ease correspondingly.

If a smooth transition is followed by a successful management of Hong Kong's autonomy in accordance with the commitments of the Chinese government in the Sino-British Declaration and the Basic Law, China's leaders will have passed their first real test in the post–Deng Xiaoping period. That will undoubtedly boost their confidence and ease the problems of political succession within China. The fifteenth National Congress of the Chinese Communist Party is due to convene in October 1997, only three to four months after the return of Hong Kong. Since the event has been presented within China as a major patriotic occasion of immense historic significance, the new leadership – and Jiang Zemin in particular – will find its prestige enhanced and its tasks made easier. They can then profess a more confident form of nationalism,

---

[2] Wang Gungwu, the leading historian of the overseas Chinese, has argued that ethnic Chinese businesspeople in Southeast Asia are still waiting for clearer signs of stability in the PRC and of its government's "capacity to adjust to new global and regional relationships." Meanwhile, he observed, the wealthiest among them with "bases in Hong Kong" have so far limited themselves to "short term investments." See Wang Gungwu, "Greater China and the Overseas Chinese," *The China Quarterly* (Special Issue: *Greater China*), December 1993, no. 136, p. 928.

reinforced by a more welcoming and less suspicious approach from the international economic community and the Western world as a whole.[3]

Conversely, if the return of Hong Kong is handled badly, leading to a major exodus of professional and wealthy residents, the damage to China will be deep and wide-ranging. Tension with Taiwan will increase if Beijing's policy of "one country, two systems" is shown to be inoperable even where circumstances are ostensibly favorable. This failure will inevitably sour Beijing's relations within the Asia Pacific region generally, and with Washington and Tokyo particularly. The ethnic Chinese communities overseas will feel that they have lost their home, their "capital city."[4] That will undoubtedly affect adversely the flow of direct foreign investment into China. Southeast Asian governments will lose confidence in their policies of constructive engagement and look for other means to balance growing Chinese power. A manifest failure by the Chinese government in Hong Kong will alarm the international financial community, leading to a reversal of investment trends and delaying considerably China's accession to the WTO.

If the reversion does not proceed smoothly, the new Chinese leadership will have failed its first test and its political standing will be noticeably damaged just at the point when the Fifteenth Party Congress is due to convene and affirm the post-Deng leadership and its program for the future. Under such conditions – with tensions increasing abroad, foreign investments declining, and the economy slowing – the leadership will likely turn inward. Truculence will be displayed abroad, and at home a harder line will be pursued in order to contain the rise in social tensions that would almost certainly follow a slowing of economic growth. The regime would almost certainly feel that its very existence was under threat.

Given how much depends on the outcome of the return of Hong Kong, it is remarkable that the event remains shrouded with so much doubt and uncertainty. This is all the more surprising in view of the fact that none of the principal parties has the slightest interest in failure. The Chinese side not only stands to lose a prize economic asset, but the survival of the regime could be at stake. The people of Hong Kong and their various groups and parties, including the Democratic Party, which has won the majority of votes in two succes-

---

[3] For an analysis of the important distinctions between the different manifestations of Chinese nationalism and their implications for the conduct of foreign relations, see Allen S. Whiting, "Chinese Nationalism and Foreign Policy after Deng," *The China Quarterly,* no. 142, June 1995, pp. 295–316.

[4] Dick Wilson, *Hong Kong! Hong Kong!* (London: Unwin Hyman, 1990), p. 31.

sive elections, have no interest in the collapse of Hong Kong. Nor do the British, whose international prestige, significant economic interests, and prospects in the region would be irretrievably damaged by failure. This chapter first seeks to explain why the outcome of reversion remains in doubt. It then considers the immediate prospects before concluding with an assessment of the probable outcome and its implications for China.

A PECULIAR NEGLECT

Curiously, the larger political significance of Hong Kong has been little discussed in Beijing. In fact, little attention has been paid to Hong Kong through the years. As a place administered by the British, but technically claimed by China, it has occupied a kind of bureaucratic no-man's-land: Hong Kong was neither a domestic issue nor a foreign affairs issue. Various local conventions and practices had evolved pragmatically over the years to manage cross-border affairs and to take advantage of the anomalous condition of the territory, while the significant issues concerning Hong Kong were kept under the strict personal control of the supreme leaders. Thus, Hong Kong was under the personal charge of Mao Zedong and Zhou Enlai; after them, Deng Xiaoping took the key decisions. It was he who controlled the negotiations with Britain leading to the Joint Declaration in 1984, and it was he who supervised the key policy issues of the transition thereafter until he became incapacitated by advanced age toward the end of 1993.

Interestingly, the official organizations that deal with Hong Kong are not part of any of the major *xitong* (bureaucratic systems) inherent in the Chinese administrative system, with the result that they are not linked with the many organizations that have developed economic interests in the territory. The Ministry of Foreign Affairs, which nominally handles negotiations with the British Foreign Office, and similar ministries elsewhere, does not have an obvious domestic constituency. The Hong Kong and Macao Affairs Office, which enjoys ministerial status under the State Council, is not linked or affiliated with any of the other ministries. Unlike its first head, Liao Chengzhi, who died in 1983, Lu Ping has not been a close and trusted colleague of the core leader, and he is not a senior figure in the party hierarchy. The Xinhua Branch in Hong Kong is also an orphan within the Chinese bureaucracy, answerable in part to the Ministry of Foreign Affairs, the formal Xinhua Agency in Beijing, and a number of different departments of the Central Committee of the Communist

201

Party. Its head, Zhou Nan, like Lu Ping, does not rank high in the Communist Party.

Moreover, unlike the case of Taiwan, which may also be considered to inhabit a kind of limbo outside the conventional domestic or external bureaucratic spheres, Hong Kong has not been the subject of prolonged, intense concern for the Chinese military and political elites. Similarly, it has not been at the core of China's national security interests or at the center of Beijing's relations with the United States. The small part that Hong Kong has occupied in Chinese political consciousness is reflected in the absence of a single institute devoted to Hong Kong in the Chinese Academy of Social Sciences and of any similar center or society at any of the higher-education institutions except for one, in Zhongshan University in Guangzhou, which focuses mainly on economics. Indeed, over the past few years, none of my various academic hosts in Beijing has been able to identify a single researcher with whom I could discuss socio-economic developments within Hong Kong, yet there was never an absence of researchers who claimed to have studied these developments within Taiwan. This void was all the more remarkable in view of the many organizations and people who had economic interests in Hong Kong, some of whom, like the Bank of China, had a cumulative experience of nearly fifty years.

In the absence of informed opinion, it is hardly surprising that myths and stereotypes about Hong Kong and its people flourish in Beijing and elsewhere, particularly in northern China. At the popular level and even among intellectuals, the view commonly held is that the people of Hong Kong are to some extent tainted by having lived under British capitalist colonial rule. They are therefore regarded as corrupt, and therefore as a corrupting influence in the mainland; they are alleged to bribe officials and to exploit disadvantaged fellow countrymen. As compatriots they are thought to have benefited uniquely from their proximity to the mainland, which is said to account for much of their prosperity. Northern people typically see that prosperity as the product of a windfall rather than the result of the industry, entrepreneurialism, and professionalism of Hong Kong's people. Much of the prejudice of the northerners against the perceived excessive commercialism and lack of intellectual interests of the Cantonese is directed still more strongly against the people of Hong Kong. In short, considerable resentment and envy exists, which is fueled by ignorance. Even professionals in Beijing exhibit an alarming lack of understanding of China's officially declared position about the concept of "one country, two systems" and how it is to be applied to Hong Kong. Many appear to believe that after the transition to Chinese sovereignty, they will be able to find work in

Hong Kong where they, too, will enjoy salaries some hundredfold more than they can earn on the Chinese mainland. All they will need is the right *guanxi* (personal connections) with the appropriate officials.

Since the establishment of the PRC in 1949, China and Hong Kong have evolved in fundamentally different ways with very little institutional contact between them. In the early years, people such as Liao Chengzhi, who were close to the senior leaders in Beijing, had extensive ties with the leading business families in the Chinese communities overseas as well as with members of Zhou Enlai's entourage, all of whom were familiar with conditions in Hong Kong during and after the Japanese occupation. However, the personal ties that had served Beijing well in the 1950s and into the 1960s were weakened during the political upheavals in China. When the elderly survivors in Beijing attempted to rebuild relationships in the late 1970s, conditions had changed; they were out of touch with the new middle class of Hong Kong and its modern lifestyle.

Although Hong Kong people were able to visit family members resident across the border, these social contacts did not impinge on the conduct of the two separate systems. The people of Hong Kong are largely made up of refugees or the children of refugees who had fled from the regime of mainland China. Their life experiences have made them different social and political beings. Their evolution under British rule has accustomed them to the rule of law and to operating in a highly complex and diverse civil society where they have enjoyed all the basic liberties of a Western liberal system, save the right to choose their rulers. They have not experienced the tumultuous upheavals of the political history of the PRC, with the callous loss of life and suffering inflicted on countless millions. Nor have they been subject to the pervasive and often arbitrary discipline of a ruling Communist party. Even the Chinese officials who are responsible for managing relations with Hong Kong often exhibit a lack of understanding of the key characteristics that underpin the territory's way of life. Xu Jiatun, the former head of the Xinhua branch in Hong Kong, complained in 1988 about his Communist colleagues back in China: "They always judge capitalism by old standards. They do not notice its changes. Had I not worked in Hong Kong for four years, I would probably have entertained the same idea as those comrades."[5] Local-born senior journalists and officials who have lived and worked for Communist publications in Hong Kong for all or most of their lives complain privately that their colleagues from the main-

---

[5] Kevin Rafferty, *City on the Rocks: Hong Kong's Uncertain Future* (London: Penguin, revised edition, 1991), p. 492.

land have a "totally different mentality" that causes them to misunderstand "even simple things" about Hong Kong.[6]

There are signs that senior leaders in Beijing are aware that something is seriously amiss in their understanding of Hong Kong. In a talk in March 1995, Li Ruihuan, a member of the Standing Committee of the Politburo of the Chinese Communist Party, publicly admitted that the leaders had a dangerously insufficient understanding of Hong Kong. He warned that "taking Hong Kong back is an unusually complicated job" with "many issues and difficulties" and that it is "inevitable that we shall fail to manage some things appropriately and well." He then famously compared Hong Kong to a 100-year-old Yixing teapot whose value lay in some sediments attached to the inside. The well-meaning but ignorant old lady who owned the pot cleaned away the sediments, whereupon her prospective purchaser pronounced the pot valueless. Li drove home his message, concluding: "If you don't understand something, you are unaware of what makes it valuable and it will be difficult to keep it intact."[7]

THE TROUBLED NEGOTIATIONS[8]

Chinese lack of expertise and understanding of Hong Kong has been compounded by the distrust and misunderstandings that have dogged their negotiations with Britain. China has refused to entertain Great Britain's claims that it is motivated by moral responsibilities toward the people of Hong Kong as anything other than hypocrisy or a smoke screen to conceal plans to abscond with the capital resources of Hong Kong and/or to destabilize the Communist regime.[9] Indeed, from the outset, Deng Xiaoping admonished his negotiators to

---

[6] From the author's interviews with various journalists and officials attached to the Xinhua News Agency and its related newspapers in Hong Kong.

[7] Li Ruihuan's address to the Hong Kong and Macao representatives to the Chinese People's Political Consultative Conference on March 13, 1995, was carried in full in the Hong Kong Communist-controlled newspaper *Wen Wei Po,* and is available in English translation in BBC, *Summary of World Broadcasts,* FE/2253/F1–4.

[8] For more extended analysis, see Michael Yahuda, *Hong Kong: China's Challenge,* op. cit., chap. 3, pp. 61–82.

[9] Sir Percy Cradock, who played a leading role in the negotiations from 1978 to 1992, and who was later to criticize Governor Patten for his handling of China, described the Chinese view as follows: "We [British] were in Hong Kong to exploit the territory and extract revenue from it. The British government exercised control over British businessmen there and manipulated the local currency for political ends, as, for example, in the financial crisis of September 1983. The negotiation would be a struggle in which the British as colonialists would prove both obstinate and devious. Deng warned against their tricks. In the end, British commercial and financial interests would need to be satisfied; on this point, they were prepared to talk. Our assurances that we

"watch those British lest they run away with the money."[10] The British have not always helped their own cause; initially, they underestimated the depth of the Chinese attachment to sovereignty, and they also took an excessively legalistic approach. Thus, they approached Deng Xiaoping, of all people, by attempting to draw a distinction between the head lease of the 1898 treaty and the crown leases that were derived from that. The futility of that subtle distinction was compounded when the initial rounds of formal negotiations began in 1982: The British tried to persuade the Chinese to allow continued British administration of Hong Kong during the transfer of formal legal mechanisms of sovereignty. It encouraged the Chinese to recognize that they could not manage Hong Kong. This was after the Chinese premier had earlier disclosed to a visiting British minister his view of how the policy of "one country, two systems" would be applied to the territory.[11]

Thus Chinese officials have treated with great skepticism British attempts to familiarize them with the inner workings of Hong Kong and the absolute centrality of the rule of law, an apolitical civil service, basic freedoms, and the free flow of information. The Chinese appear to have been puzzled by the seriousness with which Britain sought to discharge its responsibilities in preparing for the transition from the time of the Joint Declaration in 1984 to the handover in 1997. Indeed, the Chinese side has rued its agreement to settle for a Joint Liaison Group as opposed to the Joint Commission for that thirteen-year transition period. The Joint Declaration specified that the two sides would cooperate closely in the latter stage of the transition; however, in acquiescing to British insistence on maintaining effective authority to the end, the Chinese found that they had forfeited control and that they could not compel the British to "cooperate" on their terms. They had expected Great Britain, as a declining power with only economic interests remaining, to follow Beijing's wishes. The furor over Chris Patten's electoral reforms may be traced to that in the final analysis. The end result was that the one mechanism through which China could have familiarized itself with Hong Kong and its distinctive way of life was ruled out almost from the start.

---

sought only the well-being of the people of Hong Kong and recognized a moral responsibility for them were found both baffling and hypocritical." See Cradock, *Experiences of China* (London: John Murray, 1994), pp. 210–11.

[10] As told to the author in 1992 by a Chinese official closely involved in the negotiations.

[11] For details of these negotiations, see Robert Cottrell, *The End of Hong Kong, The Secret Diplomacy of Imperial Retreat* (London: John Murray, 1993)

Michael Yahuda

The beginning of the divide between Great Britain and China was occasioned by the Tiananmen killings of June 4, 1989. British Governor Sir David Wilson responded to the outcry of a million demonstrators in the streets of Hong Kong by seeking a way to retain public confidence in the city while condemning Beijing. Beijing, which had already begun to see Hong Kong less as an economic asset and more as a base for political subversion, was outraged. It fulminated against the proposed issue of British passports to 50,000 heads of family, and it denounced the Bill of Rights. It considered the proposed new airport to be a device by which the British could gain a degree of control over Hong Kong; British consent was required for any project that extended beyond the date of the reversion of sovereignty. Beijing viewed Governor Chris Patten's proposals for electoral reform in 1992, coupled with the way he introduced them, as part of a wider Western plot to destabilize Hong Kong and China. In effect, two years were lost until the looming deadline of 1997 began to induce flexibility on both sides toward the end of 1995.

THE ENDGAME

Beginning in January 1996, China was compelled to take the leading role in accordance with the Basic Law and, for the first time, address the people of Hong Kong directly. To this end it set up a Preparatory Committee (PC) of 150 members, including 94 Hong Kong residents. Although members of the Democratic Party were excluded, membership was more broadly representative than had been feared – even though Beijing had taken care to ensure that it would retain full control. The PC then went through the charade of "electing" a 400-member Selection Committee. This committee was charged with "electing" a Chief Executive to replace the Governor in 1997 and, more controversially, with "electing" members of a Provisional Legislative Council (PLC) to replace temporarily the Legislative Council elected by the people of Hong Kong in 1995. The existence of the PLC raises great difficulties: Its legality is doubtful, and, by coexisting with the duly elected Legislative Council, it threatens to undermine the effectiveness of government administration before the transition. It could impose divided loyalties on the Chief Executive designate that could weaken his standing in advance of assuming office. Upon the transfer of authority on July 1, 1997, a PLC that lacks the legitimacy of a duly elected legislature will pass laws regarding subversion and a new electoral system. Even though the PLC is slated to last no longer than a year, it could do much to weaken confidence and threaten the independence of the judiciary, and it could fail to hold the Chief Executive to account.

Clearly, a great danger exists that things could go awry, despite the common interests of all sides in a smooth transition. Nevertheless, there are grounds for cautious optimism. Conscious of the urgency of the situation – as demonstrated by the giant clock in Tiananmen Square that counts down the days, the minutes, and seconds to the handover – the Chinese have finally recognized the need to cooperate with Great Britain. Since the autumn of 1995, agreements have been reached on several outstanding matters. Also there are signs of new found Chinese flexibility in the PLC, with regard to both putative membership and its duration and role. Perhaps even more important, the Chinese side has softened its approach toward the Hong Kong Democrats. The latter represent the vast majority of the voting public; as long as Beijing dismissed them as subversives, they risked alienating the bulk of the professional and middle-class people whose work is essential if the city is to survive as a major economic and financial hub. Far from excluding them, Beijing has encouraged them to participate in the PLC, knowing that that will give that body the aura of legitimacy that it manifestly lacks. The Democrats have so far refused, as any such participation would undermine their credentials as truly elected representatives. However, they have said that they would participate in any electoral system that the PLC might establish. This suggests that some sort of accommodation might be feasible.

Beijing must also sort out its own institutional confusion. The Hong Kong Branch of the New China News Agency cannot be allowed to continue as the arm of the Chinese government without undermining the authority of the Chief Executive of the future Hong Kong Special Administrative Region (HKSAR). It must be restructured, and Beijing should address this sooner rather than later. Similarly, the functions of the Hong Kong Macao Affairs Office must be changed. Since the Chief Executive of Hong Kong will be constitutionally superior to any provincial governor and will be required to report on the work of his government to the Premier of the State Council, the Hong Kong Macao Affairs Office could perhaps be transformed into an office to assist the Premier in dealing with Hong Kong.

The Chief Executive designate should have the opportunity to acquire a thorough understanding of the governance of Hong Kong through working with the Governor, the Chief Secretary, and other leading civil servants over a period of more than six months before the formal transition. Additionally, he should have the opportunity to familiarize himself and, ideally, Beijing with the surprisingly full range of activities in which Hong Kong expresses its independent international identity – ostensibly confined to economic matters.

Hong Kong's peculiar status is recognized internationally. The governments of about ninety states are represented by consular or trade missions, and a number of sub-national governments (such as provinces and states) also maintain representative offices in the territory. Since these are nominally accredited to the United Kingdom, Hong Kong is not required to reciprocate. However, Hong Kong probably hosts more foreign diplomatic offices than most states in the world.[12] A 1992 act of Congress required the United States to treat Hong Kong as "a non-sovereign entity distinct from China for the purposes of domestic law based on the principles of the 1984 Sino-British Joint Declaration." The act further stated that the United States should "continue to fulfill its obligations to Hong Kong under international agreements as long as Hong Kong reciprocates, regardless of whether the People's Republic of China is a party to the particular international agreement." It added that Hong Kong should continue to be treated "as a separate territory in economic and trade matters." Canada had passed an act one year earlier which also gave special consideration to Hong Kong. An expert in international relations in Hong Kong observed: "Compared with other autonomous entities, Hong Kong's formal authority to conduct its external economic and cultural relations and to take part in international organizations is therefore unparalleled."[13]

Because of Hong Kong's special political position, the activities of the Hong Kong government in international affairs have been confined primarily to economic matters. Its external representatives, for example, have ignored most international political and security issues, confining themselves largely to trade negotiations and trade and industrial promotion. Hong Kong, however, did follow the British position in severing economic links with Argentina during the Falklands War, and in 1986 it imposed import restrictions on South African goods in line with British policy. Perhaps the most notable example of Hong Kong's engagement in international politics was the lobbying of the U.S. government between 1989 and 1994 to renew most-favored-nation treatment to imports from China. In this case, Hong Kong's own economic interests were

---

[12] Bernard H. K. Luk, "Hong Kong's International Presence," in Donald McMillen & Man Si-wai (eds.), *The Other Hong Kong Report 1994* (Hong Kong: The Chinese University Press, 1994), p. 435.

[13] James T. H. Tang, "Hong Kong's International Status," *The Pacific Review*, vol. 6(3), 1993, p. 208.

directly involved; however, this activity demonstrated that the growing connection between politics and economics may yet draw Hong Kong into a more active role in overlapping areas between the two.[14]

Hong Kong's disengagement from international politics has been of great significance in another sense – especially to China. During the Cold War period, its detachment facilitated its role as a gateway to the international capitalist economy. Since then, Hong Kong has been the gateway for countries that did not at first recognize the PRC – notably South Korea, and especially Taiwan. Moreover, the absence of sovereignty has enabled Hong Kong to cultivate the more informal aspects of international relationships and the various links with the overseas Chinese in Southeast Asia. Hong Kong is also a member or associate member of many international and regional organizations including the Asia Development Bank; the General Agreement on Tariff and Trade (GATT) and GATT's successor, the WTO; the UN Economic and Social Commission for Asia and the Pacific; the Asia Pacific Economic Cooperation forum (APEC); Interpol; and many others. In fact, membership in thirty such organizations has been approved by the Sino-British Joint Liaison Group.

The remaining transition period should provide an opportunity for the Chief Executive designate and his team to establish a working relationship with Beijing on these external matters. That is particularly important because, according to the existing agreements, Beijing will enjoy control over defense and foreign affairs. However, "control" may be defined in practice as allowing Beijing to subordinate Hong Kong's existing international identity and independent activities to its own ends.

CAUTIOUS OPTIMISM

It is difficult to overestimate the importance to Beijing of Hong Kong's reversion. As noted at the outset of this chapter, the process involves nearly all the key issues of China's contemporary foreign relations, and – perhaps even more pressing from the perspective of the post-Deng leadership – if mishandled, the return of Hong Kong could contribute to undermining the Communist regime. Accordingly, it is hardly surprising to note that as the deadline of July 1, 1997, approaches, China has become more flexible, and its desire to cooperate with Great Britain has become more evident. For example, the earlier attempts to polarize Hong Kong residents into either "pro-China" or "pro-British" camps

---

[14] Ibid., pp. 211–13.

have ceased, as have the public attacks upon Governor Chris Patten. Attempts have also been made to reach out to members of the Democratic Party. There can be no doubt of Beijing's intention to manage the return well.

As yet, it is unclear what these good intentions mean in practical terms from Beijing's perspective. Britain's history of negotiations with China is marked by Chinese uncertainty. Beyond setting forth some broad general guiding principles and objectives, Chinese negotiators have traditionally avoided discussion of specific content and detailed plans.[15] There is no reason to believe that this noncommittal style has changed in recent years. Indeed, currently there is no indication of whom the Chinese wish to seat on the provisional legislature, how it will operate, how long it may last, and how they envisage it coexisting with the existing Legislative Council and the Hong Kong government before, presumably, it is sworn into office upon the transfer of sovereignty. Indeed, it is not outside the bounds of possibility that China may yet be persuaded to find a face-saving way of reducing the role of the provisional legislature to negligible proportions, or of doing away with its services altogether.

In broader terms, the objectives of Beijing's leaders may stem from their desire to consolidate the political succession to Deng and to maintain social and political stability in the buildup to the Fifteenth Party Congress. The fact that there continues to be jockeying for position and arguments about the drafts of the main documents for the Congress means that in the first instance, Jiang Zemin and Li Peng (who have final responsibility for Hong Kong) want a smooth transfer of sovereignty. As Li Peng apparently told the visiting British Trade and Deputy Prime Minister earlier in 1996, China does not want to "lose face" over the transfer. The Chinese leaders want to preside over a dignified ceremony where the eyes of the assembled media representatives of the world can report a trouble-free transfer. Any "trouble" would reflect adversely upon them, not least in the view of their colleagues. The Chinese must weigh the advantages of curtailing demonstrations – the right to free assembly – against the dangers of being received as undermining the separate "system" of Hong Kong. This perception could trigger alarm among local middle-class professionals and frighten off foreign investors. Such a scenario could lead to the truly damaging consequences that would attend a mismanagement of Hong Kong.

---

[15] Sir Percy Cradock recorded the British surprise when allowed, at one point, a glimpse of Chinese planning for post-1997 Hong Kong: "Here a surprise awaited us. We had been pushing at the door of a locked room, containing, as we thought, treasures of Chinese planning. Now the door was open and the room was found to be virtually empty. There were some broad prescriptions, little else." Cradock, op. cit., pp. 192–93.

It is perhaps a calculation such as this that has prompted China to adopt more flexible approaches. Consequently, despite its manifest weakness as the outgoing colonial authority, Great Britain may retain some leverage to persuade China to adopt policies that would retain the distinctive features of the Hong Kong way of life. The first six months of 1997 should provide an unprecedented opportunity: This will constitute a probationary period for the Chief Executive designate and his team, during which they will learn how to govern Hong Kong by cooperating with both the existing government and Beijing.

Assuming that Beijing manages the actual transfer of authority well, the next important stage for Beijing's leaders will begin after they overcome the hurdle of the Fifteenth Party Congress. The following eighteen months to two years will show whether the leaders understand enough about the realities of Hong Kong to provide proper support for its institutions against the threat of erosion from across the border – by corruption, cronyism, and all the other practices for which China is well known. Most observers regard that seepage of undesirable practices as the real threat to the rule of law and to the probity of the civil service, which ultimately undergirds Hong Kong's capacity to act as an international financial center and as a source of capital flows and management knowhow to China.

There are reasons to be optimistic on this score, too; a peaceful transfer of sovereignty will mean that China's leaders can begin to reap some rewards. They will benefit from the further relaxation of tensions in the region and in their relations with Washington and Tokyo. They will also enjoy a more positive reception from the international financial and trading communities, which might become more flexible in their negotiations concerning entry into the WTO. Moreover, investment flows into China might also increase. If China's leaders then allow corrupt practices to infect Hong Kong, international companies are likely to scale down their presence in Hong Kong in favor of other regional centers that show more respect for the rule of law. That reaction will lead to reassessments of the value of Hong Kong, which could lead to an erosion of confidence commensurate with the erosion of the territory's "way of life." In other words, the dramatic effects of both rewards and constraints should induce China's leaders to sustain the key elements of the Hong Kong system.

Finally, consideration must be given to the possible impact of the future HKSAR on China. If it continues to enforce the rule of law, support an elected legislature, and promote an effective and politically neutral civil service combined with basic civil liberties, the HKSAR could be a most attractive model to many in China. It will surely not be long before Shanghai, which aims to become an international financial center in its own right, will find elements of the Hong Kong system worthy of emulation, especially as the stigma of colonialism no longer applies. As a symbol of modernization, however, Hong Kong could also attract opposition, becoming a major focal point for the next round of debate and conflict in China concerning the country's future.

In the long run, the Hong Kong issue must necessarily become central to the larger question about the nature of the modernization process in China itself. Its role as a key to deepening China's integration into the international community is very important indeed. At this stage, however, it is not possible to be more than cautiously optimistic about Hong Kong's future. Despite their manifest interest in ensuring the successful reversion of Hong Kong, China's leaders have yet to show an understanding or appreciation of Hong Kong's system, and their lifetime experience as communists and the nearly fifty years of Communist rule in China militate against their intrinsic capacity to do so.

10

Hong Kong as a Problem in Chinese–American Relations

NANCY BERNKOPF TUCKER

HONG Kong confronts American foreign policy makers with a classic foreign policy dilemma. Despite its superpower status, there appears to be no way for the United States to bring that power to bear on the issue of Hong Kong's reversion to China. The United States lacks legal standing even though its role in and commitment to Hong Kong have been significant for the past fifty years. Options are further circumscribed by widespread apathy in the United States. Yet, Americans have much to lose if Hong Kong's retrocession goes badly – not only in Hong Kong itself but also in the wider arena of regional interaction and, of course, in the difficult relationship with the People's Republic of China. So far, developments in the transition that will span the change of sovereign authorities suggest that the long-term prognosis for Hong Kong and the U.S. presence in the territory is, at best, uncertain, unstable, and troubled.

American opposition to the continued British occupation of Hong Kong as a colony after the end of the Second World War serves as an ironic backdrop to the growth of American involvement in the territory thereafter. Franklin Roosevelt had insisted during the course of the war that the phenomenon of colonialism would have to end and promised Madame Chiang Kai-shek that Hong Kong would be restored to Chinese control. However, the combination of Prime Minister Winston Churchill's obduracy on the subject and the Chinese civil war invalidated such guarantees, and British troops retrieved the colony without resistance. Almost immediately, Washington discovered that having London in charge conferred significant economic and political benefits on American merchants, soldiers, and spies.

Through the decades that followed, the precise role that Americans would play in the enclave challenged British, American, and Chinese officials. Amer-

213

icans were welcomed as sojourners and investors, but neither British nor Chinese authorities wanted them to arrogate to themselves a dominant or official role in the life of the enclave. Thus, British authorities viewed American cultural imports into the colony with some anxiety and reopened Hong Kong University in the 1940s in part to promote "British culture, British prestige, and British interests . . . in the face of growing American influence."[1] The American-sponsored embargo placed upon trade with China as a result of war in Korea had a devastating impact on the local economy – until the U.S. government stopped treating Hong Kong like a Chinese Communist port and brushing aside "the technicality of British sovereignty."[2] Washington also evoked British and Chinese fears with its continuing determination to use Hong Kong as a base for espionage against China and with the large American military presence during both the Korean and Vietnam wars. Beijing repeatedly denounced British complicity in American imperialism, and British diplomats worried that the United States would eventually provoke China into reclaiming the colony. Although Washington bridled at – and defied – some of the efforts to constrain its activities in Hong Kong, officials prized the almost cost-free access they enjoyed, unencumbered by the responsibilities of a colonial power. They ignored Chinese hostility and assiduously evaded British efforts to elicit a clearly articulated defense commitment.[3]

The habit of leaving political issues to the British and focusing American energies primarily on trade and investment lasted until the Beijing Spring and Tiananmen massacre of 1989. Even in the tense months surrounding negotiation of the Sino-British Joint Declaration in 1984, Washington played a negligible part. Although American bankers may have contributed to pressures on the British government to resolve the unsettled future of the territory so that they could extend loans and negotiate leases, British and Hong Kong interests took the lead.[4] However, Hong Kong's massive demonstrations in sympathy

---

[1] Gerald A. Postiglione, "The United States and Higher Education in Hong Kong: Preserving the High Road to China," paper presented at the International Conference on America and the Asia-Pacific Region in the Twentieth Century, Beijing, May 1991, p. 4.

[2] 446G.119/2–151 R. W. Barnett (CA) to John Allison (FE), "US Export Licensing Policy Toward Hong Kong and Macao," Box 1983, General Records of the Department of State, Record Group 59, National Archives, College Park, Maryland.

[3] For a more detailed discussion of the history of American involvement in Hong Kong, see Nancy Bernkopf Tucker, *Taiwan, Hong Kong and the United States, 1945–1992: Uncertain Friendships* (New York: Twayne/Macmillan, 1994), pp. 197–233.

[4] Frank Welsh, *A Borrowed Place* (New York: Kodansha, 1993), p. 503.

with protesters in China awoke Americans to the human rights quandary created by the agreement for the resumption of Chinese Communist control over the
colony. Although decidedly ignorant of Hong Kong politics, television watch-
ers in the United States instantly, if fleetingly, jettisoned their indifference to
Asian affairs. They lamented the impending reversion and sympathized with
those who demanded change in Hong Kong's government – which could hardly have been considered a bastion of democracy in 1989. Americans instinctively supported demands for greater representation, angering the Chinese,
who, in contrast, wanted to preserve the status quo until 1997 and refused to
accept modest British liberalization measures.

The most palpable result of this awakening was the U.S.–Hong Kong Policy
Act of 1992, introduced by Senator Mitch McConnell, a Republican from Ken-
tucky. This piece of legislation established a formal mechanism for the United
States to monitor changes in Hong Kong, putting the United States on record
regarding Hong Kong's future and attempting to support the advancement of
political rights. It formally enjoined the executive branch to deliver periodic
reports to Congress on conditions in the territory as well as to negotiate bilateral agreements with Hong Kong authorities to keep commercial, cultural, and
other ties viable beyond the transition. Further, it gave the U.S. government the
legal right to treat Hong Kong as a distinct entity after it became a Special
Administrative Region of China. However, the act did not include any remedial formula to deal with problems that the State Department might identify, short
of withdrawing all preferences and treating Hong Kong like any other Chinese
city; also, in sharp contrast with the 1979 Taiwan Relations Act, it lacked a
security dimension.

In fact, the act as passed took a more moderate approach than even cautious
early drafts mandated. Initially, McConnell had intended that the U.S. Congress oversee Chinese adherence to the provisions of the Joint Declaration to
help ensure Hong Kong's autonomy. China's protest against such interference
in its internal affairs, coupled with the recognition that, as a bystander to the
agreement, the United States could not legitimately appropriate supervisory
powers, led to broader and less specific language and responsibilities.

The Hong Kong Act, then, clearly demonstrates the problem that Washington confronts: On the one hand, it must try to protect American national interests in the economic and political future of the territory; on the other, it must be
careful neither to anger the Chinese and the British nor to transgress international law. Beyond this weak legislative initiative, the Bush and Clinton administrations have largely ignored Hong Kong. At a time when budget-cutting is

threatening to eliminate entire foreign policy agencies in Washington, the number of people able and inclined to give serious, sustained attention to Hong Kong affairs are few. That situation was only aggravated by the distractions of the 1996 presidential election and the subsequent personnel changes that disrupted work schedules and eliminated experienced officials.

An interagency task force operating in the executive branch since 1995 has worked quietly on modifying laws concerning issues such as export control and aviation. The likelihood of all treaties and agreements being extended and reworked in time for retrocession, however, appears small since few measures requiring congressional action had even been put forward at the end of 1996. The prolonged negotiations over an investment promotion and protection accord between Washington and Hong Kong – which might seem to be in the interests of both sides – suggest the complexities inherent even in the prosaic aspects of the new order.[5]

It is clear that in the volatile times ahead, Congress will evaluate developments in Hong Kong as indicators of the health of the larger relationship between the United States and China. Members of Congress, who have in the past often been critical of the Chinese, formed a bipartisan and bicameral Hong Kong Caucus early in 1996 to educate and rally their colleagues in anticipation of difficulties in the transition process. The co-sponsors of the effort, Congressmen John Porter (R-IL) and Sam Gejdenson (D-CT) and Senators Connie Mack (R-FL) and Joseph Lieberman (D-CT), intended that vigilance be supplemented by authorship of resolutions that would help protect civil liberties in the territory. However, Beijing is most likely to consider such resolutions as intrusive and contrary to Clinton administration efforts to arrest the downward spiral in Sino-American relations. Conversely, the level of tension between the United States and China will have an impact upon how smoothly the changeover proceeds. Beyond this, American policy in the region will have to be adjusted to cope with the problems that an alteration in Hong Kong's status produces for political, economic, or social stability.

The most significant and complicated arena for compromise encompasses economic interaction between the United States and Hong Kong. The United States must remain engaged in a territory that commands the talent, wisdom, and experience to have become the eighth largest trader, the fourth largest international banking center, and the world's largest container port despite its

---

[5] Nigel Holloway, "No Guarantee," *Far Eastern Economic Review*, Oct. 10, 1996, p. 63.

diminutive size and anomalous status.[6] In jeopardy are not only holdings in the colony, but also trade and investment via Hong Kong inside the People's Republic of China as well as the headquarters of companies that do business throughout East and Southeast Asia. The American Chamber of Commerce of Hong Kong is the largest chapter of that organization outside the continental United States. There are some 1,200 American companies in Hong Kong, employing 250,000 workers, including 198 regional headquarters and 228 regional offices, as well as almost US$14 billion in investments.

With so great a stake in the territory, Americans are determined to remain. Chinese and British negotiators have tried to reassure Hong Kong residents and the world community through their Joint Declaration, which promised that Hong Kong would be allowed to keep its existing system for fifty years after the turnover. To businesspeople from the United States, such guarantees, combined with multiplying opportunities, appear to justify considerable risk.

The health of Hong Kong's economy is not contingent solely upon developments in the territory. The most obvious source of controversy may be the question of American most-favored-nation (MFN) trade treatment for China, which must be renewed by the U.S. Congress on an annual basis. Ending MFN status would be costly for Hong Kong, which forecasts the loss of 90,000 jobs and a 1.5 percent drop in projected growth of its gross domestic product. Representatives from Hong Kong have made annual pilgrimages to Washington to argue on behalf of unconditional MFN for China ever since the Tiananmen crackdown induced Congress to consider economic sanctions as punishment for China's government. In 1996 these representatives included not only Governor Chris Patten and Hong Kong's Chief Secretary Anson Chan, but also the leader of the Democratic Party, Martin Lee, who has been under almost constant fire from Beijing for his political activism.

Continuation of MFN treatment, however, depends on issues which go well beyond the welfare of Hong Kong and over which the people of Hong Kong have little influence. So long as some powerful members of the U.S. Congress view MFN as a mechanism for eliciting better behavior from the Chinese Communists, and from the executive branch of the U.S. government, efforts to make MFN permanent will continue to founder and Hong Kong will remain in jeopardy. After reversion, when there are no more independent authorities to argue Hong Kong's case in Washington, Congress may worry less about safeguarding its economy.

---

[6] Michael Yahuda, *Hong Kong: China's Challenge* (New York: Routledge, 1996), p. 42.

The fight then will rest more heavily on the shoulders of the American business community in Hong Kong. The American Chamber of Commerce busies itself each year with the lobbying circuit in the United States as the springtime MFN debate heats up. A Chamber delegation visiting Washington, D.C., in 1996 emphasized Hong Kong's vigorous business climate and importance as a financial center, urging Congress not to damage business prospects there as a result of tensions between Washington and Beijing.

Of course, the strength of American trade with and investment in Hong Kong goes beyond the MFN status of China to the continuation of a laissez-faire environment and the rule of law in the territory itself. Businesspeople have been willing, when pressed, to compromise their principles in the People's Republic of China, recognizing that they function in a context where few precedents exist and regulations often change. The celebrated dispute between Beijing and McDonald's, which forced the hamburger chain to give up a prime location in the heart of the Chinese capital, reverberated through the American business world without driving executives out of China en masse. However, Hong Kong's traditions are firmly rooted, and entrepreneurs do not wander in uncharted territory. The willingness of American businesspeople to remain in Hong Kong will follow from the perpetuation of a level playing field unencumbered by Beijing's interference, whether in the form of discriminatory controls or sweetheart deals for pro-Beijing enterprises. Americans will insist upon the sanctity of contracts and access to legal redress. Restrictions such as the threatened curbs on dissemination of economic information inside China, announced in the winter of 1996, demoralized businesspeople in that country, but they would be devastating in Hong Kong.[7]

Beijing recognizes this fact. China's pledge to maintain a high degree of autonomy in Hong Kong is meant nowhere more sincerely than in the economic arena. The retrieval of Hong Kong has profound symbolic meaning for China, where its return will significantly lighten the century-old burden of imperialist humiliation. In practical terms, however, Hong Kong is important for the economic benefits that could flow from a smooth transition to Chinese rule.

The key will be the ability of Chinese officials to refrain from tampering with Hong Kong's economic system. This hands-off strategy will be difficult, however, for bureaucrats accustomed to participation in local economic activity. Already, corruption, endemic inside the People's Republic of China, has spread

---

[7] Steven Mufson, "China Curbs Foreign News Services," *Washington Post*, Apr. 16, 1996, pp. 1D, 3D.

into the colony, where rigorous law enforcement since the mid-1970s had all but eradicated corrupt practices. Beijing has also put heavy pressure on providers of basic services to accept mainland domination, compelling Swire Pacific, Ltd., for instance, to reduce its holdings in Cathay Pacific airlines to a minority share by selling at bargain prices to Chinese interests. Restraint may prove impossible if Hong Kong's more advanced and more liberal commercial order threatens Chinese assumptions and procedures inside the mainland. Abstinence could also be severely strained by a harshly restrictive American approach to trade issues such as textile quotas and the export of sensitive materials. Moreover, although the development of Shanghai today comes with considerable investment by, and guidance from, Hong Kong, and although its business environment is hardly free, Chinese officials could turn to Shanghai as a substitute if they come to see Hong Kong as dangerously unmanageable.

Among the factors likely to challenge the patience and fortitude of China's leaders will be the clash of cultures between China and Hong Kong and the resulting conflicts over human rights issues. Run as a colonial territory for more than a century, Hong Kong did not enjoy a democratic government prior to the 1990s. Disinclined to broaden local representation that might conflict with their metropolitan interests, the British also understood that Beijing objected to measures which could dispose the population toward independence rather than reunification with the People's Republic of China.[8] But the unspoken pledge to refrain from significantly altering political conditions in the colony was undermined by the events at Tiananmen in 1989. Some 20 percent of the Hong Kong population took to the streets in support of the demonstrators inside China; after the brutal suppression of the Beijing Spring, they demanded a greater voice in Hong Kong's affairs. Having come to believe that the reform era under Deng Xiaoping signified a more modern and more politically liberal China, the people of Hong Kong were horrified by the surviving potency of Communism and authoritarianism. Suddenly, their future under Chinese rule appeared frightening. As American legal expert Jerome Cohen has observed:

> It is difficult to overestimate the impact of Tiananmen on Hong Kong perceptions of the Joint Declaration, the Basic Law, and the entire constitutional house of cards that had been so elaborately constructed. . . . Tiananmen showed not only the deliberately disproportionate savagery of a regime determined to stay in power, but also the

---

[8] Deng Zhiduan, "Beijing's Policy on Hong Kong," in Hao Yufan & Huan Guocang (eds). *The Chinese View of the World* (New York: Random House, 1989), pp. 289–90.

Nancy Bernkopf Tucker

regime's blatant manipulation of the forms of law in evident violation of their substance, even before the killing started.[9]

British politicians who had earlier consoled themselves with the recognition that history made reversion inevitable unexpectedly felt the need to prepare Hong Kong's people for their new situation by giving them a heritage of democracy. In this effort, not surprisingly, they received considerable encouragement from Washington. Governor Sir Edward Youde and his successor, Sir David Wilson, set about replacing benevolent despotism with strengthened individual rights. When Governor Christopher Patten arrived in 1992, the pace accelerated; he focused on a more representative system, including expanding eligibility to vote for the Legislative Council and lessening the influence of narrow interest groups. Patten also launched a program to improve educational institutions, social services, and environmental protection. The American press was quick to applaud his new policies (some proudly pointed to Patten's political training as a volunteer in the New York City mayoralty campaign of John V. Lindsay in the 1970s).[10] Whereas China rapidly became harshly critical of Patten, many Americans cheered him forward.

Despite promises to maintain the existing system for fifty years, Beijing immediately began to demonstrate its determination to curb freedoms in Hong Kong. The most glaring example was its decision to abolish the Legislative Council, which, according to the U.S. Department of State, had been chosen in "elections [which] were fair, open, and resulted in the most representative and democratic legislative body in Hong Kong's history."[11] When one single dissenter cast a vote in the Preparatory Committee favoring retention of the Legislative Council, Lu Ping, head of Beijing's Hong Kong and Macao office, disqualified him from any further role in either the transition or the future government. Moreover, Chinese leaders made their position official only one

---

[9] Jerome A. Cohen, "Hong Kong: Domestic Politics/Socio-Economic Developments and Implications for the United States and the PRC," in David M. Lampton & Alfred D. Wilhelm, Jr. (eds), *United States and China Relations at a Crossroads* (Lanham, Md.: University Press of America, 1995), pp. 134–35.
[10] Barbara Basler, "For Hong Kong, a New Governor, and a Much Different Style," *New York Times*, June 14, 1992, p. 7. On the course of electoral reforms see Welsh, *A Borrowed Place*, op. cit., pp. 515–19, 528–31.
[11] U.S. Department of State, "Hong Kong Policy Act Report as of March 31, 1996," Washington, D.C., 1996, p. 18.

day after Taiwan held the first fully democratic presidential election in Chinese history.

Beijing also attacked the integrity of the non-political civil service (by demanding access to personnel records), political participation by the main opposition political party, and the legal system. It called the sanctity of the Court of Final Appeal into question, although it did surrender its "post-verdict remedial mechanism," which would have politicized all decisions of the Court by transferring ultimate legal authority to Beijing. The Chinese nevertheless limited the participation of foreign judges and refused to allow the Court to begin functioning before July 1, 1997, lest it compile precedents in an environment unfettered by Communist control.

Human rights organizations in both Hong Kong and the United States have expressed concern regarding future freedoms in the territory. Although in the Joint Declaration and the Basic Law, China guaranteed that adherence to the International Covenant on Civil and Political Rights would be maintained, it subsequently declared that it would not abide by the requirement to report biannually to the United Nations Human Rights Committee on Hong Kong's behalf. Moreover, Beijing attacked Hong Kong's Bill of Rights, which incorporated the Covenant's principles into Hong Kong law, asserting that it was incompatible with observance of the Basic Law. In January 1997 China's 150-member Preparatory Committee for Hong Kong met in Beijing and agreed to scrap not only the Bill of Rights, but also the existing electoral system and privacy laws governing access to personal data. To assure political quiescence, the Committee accepted proposals to ban peaceful demonstrations unless approved by the Hong Kong police and prohibited ties to overseas political organizations. Although proud to be reclaiming Hong Kong from British imperialism, Beijing, six months before retrocession, had decided to return the territory to a legal status comparable to that of the darkest days of autocratic colonial control.

In reality, Beijing does not need to take formal action in order for freedom in Hong Kong to erode. The media, for instance, began to censor themselves without any formal prohibitions by Communist leaders. Columns and political cartoons have been dropped from newspapers, and commentary on issues that might distress Beijing has diminished. Lu Ping declared to CNN on May 31, 1996, that in the future the press in Hong Kong must not write about the independence of Taiwan. Perhaps uncomfortable with delivering such a bald warning, he (laughably) paralleled China and Taiwan with the United States and Hawaii, erroneously insisting that the American press is not allowed to write about independence for Hawaiians either. Even though Lu's remarks caused considerable outcry in Hong Kong, in October Foreign Minister Qian Qichen reiterated Beijing's determination to limit political commentary in the Hong Kong media after retrocession.[12]

Optimists have insisted that Beijing's desire to preserve the economic advantages of Hong Kong protects the territory from radical change and repressive policies. On the other hand, the link between politics and economics has always been powerful, and China's leaders have been willing to compromise prosperity to protect political control. Therefore, they have been loath to deal with difficult questions surrounding reform of domestic state enterprises, not only because they fear the unrest which would follow massive unemployment, but also because they are reluctant to surrender their ideological predispositions. Indeed, the central government sacrifices tax revenues from what could be profitable businesses, and it invests heavily in inefficient, money-losing factories. In the first three months of 1996, in fact, these enterprises lost US$361 million.[13] The increasing emphasis on "spiritual civilization," as Jiang Zemin struggles to consolidate his power, reinforces the message that Beijing will abandon rational business practices when politics dictate. This fact was clearly reflected in the closing document of the Plenum of the Communist Party's Central Committee in the autumn of 1996, which asserted that "at no time can we sacrifice spiritual values in the name of momentary economic development."[14]

Similarly, the growing confidence evinced by Chinese leaders regarding their mastery of the capitalist economic system and their understanding of the requirements for success in Hong Kong bodes ill, given the nature of their conclusions. Jiang Zemin reportedly told *Le Figaro* that Hong Kong's prosperity "cannot be attributed, as some have suggested, to an independent judiciary and a free system of the press."[15] Although Frank Ching of the *Far Eastern Economic Review* did not join *Fortune* magazine in proclaiming "The Death of Hong Kong," he warned that "the entrepreneurial spirit of Hong Kong . . . was

---

[12] Philip Bowring, "Threats to Hong Kong's Free Press," *International Herald Tribune*, June 6, 1996, p. 8; Kathy Chen, Urban C. Lehner, & Marcus W. Brauchli, "China's Foreign Minister Issues Warnings," *Wall Street Journal*, Oct. 16, 1996, p. A17. On the question of independence for Hawaii, Lu Ping should read the editorial "Back to the 49 States?" *Washington Post*, Sept. 23, 1996, p. A18.

[13] Steven Mufson, "China's Leaders Jostle for Control," *Washington Post*, Aug. 17, 1996, p. A18.

[14] Steven Mufson, "China's Communists Put Spiritual Above Economics at Party Session," *Washington Post*, Oct. 11, 1996, p. A30.

[15] Frank Ching, "Danger Signals for Hong Kong," *Far Eastern Economic Review*, Oct. 17, 1996, p. 36.

only able to operate successfully in an environment where rule of law held sway, and where information and ideas were freely available. For China to conclude that these elements are unimportant could lead to tragic consequences." Indeed, in January 1997, President Clinton questioned whether Hong Kong could "exist, with all of its potential to help China modernize its own economy and open opportunities for its own people, if the civil liberties of the people are crushed."[16]

Security issues surrounding the retrocession of Hong Kong are equally as diverse and divisive. If the Chinese takeover goes smoothly – not only in the near term but over the subsequent months and years – it will enhance China's stature and calm some of the fears that people in Macao and Taiwan might harbor concerning reunification with the mainland. However, if the transition goes badly, the impact will be far more extreme. The possibility of peaceful unification between China and Taiwan would diminish precipitously, and the desire among those living on Taiwan for a declaration of independence would increase along with the danger of war. What the U.S. government would do in such an eventuality remains unclear.

The United States has intentionally followed a policy of ambiguity in the Taiwan Strait since the 1950s, when President Dwight D. Eisenhower came to believe that it was the best way to curb Beijing's urge to seize the island. More recently, perpetuation of the policy came to be seen as vital – not only to block Chinese aggression, but also to inhibit those in Taiwan who might take advantage of American guarantees to declare independence. The 1979 Taiwan Relations Act, which provides for the conduct of informal relations between Washington and Taipei, included an assurance of arms sales to allow Taiwan to defend itself, but no explicit pledge to send American forces if war develops between Taiwan and China.

In the 1990s the American people have increasingly expressed their lack of enthusiasm for committing U.S. armed forces to foreign engagements. On the other hand, it is difficult to imagine that the United States would ignore the fate of a thriving democracy – long nurtured by American government, religious, and business interests – if it were attacked by one of the few remaining Communist

---

[16] Frank Ching, op. cit.; Louis Kraar, "The Death of Hong Kong," *Fortune*, June 26, 1995. Li Rui-huan, a member of the Standing Committee of the Politburo, asserted in March 1995 that Chinese leaders did not understand what made Hong Kong successful and, as a result, "it will be to keep it intact." However, Li had no supervisory responsibility for the territory. Yahuda, *Hong Kong*, op. cit., pp. 3, 56. Regarding the lack of background studies on Hong Kong, see Deng Zhiduan, "Beijing's Policy," op. cit., p. 305. Text of Clinton's press conference, *Washington Post*, Jan. 29, 1997, p. A12.

dictatorships in the world. The lack of clarity in Washington's planning is therefore understandable. To a significant degree, the response would be conditioned by the circumstances under which conflict broke out. If provoked by Taiwan, Americans would be less likely to welcome taking a strong hand than if they perceived Taiwan as a victim. And seeing Taiwan as a victim may in part follow from developments in Hong Kong.

Of course, the balance might shift if groups or individuals from Taiwan were to take initiatives in Hong Kong that would make it more difficult for the Chinese to normalize their control of the territory. Financial support for dissidents, or other similar measures, would strike the United States as reckless. Indeed, Taiwan itself would have much to lose given that its trade, its US$15 to US$20 billion in investments, and its transportation ties to China have depended heavily on Hong Kong's mediation. From Washington's perspective, the retrocession of Hong Kong actually provides an opportunity for Taiwan and China to resolve their continuing differences over the so-called *santong* (three links), substituting direct transportation, communication, and trade for the cumbersome third-party channel through Hong Kong. For Taipei to disregard opportunities to better relations at the same time as opponents of reunification work to undermine a peaceful transition for Hong Kong would doubtless alienate American officials, who will have to cope with the consequences.

Instability in Hong Kong threatens U.S. security interests apart from the Taiwan factor. Americans constitute the second largest expatriate community in Hong Kong (after Filipinos), numbering about 37,000, and their safety must not be endangered. Of course, were Americans to be physically threatened, that would most probably mean that the 6 million citizens of Hong Kong would also be in jeopardy, sparking a new refugee crisis in the region. More than 500,000 Hong Kong residents have obtained foreign passports which would enable them to flee to the United States, Canada, Australia, New Zealand, or Great Britain. The United States liberalized its laws in 1990 in response to Tiananmen, passing an Immigration Act that increased Hong Kong's quota, protected it as a category separate from that of China after 1997, and changed procedures to allow visas issued by the U.S. Consulate in Hong Kong to remain valid until 2002. In this way, American officials and members of Congress hoped they could prevent an outflow of the most highly educated and cosmopolitan residents, whose skills will continue to be needed by the business community, civil service, and other institutions.

The rest, however, have been denied an easy departure. The status of British Dependent Territory Citizenship does not entail a right of abode in the British

Isles; in a crisis, desperate Hong Kong residents will likely set sail for the shores of America's friends in the region (Taiwan, Japan, and states of Southeast Asia), bringing along enormous economic demands and risks of infiltration and sabotage.[17] This would generate strains at least as discordant as those posed previously by Vietnam's boat people. Washington proved reluctant to open its doors to the Vietnamese refugees, but for years opposed involuntary repatriation, angering governments which were forced to host the Vietnamese. A similar scenario resulting from a Hong Kong diaspora would again place the American government in the difficult position of championing fugitives from Communist tyranny while those same aliens jeopardized the welfare of sanctuary states.

Pressures severe enough to provoke a refugee crisis would also aggravate existing law enforcement problems. Only a stable environment can reduce the influence and incidence of organized crime, drug trafficking, counterfeiting, money laundering, credit card fraud, and illegal immigration of mainland Chinese to the United States. Cooperation between the Hong Kong authorities and U.S. agencies, including the FBI and the Secret Service, would be undermined by a breakdown in local order and an erosion of trust between Washington and Hong Kong.[18]

More broadly, a perception among China's neighbors that Beijing had proven unable or unwilling to deal with Hong Kong through means other than militancy and oppression would be likely to weaken confidence in the future of the region. China already is seen as an unpredictable and dangerous power; its claims to islands in the South China Sea, among other issues, produced the foolhardy and destabilizing Mischief Reef Incident of February 1995. The potential for an economically draining arms race in the region would only accelerate if retrocession goes badly; so, too, would the desire on the part of the members of the Association of Southeast Asian Nations to retain U.S. military forces in the area. Similarly, Japan's enthusiasm for its alliance with the United States would escalate if China behaves badly in Hong Kong.

Tensions between the United States and China necessarily play an important role in the future of Hong Kong and the way in which developments in Hong

---

[17] On the British immigration issue, see Frank Ching, "One Country, Two Systems: The Future of Hong Kong," in Anthony J. Kane (ed.), *China Briefing, 1990* (Boulder, CO: Westview, 1990), pp. 115, 120–21.

[18] China's inclination to sustain U.S.–Hong Kong cooperation in these areas is likely to be encouraged by the growing ties between Chinese and American law enforcement agencies. Richard W. Mueller, "America's Long-Term Interest in Hong Kong," *Annals of the American Academy of Political and Social Science,* September 1996, pp. 150–51.

Kong reflect upon the broader relationship. Popular American disillusionment and anger with Beijing have characterized views of China since Tiananmen. Because that shocking event was followed soon after by the end of the Cold War and the collapse of the Soviet Union, strategic imperatives – which, in the past, had led the United States to ignore Chinese behavior – no longer sufficed to excuse arbitrary policies. Disputes over trade and proliferation further heightened anxiety, as did Chinese projection of force in the South China Sea. Moreover, Beijing's suspicion that the United States is trying to fragment China to ensure its weakness, however erroneous, renders China less cooperative. This is coupled with Beijing's apparent belief, during the first Clinton administration, that it could with impunity manipulate and embarrass the White House and State Department. On the American side, a belligerent Republican Congress determined to reduce U.S. commitments abroad and to shun Communist regimes has not only diminished the chances that reconciliation will come from the United States, but also heightened the prospect of new provocations.

The implications for Hong Kong, of course, are unfortunate. Although not directly involved in the disputes raging between Washington and Beijing, Hong Kong will almost inevitably be caught in the crossfire should either side adopt sanctions incautiously. During the March missile firings in the Taiwan Strait that brought U.S. aircraft carrier groups to the area, the Hong Kong stock market fell precipitously.[19] Furthermore, Washington could hardly expect to intercede with Beijing to preserve Hong Kong's freedoms in a hostile climate.

The growth of nationalism in China renders the Hong Kong situation increasingly sensitive because that nationalism stirs defiantly patriotic emotions. The government in Beijing erected an immense digital clock in Tiananmen Square to count down the approach toward reversion. At midnight on June 30, 1997, a century of humiliation will be expunged, countrymen will be retrieved from imperialism, and China's greatness will be reinforced. As part of the handover ceremonies, Beijing has announced that it will march 6,000 soldiers into the territory in a display of strength heightened by air force and naval maneuvers. This has been only a part of the wider emphasis on nationalism that China's leaders have used in recent years to take the place of a largely discredited Communist ideology. Although popular support may be difficult to generate for the old

---

[19] The drop stemmed also from a slide in the Dow Jones average in New York, but analysts considered the Taiwan factor to have been a key to Hong Kong's performance. Edward A. Gargan, "Hong Kong Stocks Plunge 7.3 %, Rattled by U.S. Bond Prices and China," *New York Times*, Mar. 12, 1996, p. D8.

virtues of abstinence, egalitarianism, and self-sacrifice, pride in the achievements of a rapidly prospering and increasingly powerful China comes easily.

That the rising tide of nationalism also entails some vigorous anti-Americanism makes the phenomenon particularly troubling for the United States. A 1995 survey conducted by the Beijing publication *Zhongguo Qingnian* (*Chinese Youth*) reported that 87 percent of respondents thought that the United States was the "most unfriendly country" toward China. Further, some 57 percent reciprocated those sentiments, making the United States allegedly the country least liked by Chinese youth.[20] More recently, the controversial book *The China That Can Say No* and the popular television soap opera *Foreign Babes in Beijing* attacked Americans for their moral and spiritual degeneracy, evidence of which Chinese authorities might easily find in the Hong Kong red-light districts catering to American servicemen on shore leave.

This kind of anti-American attitude makes it more difficult for China to contemplate or justify compromise with the United States on Hong Kong issues. For instance, Chinese leaders may have promised to live with an autonomous Special Administrative Region, but they never conceived of tolerating forces within the territory that would challenge their control inside China. Therefore, in response to the escape of political dissident Wang Xizhe in October 1996, they declared that Hong Kong's role as a sanctuary and conduit for flight to the United States must end. Although they have accepted the pegging of Hong Kong's currency to the U.S. dollar and declared that they would defend it, this means that a currency will exist in Hong Kong that not only is different from the currency of the rest of China, but also, in essence, is hostage to the U.S. Federal Reserve. And, although Chinese military leaders have approved ship visits by the U.S. Navy, they may not approve of having American warships at anchor in Hong Kong on anything like the routine and frequent basis of the British era.

In the end, it is crucial to Hong Kong's future that relations between the United States and China be, if not close, at least amicable. So long as the tensions of a broader conflict do not impinge on conditions in the Special Administrative Region, chances of a successful adaptation to the new circumstances will be greater. During the difficult year of 1996, Chinese officials overlooked other confrontational issues and indicated an unprecedented willingness to discuss Hong Kong with Americans, making clear that they accepted a legitimate role

---

[20] "Survey Results of Chinese Youth Attitudes Viewed," *Foreign Broadcast Information Service*, FBIS-CHI-95–184, Sept. 22, 1995, p. 18.

Nancy Bernkopf Tucker

for the United States in the territory. At the same time, they refused to engage in any dialogue regarding the specifics of local administration, simply assuring their interlocutors that everything would proceed smoothly.[21]

To some observers in Hong Kong, Washington's desire to repair tattered relations with Beijing may not be an unmitigated blessing. Martin Lee has made clear his dissatisfaction with the Clinton administration's unwillingness to take a tough line with China regarding the impending dissolution of the Legislative Council. Emily Lau, like Lee an elected representative to that Council, laments Clinton's embrace of Chinese dictators he once appeared to abhor. If the United States quietly accepts Beijing's insistence that on July 1, 1997, Hong Kong will become an internal affair, then, according to Lee, it "will go down the drain like Tibet." Moreover, he warns, "By failing to speak out, the United States is sending a very negative message to the Hong Kong people."[22]

In reality, the United States has few policy alternatives. Efforts at oversight must be balanced by the reality of Chinese power and determination. In contemplating its approach to China on issues such as proliferation, trade, and human rights, the United States should regard the interests of Hong Kong as an important variable. In the past, Congress and the White House have listened with compassion to Hong Kong's representatives when troubled U.S.–China relations threatened the viability of the colony. That disposition to consider Hong Kong as a community that merits special consideration must not change. Beyond this, the United States can maintain a large and continuous presence in the territory, ensuring that cultural and economic contacts retain their centrality. Media attention, which, as the American Assembly has warned, could magnify missteps and thereby harm U.S.–China relations, will also play a role as a positive guarantor of the continuing health and viability of Hong Kong as both an international and a Chinese city.[23] The American position in Hong Kong has always been unofficial and unusual. After June 30, 1997, that reality will not change. Relations pursued cautiously but with conviction should assure that the informal, sizable, and valuable American presence will neither erode nor be altered significantly.

[21] Testimony of Winston Lord, Assistant Secretary of State for East Asian and Pacific Affairs, Department of State, Hearings of the East Asian and Pacific Affairs Subcommittee of the Senate Foreign Relations Committee, July 18, 1996.
[22] Michael Dobbs, "Hope on the Road to Hong Kong," *Washington Post*, Dec. 10, 1996, p. A22.
[23] American Assembly, *China–U.S. Relations in the Twenty-First Century: Fostering Cooperation, Preventing Conflict*, New York, November 1996, p. 18.

11

Post–July 1997 Challenges

KENNETH LIEBERTHAL[1]

THE Basic Law, the constitution for post–July 1997 Hong Kong, carefully balances the requirements of maintaining Hong Kong as a separate political, economic, and social system against the need to assert Chinese sovereignty.[2] The resulting mix of elements may succeed in attaining both goals. It requires that the *Chinese* in Hong Kong play the predominant political role there, and that they generally be individuals who have not acquired right of abode elsewhere. It also gives tremendously important prerogatives to Beijing in terms of appointing – or approving the appointments of – key individuals, conducting the Special Administrative Region's (SAR's) foreign and defense policies, and retaining the authority to amend the Basic Law in the future. Yet it contains numerous provisions that explicitly assure continuation of Hong Kong's distinctive system in everything from legal affairs to social issues such as freedom of religion and freedom of the press. Only future developments will tell whether the Basic Law will be implemented in a way that preserves Hong Kong's system.

The Western media, when discussing this issue, have tended to focus on a small number of very high profile issues, such as the choice of a Chief Executive, China's decision to replace the legislature, and potential curtailment of freedom of the press. These issues unquestionably are important, and they war-

---

[1] Kenneth Liberthal is the Arthur Thurnau Professor of Political Science and the William Davidson Professor of Business Administration at the University of Michigan. He has previously served as the director of the university's Center for Chinese Studies. His most recent book is *Governing China: From Revolution Through Reform* (New York: W.W. Norton, 1995).

[2] The Basic Law was adopted on April 4, 1990, by the Seventh National People's Congress of the PRC. Its text is widely available.

229

rant serious attention. If the People's Republic of China (PRC) should significantly curtail press freedom, for example, this would badly shake confidence in China's ability to keep its word when dealing with the sophisticated, open society of Hong Kong. The guarantee of press freedom in the Basic Law is clear and unequivocal.

Much of the commentary on the future of Hong Kong assumes that China will take advantage of gray areas and loopholes to act to Hong Kong's disadvantage. Beijing's leaders evidence deep concern about political stability and would be loath to see the vibrant freedoms of Hong Kong "infect" thinking on the mainland side of the border. Public political activities in Hong Kong targeted at mainland leaders and policies are particularly sensitive and might provoke repressive responses. Comments and actions by some mainland leaders in the approach to Hong Kong's reversion provide legitimate reason for worry.[3] However, it is also a safe assumption that Beijing will bend every effort to make the "one country, two systems" formula work. The PRC has huge interests riding on the success of this experiment, as other chapters in this volume detail. Making Hong Kong's reversion a success will be one of the most important items on the leaders' agenda for 1997. Indeed, probably no other issue will absorb as much of Beijing's leaders' time during that year.

Hong Kong is unlikely, therefore, to confront catastrophic challenges to its well-being, barring unanticipated domestic turmoil in China. *The most serious obstacles to Hong Kong's well-being are, rather, to be found in the inevitable difficulties of making two very distinctive systems deal effectively with each other.* There is no question that the PRC will have the upper hand when it comes to contacts with Hong Kong, and there are aspects of Hong Kong that are well understood in Beijing and that cause consternation there. China understands, for example, that Hong Kong is a remarkably free society; it will want various assurances that the citizens of the Hong Kong SAR will not try to export their model of society to the mainland. Another dimension of the problem concerns the limitations on Beijing's real grasp of the dynamics of Hong Kong itself, and significant failures in China to understand the realities of Hong Kong can *unintentionally* produce major problems, even assuming Beijing seeks in good faith to assure Hong Kong's success. In this context, it is sober-

---

[3] In October 1996, for example, Foreign Minister Qian Qichen asserted that the Hong Kong press would not be free to print "rumors" about mainland leaders. Other mainland actions earlier in the year reflect an intolerance for dissenting opinion.

ing to consider how fundamentally different the Hong Kong and Chinese systems of rule are.

In almost every sphere, from the role of the civil service to the functions of the courts to the government's role in the economy, mainland experience and norms bear little likeness to those in Hong Kong. Arguably the most important element in Hong Kong's economic success, for example, has been the government's ability to restrain itself from interfering excessively in the workings of the market. A combination of laws, transparent regulations, and market forces has framed business and financial activities in Hong Kong, and the results have been very impressive. This record has permitted the people of Hong Kong to have confidence in the rules that govern property and transactions, and they know from experience that they can resort to an independent, relatively high-quality legal system if they feel they have suffered from breaches of that system. China has also achieved remarkable economic progress, but it has done so on premises that differ in almost every essential from those undergirding the Hong Kong system. Even ardent reformers in the PRC, for example, do not think in terms that resonate with the government/market relationships taken for granted in Hong Kong.

The differences in systems and perspectives are so basic that Hong Kong will have to make major, long-term efforts to improve China's understanding of Hong Kong's chemistry. The Hong Kong SAR will also have to rely to a significant extent on those whom it has sensitized in Beijing to protect it from the activities of many others in both the Center and the provinces who deal with Hong Kong.[4]

Educational efforts directed at the PRC, while crucial, will themselves prove insufficient. Even if the major issues that have received so much public scrutiny to date are handled very well, the Hong Kong SAR government will still face a series of challenges that will require careful preparation and, in some instances, substantial adaptation of existing practices. We know a great deal about how China itself operates, hence about the specific challenges Hong Kong will face and the specific changes that are likely to occur. The following overview does not aspire to comprehensiveness but seeks to present in summa-

---

[4] Beijing is sensitive to the problems that can arise from excessive, undisciplined provincial interference in Hong Kong's affairs. Reportedly in the early fall of 1996, Beijing issued a directive to all provinces that prohibits any activities in Hong Kong without prior approval from the Center. (Personal communication with the author.)

ry fashion six significant challenges the Hong Kong SAR government will need to address in order to thrive after July 1, 1997.

CHALLENGE #1: LOBBYING BEIJING

The new Chief Executive (CE) will play a critical role in shaping the relations between Beijing and the Hong Kong SAR. He has formal responsibility for regular reporting to and consultation with Beijing, and many of his important decisions, such as appointing the key officials under him, are subject to approval from the Center. The first CE must be successful in earning the trust of both the people of the Hong Kong SAR and the leaders of the PRC if the "one country, two systems" formula is to have a good chance of succeeding. Indeed, securing the trust of both sides is probably the single most important task confronting the new CE upon assuming office in mid-1997.

In this context, it is striking to see how little is detailed in the Basic Law concerning the kind of access the new CE will enjoy in Beijing. Will he have to report through the Hong Kong and Macao Affairs Office (the *Gang Ao Ban*)? Will he have direct access to the Premier? To the General Secretary?[5] In rank-conscious China, will he be given the rank of Minister or of Vice Premier? It will be far more difficult to build trust if the CE is not able to develop personal ties with the highest-ranking leaders of the PRC.

The access issue is very important because an array of offices in Beijing will be involved in governing Hong Kong, and the relationships among them are not at all clear at this point. To date, the two key offices have been the New China News Agency (NCNA), whose Hong Kong office has taken on the stature of a shadow government there, and the Hong Kong and Macao Affairs Office. However, relations between these bodies have not been smooth. With reversion in July 1997, moreover, the PRC's Ministry of Foreign Affairs will establish its own office in Hong Kong to take charge of foreign affairs work there, but the boundaries on what exactly constitutes "foreign affairs" in this totally international polity have not been clearly drawn.[6] In short, beneath the very highest levels in Beijing, there is a welter of bodies with at least potentially competing interests that seek an active role in dealing with Hong Kong.[7] It will be very

---

[5] Reportedly, as of late 1996 Jiang Zemin personally heads China's Leadership Small Group on Hong Kong.
[6] The building that will house this office is currently under construction near the U.S. Consulate.
[7] It is possible, in addition, that Beijing will dispatch some people to Hong Kong to oversee various parts of the SAR's operations, even though the Basic Law appears to prohibit such a move.

important for the CE to be able to go over the heads of these bodies directly to the top Chinese leadership if he is to become the key person structuring the SAR's relations with the Center.

This problem must be seen against the reality that the CE is not the only representative from Hong Kong who will have regular access to Beijing. The Basic Law provides for Hong Kong SAR representation in the National People's Congress (NPC), and on its Committee for the Basic Law of the Hong Kong SAR, but no information is provided about the means to select the individuals who will serve on these bodies. Quite likely, they will be chosen by Beijing either directly or indirectly. In addition, Hong Kong already has "representatives" on the Chinese People's Political Consultative Conference (CPPCC) and presumably will continue to have such representation there.[8] Hong Kong's leading businesspeople have had regular access to the top Chinese leaders, and they, too, may provide an alternative source of information about developments and prospects in the SAR.

In this context, it is important to think about the institutional presence that Hong Kong will have in Beijing to supplement the efforts of the CE. All the attention that has been given to the CE in Hong Kong as the key individual who will represent Hong Kong to Beijing has inadvertently obscured the importance of developing a serious, permanent lobbying effort in the capital, under the control of the executive branch. Such an effort will not simply take shape of its own accord. In this, the Hong Kong SAR would do well to heed the efforts of China's various provinces.

The decentralization that has accompanied the reforms since the late 1970s has effectively put considerable decision-making power in the hands of China's provincial leaders. They have, in turn, worked assiduously to expand their room for maneuver in the system, even as they have simultaneously sought additional resources – in physical, monetary, and policy terms – from the Center. Partially reflecting the fact that the new system is quite fluid and not institutionalized, all provincial units, and some large municipalities, have set up extensive lobbying operations in Beijing. Each has its own office in the capital. Part of the work of these offices is to help make arrangements for provincials who come to the capital on business. A major part of their work would be familiar

---

[8] Article 21 of the Basic Law governs NPC representation, and Articles 17, 158, and 159 reference the Committee for the Basic Law of the Hong Kong SAR. The Basic Law does not mention the CPPCC, and there is no indication of how future Hong Kong "representatives" to that body will be selected.

to Washington lobbyists representing state governments in the American political system. They keep close tabs on developments in the capital that might have an impact on their province's interests. They develop special ties to the officials in ministries and other agencies whose decisions have special importance for their affairs (e.g., the Ministry of Coal Industry, in the case of Shanxi Province). They cultivate contacts in the NPC committees and in the State Council and Party apparatuses. Also, they provide information on their province to all who request it (and probably to quite a few who have not requested it).

When the SAR establishes its own office in Beijing, the staff must be carefully selected. They must be people who understand Hong Kong thoroughly and yet can deal comfortably with the generally northern leadership in Beijing (very few individuals meet this requirement). They must learn about the exercise of power in the capital without becoming involved in the internal politics of the mainland government. They will have to maintain strong ties to and communications with Hong Kong. Indeed, given the importance of this office, careful attention must be paid to working out its avenues of communications and reportage back home.

In short, Hong Kong is going to become a "player" in the Chinese system, regardless of the "one country, two systems" framework. As such, it will need to develop an *institutionalized capacity* to play the game well in Beijing. That cannot be a job solely for the CE. A substantial office, with highly skilled staff that can grab the ear of the important officials in both Hong Kong and Beijing, will be an important component of a successful post-1997 Hong Kong.

CHALLENGE #2: DEVELOPING COUNTERPARTS TO BEIJING
GOVERNING BODIES

After July 1, 1997, very extensive contacts will develop between official bodies in Hong Kong and major government units in Beijing. Given the very close connections between the Hong Kong and PRC economies, for example, Hong Kong very likely will want to work closely with Beijing to develop common approaches – compatible standards, methodologies, and categories – to deal with key issues. Currently, for instance, the classification systems used to describe economic activities differ almost completely between the PRC and Hong Kong, as do economic accounting methods. Environmental protection efforts will require the kind of clear communication between regulators on both sides that demand the development of standard definitions, measurements, and methodologies. This is not to suggest any challenge to the "two systems" premise, but rather simply to point to the kind of practical pressures that will inexorably be felt to move toward better information sharing and coordination.

This set of issues raises the question of how most effectively to achieve appropriate coordination between the Chinese and SAR governing agencies. One model would call for trying to achieve increased symmetry between the jurisdictions of certain government agencies in the SAR and their counterpart agencies in Beijing. Beijing itself did roughly the same thing during the early 1950s, when it modeled much of its institutional structure (especially in the economic realm) after that of the USSR in order to facilitate the massive transfer of aid and technology that took place during the height of the Sino-Soviet alliance. The same logic has dictated provincial organizational structures in China, which closely parallel those of the Center.

Hong Kong might make a conscious effort in some instances to develop governmental bodies that are direct counterparts of existing Beijing units. Developing bodies with jurisdictions roughly similar to those with whom they are working in the capital would facilitate communications and liaison. Hong Kong of course is not in a directly comparable position; however, it, too, might benefit if it can achieve a better "fit" institutionally with its Beijing counterparts. The basic practicality of adapting some of its bureaucratic structure to parallel more closely that of pertinent units in Beijing should receive active consideration.

There are also considerable problems with this approach to coordination. Hong Kong itself has only about fifteen departments (dubbed "policy branches") equivalent to the ministries and commissions of Beijing.[9] As a small entity, Hong Kong might find it a very strange "fit" indeed to mimic Beijing's administrative structure in any but a very select number of cases. More broadly, Hong Kong's current system relies heavily on coordination at the central level, and it would upset this arrangement considerably if Hong Kong departments were to develop extensive direct working relations with their *duikou jigou* (counterpart organs) in Beijing.

Perhaps, therefore, the Hong Kong SAR should designate one department, such as the Constitutional Affairs Branch, to take charge of efforts to coordinate between the various SAR departments and their Beijing counterparts.

---

[9] These policy branches are underpinned by seventy-one executive departments and agencies.

Other approaches to this issue may, on examination, prove more effective. The basic point is that this issue is very significant, and, as its importance will grow rapidly after July 1, 1997, it warrants explicit attention and planning.

This, indeed, is part of a broader question of coordination with governmental units at various levels of China's national hierarchy. For practical reasons, most of the experience to date has occurred with Guangdong. Here, the police and customs have set up liaison groups with their Chinese counterpart organs, and every three to four months there is an Infrastructure Coordinating Committee meeting with the Guangdong side. This approach suggests that coordination can be best handled through ad hoc arrangements or through bodies that meet only occasionally. However, to structure such ties with a plethora of other provincial and municipal level units might quickly prove unworkable.

The Hong Kong SAR therefore needs to think through the nature of its formal ties with sub-national governmental units in China. It may prove wise to consider establishing government offices in at least some mainland provinces and municipalities. In addition, Hong Kong's Trade Development Council may set up offices in various mainland localities to facilitate trade and increase understanding of Hong Kong. The biggest problem here may be one of reciprocity, as the SAR will need to protect itself from being inundated with bodies representing provincial and sub-provincial units, each anxious to develop access to the SAR's wealth. Currently, the Basic Law provides that no province can establish an office in the Hong Kong SAR without explicit approval of the Center; however, such approvals might prove irresistible if the SAR itself proves willing to deploy representatives to various parts of the interior.

CHALLENGE #3: MODIFYING THE CIVIL SERVICE

Hong Kong now enjoys one of the best civil service systems in the world. Its officials are remarkably highly trained, well paid, loyal, and honest. The civil service, moreover, staffs a far greater array of positions than is the case in the American system. In America, cabinet and sub-cabinet posts are staffed with political appointees; in Hong Kong, these positions are filled by members of the civil service. Standards of promotion are rigorous, and careers are structured to give high-ranking civil servants broad experience in government. Salaries are kept high enough to reduce temptations of corruption to a minimum, and extensive efforts are made to assure that corruption is curtailed.

The Hong Kong civil service is far more professional than its Chinese counterpart. Beijing has been working since the 1980s to upgrade the standards of its own civil service by changing the nature of hiring, creating a norm of retirement, upgrading formal training, and adopting pertinent laws to govern development of the civil service. Unfortunately, these efforts have had limited success, perhaps because the country is so large, the nature of the task so complex, and the educational levels so much lower on average.[10]

As of 1996 the PRC's civil servants have been subjected to loyalty tests, and promotions continue to be vetted as much on the basis of political attitudes as on professional competence. By all accounts, the civil service in China harbors substantial corruption. In short, Chinese officials have had no experience with the kind of professional civil service that the Hong Kong SAR will inherit. Also, there is little reason to believe that leaders and bureaucrats in China will trust the Hong Kong civil service, which was developed under the British system.

Almost certainly, there will over time be pressures to modify aspects of Hong Kong's civil service system. Despite explicit assurances to the contrary in the Basic Law, pressure will likely develop for changes in training, promotion procedures, and (conceivably, although less likely) recruitment. The intent will be to make the system work better for various actors in the PRC. Pressures on promotion, for example, will likely take the form of individual requests to accept friends and relatives of powerful mainland players and broader efforts to assure that the most loyal civil servants are prompted, regardless of their relative administrative capabilities. The Basic Law already provides for Beijing to approve the appointment of civil servants at the highest level, upon the recommendation of the CE.

Given the likelihood of such pressures, the Hong Kong SAR must consider where to draw the line in adapting to requests from the mainland. This will likely become a highly sensitive matter, as the personal interests of key players on the mainland may become engaged in this issue. It will therefore be important for Hong Kong to make a concerted effort to educate the public and the mainland on the importance of maintaining the professional integrity of the current civil service – and on what practices must be maintained in order to do so. Such perspectives may be so deeply ingrained in the Hong Kong government that it

---

[10] John Burns provides pertinent background in his "The Chinese Civil Service Reform: The 13th Party Congress Proposals," *The China Quarterly,* 120, December 1989; pp. 739–70. The Provisional Regulations on Civil Servants were enacted in 1993, but the first nationwide examination for civil service recruitment will be held only in 1997.

is difficult for the pertinent officials to appreciate the extent to which even top leaders on the mainland are ignorant of these essentials. The Hong Kong lobbying arm in Beijing, discussed above, might take this as one of its early priorities, as should the CE himself.

The tradition of political supervision is so deeply ingrained in the Chinese system that it is naive to think that it will not carry over in some form into post-1997 Hong Kong. Indeed, on the mainland the government and military are viewed as arms of the Chinese Communist Party, with the party itself as the ultimate source of political power. The reforms have changed much of the substance of party decisions; however, the notion of a political party at the core of the system, and of political considerations taking priority, remains an essential part of the mainland system.

Remarkably little has been written about the Communist Party in Hong Kong, especially considering all the attention given to post-1997 Hong Kong in recent years. What will be the role of the party in the SAR? What type of decision-making structure will the SAR Communist Party structure have? Will its membership be made public? What will be its reporting lines: to the Guangdong provincial party committee; to the Central Committee in Beijing; to the International Liaison Department at the Center? Will top members of the SAR be required to join the party? If not, what kind of liaison will they have with it? Will the party be allowed to penetrate the civil service? Will it set up organs that parallel those of at least some government departments? Will individuals selected to represent the SAR in the NPC and the CPPCC be predominantly Communist Party members? To refer to an issue raised above, will the party gain any role in hiring and promotions within the civil service?

The mainland's experience suggests the salience of all of these issues, yet inquiries to date have produced no hint of the role Beijing envisions for the Communist Party in the Hong Kong SAR. Very likely, its ultimate role is still unclear even to those in Beijing who are most concerned with planning for the SAR. Indeed, the limited evidence to date suggests that Beijing has ample reason to question the discipline and docility of its party members in the SAR. From Xu Jiatun on down, it appears that prolonged residence in Hong Kong has tended to give Communist Party members a distinctively Hong Kong perspective.

Nevertheless, a Hong Kong Communist Party apparatus already exists, and it certainly will play some role in the SAR. This will require accommodations in Hong Kong and perhaps some serious discussions with Beijing. It is a subject that should command more attention than has been the case to date.

CHALLENGE #5: DEALING WITH POLITICAL SUBVERSION

Every society must be concerned with the nature of its police force and with handling political subversion. In Hong Kong the establishment of the SAR produces special requirements in this regard.

A large percentage of Hong Kong's population left China because of their dissatisfaction with one or another aspect of life there. Many have developed a very distinctive Hong Kong identity and harbor various doubts about their future under active PRC sovereignty. The *New York Times*, for example, reported on October 29, 1996, that surveys in Hong Kong indicate that fewer than 50 percent of the population feels comfortable with the prospect of reversion to active PRC sovereignty in 1997. Taiwan has long had a core of supporters in Hong Kong and undoubtedly has agents in place there. The substantial international presence in Hong Kong, including foreign consulates that have long acted as listening posts to monitor developments on the mainland, adds to the political mix in the SAR.

The focus of past efforts by the Hong Kong intelligence and police apparatuses has been fixed on protecting Hong Kong from PRC operatives. This focus undoubtedly will change radically. The new targets are likely to be some combination of Taiwanese subversives, foreign agents, and Hong Kong liberals such as Martin Lee. Dealing with subversion is always a secret effort in which the rules of the game can be quite dicey. The radical shift in effort is one that will inevitably cause consternation and produce some difficulties.

Indeed, a major shakeup of the security apparatus has been under way for some time. Files must be purged to protect those who cooperated in past efforts against the PRC. Agents must in many instances be terminated and replaced with others who are more useful in the efforts against the new targets. Given the individuals and types of information involved, this process is complicated and could cause problems.[11]

Inevitably, the State Security Ministry and the Public Security apparatus will increase their ties with the Hong Kong authorities. This has already occurred

---

[11] Provisions in the Basic Law for continuity of personnel should protect the police and security apparatuses from a PRC-directed wholesale housecleaning, though – at least in the short term.

quite extensively as Hong Kong has vastly expanded its contacts with Guang-dong Province since the early 1980s. One likely consequence of this set of developments will be increasing pressures for the SAR security people to engage in corruption, as some mainland authorities accustomed to having their way will try to make Hong Kong a more effective part of their networks of criminality. This is not to suggest that all mainland security people are corrupt – that certainly is not the case. However, corruption in this part of the PRC sys-tem is sufficiently widespread that it is prudent to assume that this will become a potential source of pressure in the counterpart units in Hong Kong. The Hong Kong SAR government, in the midst of a major revamping of its security appa-ratus, will have to determine the nature of the effort it will want to make in this very sensitive sphere.

In addition, the issue of subversion inevitably focuses attention on Taiwan's presence in Hong Kong, which, in turn, is connected to other important issues. The Hong Kong SAR's experience will certainly provide an important context for Taiwan's future considerations about its direct ties with the PRC. On a con-crete level, Taiwan to date has conducted its affairs in Hong Kong through the China (*Chung Hwa*) Travel Service. It is not yet clear whether this arrangement will change under the SAR. More broadly, how Taiwanese issues are treated in the SAR's press will provide one potentially very significant test of press free-dom. Beijing's attitudes and actions will be shaped, however, at least in part by concerns over political stability and the potential for subversion. Again, this is an issue that will require careful thought on the part of the SAR government.

CHALLENGE #6: SHAPING THE GOVERNING INSTITUTIONS

For all the attention paid to forecasting Beijing's choice of the CE and to Bei-jing's decision to replace the Legislative Council (Legco) with a transitional body of its own choosing before holding new legislative elections, the exact functions of the major governing institutions in the wake of the July 1997 rever-sion remain remarkably vague. Every political system operates in a fashion that differs in its dynamics from the broad constitutional provisions that undergird it,[12] and the future Hong Kong SAR government will prove no exception to this general phenomenon. Some things can be said with confidence, though.

---

[12] In the Basic Law, Chapter IV spells out in broad terms the jurisdictions of and relations among the executive, legislative, and judicial branches and the district organizations.

First, the CE will face a daunting task in maintaining the confidence of both Beijing and the people of Hong Kong. He will have to work well with Beijing, as Hong Kong's long-term well-being depends on that. However, as suggested above, there will be many issues on which the CE will have to show some backbone in resisting pressures from the mainland, and all sides will watch carefully both his style and substance in doing this. This individual can prove to be an authoritarian CE, or he can manage his post in a fashion that encourages institutional adaptations to foster an increasingly democratic society in Hong Kong. The extent to which he develops a strong lobbying office in Beijing rather than relying primarily on personal diplomacy, the extent to which he encourages the civil service to play a strong role in managing issues and protects his top appointees from pressures from Beijing, and the extent to which he works with the legislature rather than tries to marginalize it – all these factors will provide major benchmarks in the shaping of this new position.

Second, the institution of the legislature itself will have to define its role. Legco has specified powers, most notably regarding the government's budget; until recently, however, it was not a major organ of independent power. Recent British initiatives to make Legco more representative and to broaden its role have taken place under the shadow of disapproval from Beijing. The Basic Law provides for gradual expansion in democratic elections to Legco, and developments in recent years suggest that the people of Hong Kong are interested in seeing the legislature assume a more important role.[13] The ultimate assertiveness of Legco has already become a very sensitive issue, and it is not difficult to imagine quite different future scenarios. It will take skillful leadership in both the executive and legislative branches to find a division of labor and balance of initiative that suits Hong Kong's situation well. This situation is made particularly sensitive by Beijing's plan to replace the pre-reversion Legco with a provisional legislature before holding new elections.

The court system is also going to experience change. This is another realm in which the system in the PRC differs so fundamentally from that in Hong Kong that even good intentions on all sides cannot guarantee the smooth resolution of issues. Hong Kong has long been a society that practices the rule *of* law, while China after the Cultural Revolution has evolved increasingly from rule *without* law toward rule *by* law. That is, to a growing extent on the mainland a legal system is utilized to help the government shape the economy and

---

[13] An increasing percentage of eligible voters has turned out for elections, even as the number of eligible voters has expanded in the 1990s.

society in the ways it sees fit. There are some very small glimmers of movement toward a legal system that can actually restrain political power on the mainland, most notably in recently conferred rights that permit citizens to sue the government itself. However, currently the mainland remains overwhelmingly a system in which political power bends the law to its needs, rather than one in which the law serves as an absolute constraint on the exercise of political power. On this crucial issue, Hong Kong has long operated in a diametrically opposite fashion, and this has been one of the keys to Hong Kong's success. Unfortunately, very few Chinese on the mainland understand the dynamics of a society characterized by the rule of law.

The high quality of its legal system has been one of the major competitive advantages Hong Kong has offered in Asia; inevitably, any developments that could erode this advantage will be closely scrutinized. Some developments are already clear. Early retirements are producing a loss of many good judges, and senior people are not readily available to replace them. The Hong Kong SAR will have its own Court of Final Appeal, but this body will include only one foreign judge, and there are concerns about the quality of people available to serve on the Court. Hong Kong may find it difficult to convince the outside world that its Court of Final Appeal works as well as the Privy Council in the United Kingdom, which has to date served as the final appellate court for Hong Kong cases.

Certain substantive issues will be closely watched by people inside and outside of the SAR. How will things be handled when civil liberties cases arise on which the PRC has strong views, based on China's perceived need for stability? Will the system bend to permit various types of special considerations for individual litigants who are well connected politically on the mainland? In the application of law to economic issues, might pressures be brought to bear to overlook improper behavior by some politically powerful PRC-invested firms? What is at stake here is not a wholesale change in the substance or application of law in Hong Kong but rather how things are handled at the margin. The challenge is not likely to be one of a frontal assault but rather of a gradual decay of rigor and fairness – and therefore a gradual loss in necessary confidence in the court system among potential Hong Kong and international litigants.

The institutional dynamics and boundaries of all three major branches of government – the executive, the legislature, and the judicial system – are still somewhat uncertain in the Hong Kong SAR. Much will, of course, be worked out in practice, as issues arise and decisions are made. However, at this point the gray area is sufficiently large to allow for significantly different outcomes, even within the constitutional framework that has been laid.

CONCLUSION

The above overview points to a simple conclusion: The major challenges to Hong Kong, assuming that no political or social earthquakes occur in China, may take the form of various pressures to adapt current practices in order to work more effectively with the mainland. Some of these adaptations may prove difficult and painful, and more attention needs to be devoted to preparing for them. In some spheres, such as the future role of the Communist Party in Hong Kong, there is still too little information to provide a solid basis for judgment. The danger lurks as much in the ignorance on the mainland concerning the special chemistry that has been critical to Hong Kong's success, as in the purposeful mainland initiatives to curtail the freedoms enjoyed to date by Hong Kong's citizens.

The above analysis is limited to Hong Kong's governing institutions and ignores broader issues that may emerge from the business community and society in general. Overall, the Hong Kong business community long ago adapted to dealing with its Chinese counterparts, and the economies on the two sides of the border have already become almost wholly integrated.[14] If the PRC maintains sufficient vigilance to keep Chinese nationals from coming across the border in great numbers,[15] the manufacturing side of the Hong Kong economy may function somewhat differently but basically should continue to succeed as long as the economy of South China is also growing satisfactorily.

Some economic changes of significance will, of course, occur. Hong Kong's role as an international financial center may decline somewhat, as the legal system in the SAR – a system that has been so attractive to multinational corporations in the recent past – begins to decline. Naturally, if Beijing should make the mistake of utilizing its political leverage to change the regulatory environment in order to provide privileged conditions for mainland Chinese capital in Hong Kong, this will seriously damage the business environment in the SAR.

Other issues, such as those concerning freedom of the press and protection of various civil liberties, will prove crucially important for maintaining necessary confidence in Hong Kong. This modern, international city has for a long time taken for granted freedoms that still lie far in China's future; therefore, it

---

[14] For example, more than 80 percent of the employees of Hong Kong manufacturing firms live and work in Guangdong Province.

[15] The Basic Law leaves the decision to Beijing to determine how many PRC nationals may cross the border and reside in Hong Kong. Beijing is obligated only to "consult" with the Hong Kong SAR government on this important matter.

243

will require tremendous self-discipline for China to keep from taking actions that damage the SAR's modern social fabric. Whether China is capable of developing a fully modern system itself is a less crucial question than whether China can exercise the self-restraint necessary to permit an already highly successful modern system on its periphery to continue to thrive. If the answer is negative, the implications for the PRC's future ties with Taiwan are devastating.

It is especially in the areas of human rights and judicial and press freedom that the international community is likely to put the Hong Kong SAR under a microscope. Every perceived PRC transgression will receive intense scrutiny as well as negative publicity. There is some danger that such public condemnation might stoke nationalist resentments in Beijing, which could, in turn, make the situation worse.

The above analysis suggests strongly that, even under the best of circumstances, the Hong Kong authorities should undertake a major, sustained effort to communicate as effectively as possible to mainland officials a basic understanding and appreciation of the ways in which Hong Kong operates. In doing so, the Hong Kong SAR government will be competing with a cacophony of other voices, not least those of major Hong Kong businesspeople. Few things are more alien to Beijing than the idea of letting major investments fail, allowing the market to work freely or permitting a civil service to operate without close political supervision.

Nevertheless, considerable reason for optimism exists, given the enormous stakes all parties have in making the Hong Kong SAR a success story. The biggest challenge is likely to take the form noted above, in which the Hong Kong SAR government must make significant adjustments to ensure that the "one country, two systems" formula works well. A concerted, sustained effort to think through the probable pressures and necessary adaptations should increase the chances that the Hong Kong SAR will meet this challenge effectively.

Index

Index

Index

Wilson, Sir David, 206, 220
Woo, Peter, 39, 90
World Trade Organization (WTO),
    130–1, 132, 199, 209, 211
Wu, Anna, 94
Wu, Changqi, 4
Wu, Gordon, 55, 123

Xiamen, 121–2
Xinhua. *See* New China News Agency
Xu Jiatun, 203, 238

Yahuda, Michael, 5
Yam, Joseph, 147

Yang, Sir Ti-liang, 181
Yantian, 21
Ye Xuanping, 108
Youde, Sir Edward, 220
Yuan, 16, 17, 20
Yung, Larry, 105

Zhang Junsheng, 158
Zhanjiang, 187
Zhao Jihua, 57, 81n.20
Zhongguo Qingnian (Chinese Youth), 227
Zhongshan University, 202
Zhou Enlai, 201, 203
Zhou Nan, 158, 202

Printed in the United States
By Bookmasters